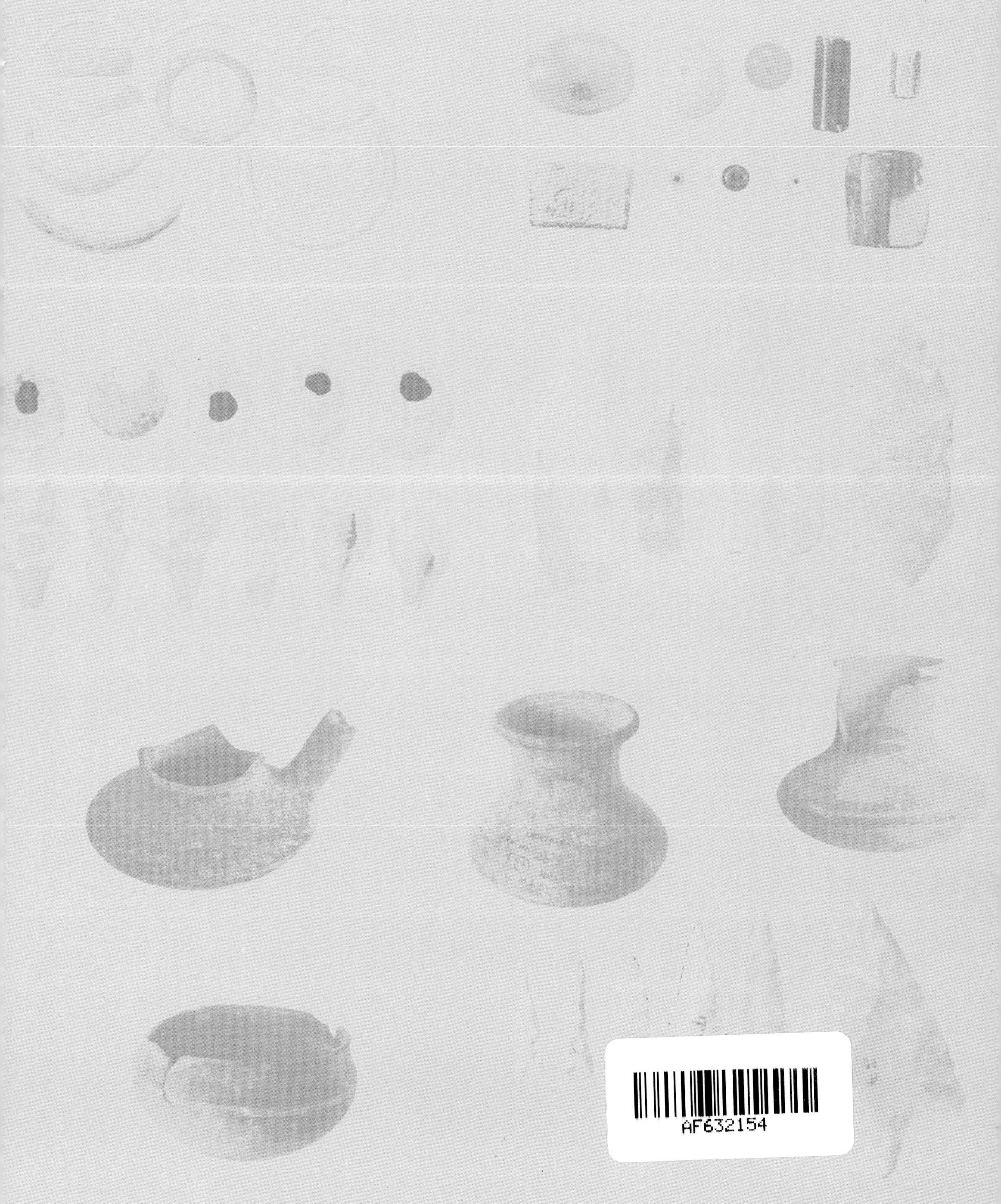

Art & Archaeology of India
Stone Age to the Present

B.S. Harishankar

With Contributions from

A.P. Khatri
V. N. Misra
S.P. Gupta

Indraprastha Museum of Art & Archaeology, New Delhi

D.K. Printworld (P) Ltd., New Delhi

First Published : 2003

ISBN 81-246-0253-0

Price: Rs.700/-

Published with the financial assistance received from the Deptt. of Culture, Govt. of India.

Cataloging in Publication Data — DK
Harishankar, B.S., 1966 –
Art & Archaeology of India.
Includes bibliographical references (p.)

1. Art — India — History. 2. India — Antiquities.
I. Title.

CATALOGUE OF THE INDRAPRASTHA MUSEUM OF ART & ARCHAEOLOGY

Published by: Director, Indraprastha Museum of Art & Archaeology
B–17, Qutab Institutional Area, New Delhi –110016.
Tel: 26523728. Telefax: 26960654. Email: iasnewdelhi@rediffmail.com

D.K. Printworld (P) Ltd.
F-52, Bali Nagar, New Delhi –110015
Tel : (011) 2545-3975; 2546-6019. Fax : (011) 2546-5926
E-mail: dkprintworld@vsnl.net Web: www.dkprintworld.com

Design/Print: VAP, H-24, Green Park Extension, New Delhi–110016
Tel : 26196787. Email: vap_enterprises@ yahoo.com Web: www.vaponline.com

Art & Archaeology of India
Stone Age to the Present

Catalogue of the Indraprastha Museum of Art and Archaeology

Preface

During the short period of around five years of its existence, the Indraprastha Museum of Art and Archaeology, established by the Indian Archaeological Society under a trust, has made a sizable collection of art and archaeological materials. This collection is varied, touching a number of periods of Indian history. In fact, a small collection belongs to other countries as well which throws light on the history and archaeology of those countries located in West Asia, Africa and Europe. There are prehistoric artifacts and protohistorical antiquities. There are a great number of fossils of several extinct animals, plants and wood. There are skulls of apes and human beings. There are Persian manuscripts and documents, painted and unpainted, and works of art of Historical Period. There are contemporary paintings and objects of decorative arts as well.

The prehistoric materials in the form of stone tools and implements belong to Palaeolithic, Mesolithic and Neolithic periods, while the protohistoric materials in the form of pottery and other artifacts, belong to the Chalcolithic cultures and the Indus-Saraswati Civilization. The remains of the Historical Period belong to the Buddha's Period, 6th–5th centuries B.C. as well as Maurya, Sunga, Kushana, Gupta, and Medieval periods. There are oil paintings, water colour paintings, pastel colour paintings and etchings, both old and contemporary. There are also stone sculptures, terracottas, ceramics and objects of other materials.These have been listed at the end in the form of a handlist. But around 3000 more objects still remain to be studied which will require one more catalogue.

An introduction gives a short account of the prehistoric and protohistoric cultures of India to which our collections largely belong. It includes an introduction to Human Evolution by Prof. V.N. Misra, former Director, Deccan College, Pune. It also includes an article on the fossil remains from the Narmada basin, and one article on pre-human hominid remains found in the Siwaliks by Dr. A.P. Khatri, one of India's most eminent prehistorians. I have also added a note on Indian art. All this has been done to make the publication useful for researchers and students. It also gives some account of the excavations conducted by the Indian Archaeological Society at Drupad-ka-Qila (Kampilya) Sanjan and Kamrej, the first site is located in Uttar Pradesh while the other two in Gujarat. A part of the materials collected from these excavations are housed in the Museum.

The Indraprastha Museum of Art and Archaeology has some supporting departments made available to it by the Indian Archaeological Society which is the parent body. There is a fully computerized library of about 5000 books on history, art and archaeology. It provides photocopy facilities to research scholars at nominal cost. The Museum also has a Lecture Hall, a Seminar Room and a Committee Room for Research and Educational purposes. There is a Photo-Division and a Division for Graphics to prepare visual materials to illustrate the publications.The Photo-Division has a Digital Video-Camera to make small documentary films, primarily for teaching but also for giving training in the subjects of art, architecture and archaeology. The teaching and training programmes are conducted on the campus not only by the Museum but also by the Centre for Research and Training in History, Archaeology and Palaeoenvironment, which, like the Indraprastha Museum of Art and Archaeology, was established by the Indian Archaeological

Society. The Society's third wing, the 'Heritage Helpmates', engaged in conservation and preservation of monuments, works of art as well as establishing new museums, also supports the activities of the Museum.

The Indraprastha Museum of Art and Archaeology has a full-fledged programme of publications, both popular and research nature. It has already brought out two major publications: (i) *The Elements of Indian Art,* and (ii) *Cultural Tourism in India,* both financially supported by the Deptt. of Culture, Govt. of India.

The Indraprastha Museum of Art and Archaeology is the product of a vision fuelled by mission and determination of heart and mind of the founder-fathers of the Indian Archaeological Society. The Museum is, therefore, also developing as an advanced research institute in the field of art and archaeology. Its office-bearers are the research guides for the Ph.D. degree. This initiative involves setting up specialized laboratories to give solid scientific basis to the research projects of the Museum.

Those who have contributed to the foundation and growth of this Museum are many, but mainly Shri K.S.Ramachandran, Treasurer, and Shri K.N.Dikshit, General Secretary of the Board of Management of the Indian Archaeological Society. But for their most active support we would not have realised our dream of establishing this museum. Dr. B.S.Harishankar, one time our Research Associate and also Asstt. Director (Honorary) of the Museum, deserves all our appreciation for authoring this catalogue.

Here we gratefully acknowledge the financial assistance that the Deptt. of Culture, Govt. of India, gave to the Museum to publish this Catalogue. We also thank Shri Tejas Garge, Ms. Mahua Bhattacharyya, Ms. Anuja Geetali and Sarvashri M.S. Mani, Jassu Ram and Lakshmi Narain of our Technical Divisions, Graphics, Art and Photography, respectively, as well as Sarvashri Rakesh Datta, Himanshu Joshi, Manoj Harbola and Arun Datta of the other Departments for their help in preparing the manuscript of this catalogue.

At the end, I take this opportunity to put on record the donation of one of the largest personal collections of Stone Age tools from many parts of India and abroad as well as Palaeontogical materials, the animal, wood and plant fossils, from the Narmada and other valleys by Dr. A.P. Khatri who has been and still is one of the greatest signatures in the field of researches connected with the Indian Prehistory. He will be preparing a separate catalogue of his collection donated to the Museum which we will be only too happy to publish. In the meantime Ms. Gency Choudhury, our Reserch Associate in the museum, is assisting him and doing the preliminary academic work. Our grateful thanks to both of them and also to Mrs. Khatri, her son, daughter and daughter-in-law since all of whom gladly agreed to make this priceless collection donated to the Museum.

We will fail in our duty if we do not record our great appreciation of the works done by Sri Praveen Mehta and Mrs. S. Davra of the VAP Enterprises in connection with the publication of this catalogue.

New Delhi

S.P. Gupta
Chairman and Director

Contents

Stages of Human Evolution

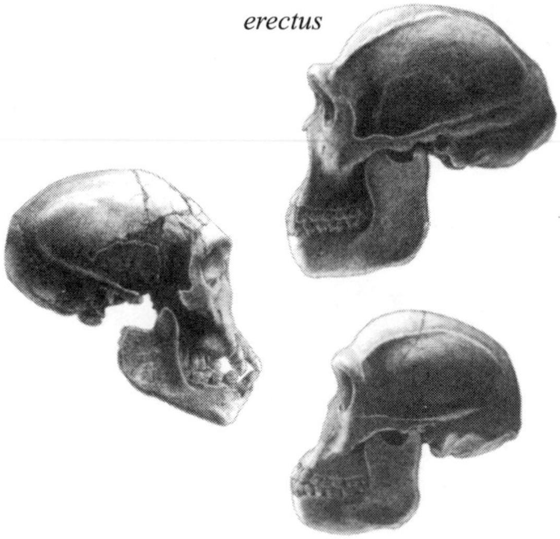

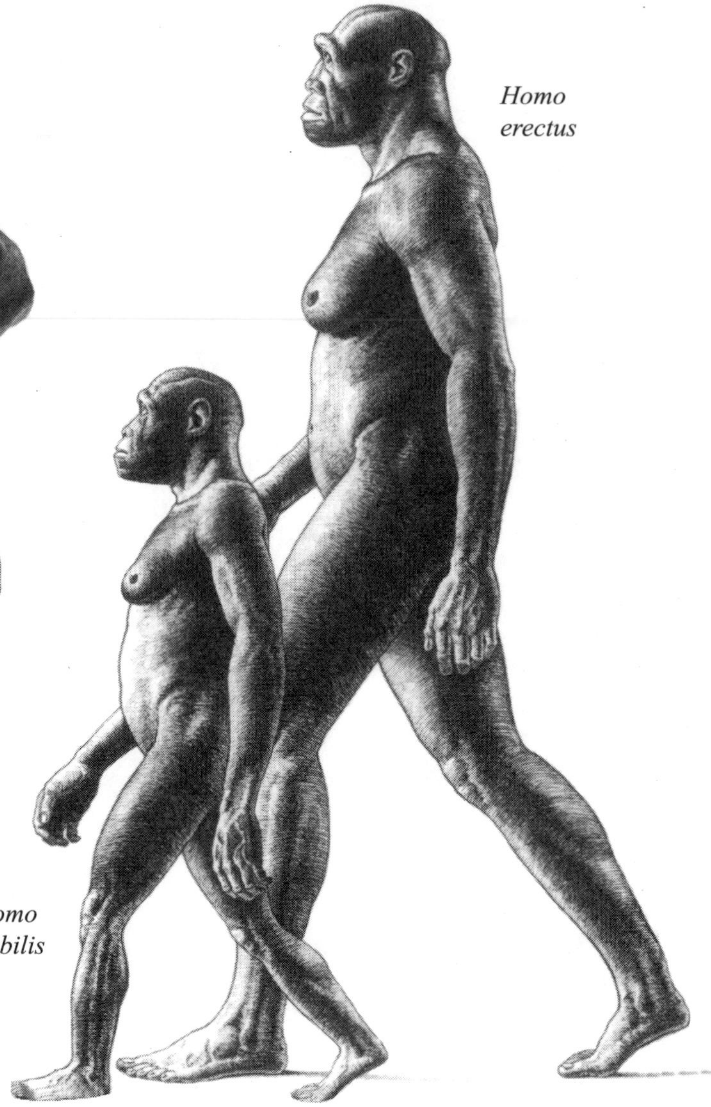

The new Dmanisi skull has a mosaic of features from other species. H. erectus is in bold; H. habilis, is spotted boxes.

Chronology of Human Evolution

A tree for the genus *Homo....*

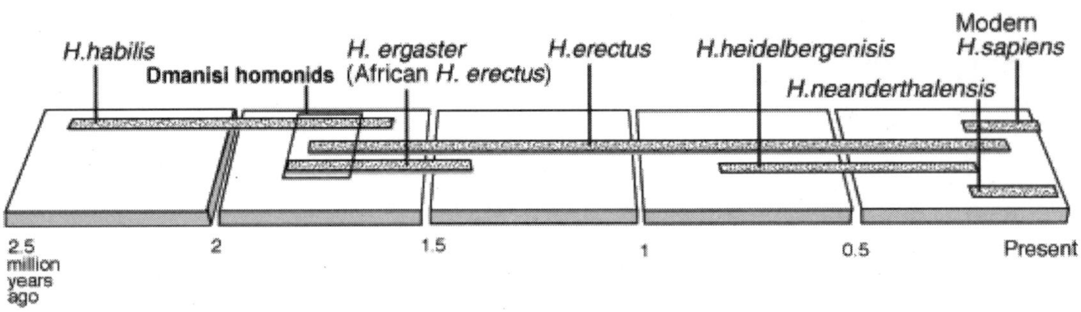

..... or a single branch?

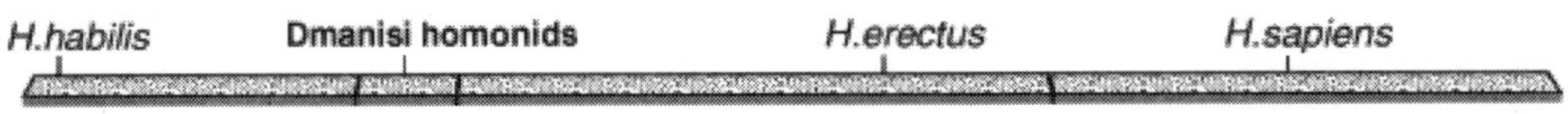

INTRODUCTION

The Early Fossil Hominids and Related Apes of Siwalik Foothills of the Himalayas
(Stages of Pre-Human Evolution)

IT IS NOW GENERALLY AGREED THAT THE KEY TO understanding the basic problems related to the ancestry of the Pleistocene hominids in Africa and Asia lies in pinpointing exactly how the separation between pongids and hominids took place in the Miocene/Pliocene period. To this age belong the Siwalik foothills of the Himalayas in India and the Rusinga Island and Fort Ternan deposits of Kenya. The first discovery of primate fossils in the Siwaliks dates back to the 1830's, while studies of the African dryopithecines began in the 1950's, recent taxonomic assignments and re-evaluation of the old material from these two areas place most of it in the Dryopithecinae, while a few specimens in both areas belong to the genus *Ramapithecus*, established by Lewis in 1934. It is now generally agreed that *Ramapithecus* is the earliest human ancestor yet known: it lived fourteen to fifteen million years ago, in the late Miocene or early Pliocene period, in Africa and Asia. I shall review the present status of the Siwalik hominoids under the revised taxonomic regrouping and shall bring together material that has come to light during the past twenty-five years.

The following abbreviations are used here:

1. AMNH: American Museum of Natural History, New York
2. BMNH: British Museum of Natural History, London
3. NMNHP: National Museum of Natural History, Paris
4. GSI: Geological Survey of India, Calcutta
5. CMN: Coryndon Museum of Natural History, Nairobi
6. YPM: Yale Peabody Museum of Natural History, New Haven
7. NMK: National Museum of Kenya, Nairobi

Historical Review

The first mention of primate specimens from the Siwalik Hills of India goes back to 1837. A right astragalus of *Presbytis palaeindicus* (BMNH1539) and a mandible of *Papio falconeri* (BMNH 15709) leist primate specimens of the Siwaliks of which we have a record. The astragalus was mentioned in the *Transactions of the Geological Society*, London (1937) Series 2,5: 499–502 and the mandible was recorded by H. Falconer and P.T. Cautley in the *Journal of the Asiatic Society of Bengal*, 6: 354–360. Falconer and Cautley's (1831–1868) and Richard Lydekker's (1876–1886) classic contributions and exhaustive monographs on the Siwalik vertebrate fauna described additional primate specimens. But all of these specimens were fossil monkeys (Cercopithecidae).

The real research on anthropoid apes commenced in 1910 with the publication of Pilgrim's classic paper "Notices of new mammalian genera and species from the Tertiaries of India." Here for the first time *Sivapithecus indicus, Dryopithecus punjabicus*, and *Semnopithecus asnoti* were mentioned. In 1915 Pilgrim established two additional species of *Dryopithecus* (D. *chinjienses* and D. *giganteus*) and the new genus *Palaeosimia*, with the specific name of *rugosidens*. Almost all the primate specimens were discovered by M. Vinayak Rao, a sub-assistant of the Geological Survey of India, at several localities, particularly Chinji and Hasnot in the Salt Range and Haritalyangar in the Simla Hills. In 1927, Pilgrim described seven more hominoid specimens from the Siwaliks and established five new species: *Sivapithecus orientalis, Sivapithecus himalayensis, Sivapithecus middlemissi, Palaeopithecus (?) sylvaricus, and Hylopithecus hysudricus*. Of the seven Siwalik specimens he described in 1927, four (D. 196, 197, 199 and 200) were discovered by Pilgrim himself at Haritalyangar. Specimen D. 198 was collected by C.S. Middlemiss. The other two specimens, which were isolated molars, came from the Salt Range and were given to Pilgrim by C. Forester. Forester later deposited those specimens in the British Museum, London. The specimens collected by Falconer, Cautley, and Lydekker also went to the British Museum, while the collection made by Pilgrim and Rao became the property of the Indian Museum, Calcutta. In 1922, the American Museum of Natural history of New York sent out a Siwalik expedition under Dr. Barnum Brown (Brown's collection of Siwalik vertebrate fauna was described by Colbert in 1935). Brown found three primate specimens on which were established three new *Dryopithecus* species; these were named *D. pilgrimi* (AMNH 194111), *D. cautleyi* (AMNH 19412), and D. frickae (AMNH 19413), in honor of Pilgrim, Cautley, and Mrs. Henry Clay Frick, who provided funds to the American Museum for the Siwalik expedition. The *D. pilgrimi* specimen was collected from Ramnagar (Jammu), while the other two came from Hasnot in the Salt Range, West Punjab. These three specimens were described and discussed exhaustively by Brown, Gregory, and Hellman (1924) and by Gregory and Hellman (1926).

In 1931–1933 the Yale North India Expedition under G. Edward Lewis secured further collections of primate fossils from Hasnot and Haritalyangar and established four new genera and species: *Indraloris lulli* (1938), *Ramapithecus brevirostris* (1934), *Ramapithecus hariensis* (1934), and *Sugrivapithecus salmontanus sivalensis*. Lewis named them after Indian gods, mythological heroes, and characters of the Indian epic Ramayana. The type specimens on which these new genera and species were established are in the Yale Peabody Museum, New Haven; their register numbers are YPM 13802, 13799, 13807, 13811, 13814, and 13806, respectively. The specimens of *Sugrivapithecus* and *Ramapithecus* (13811 and 13814) were obtained from Hasnot, in the Salt Range, while the other four specimens were collected from the Haritalyangar area in the Simla Hills.

In 1935, Helmut De Terra led the Yale-Cambridge India Expedition to the Siwalik Hills. The specimens were ultimately divided between the Yale Peabody Museum and Cambridge University, London. N.K.N. Aiyengar, a fossil collector with the Geological Survey of India, who was attached to the expedition, recovered seventeen new hominoid specimens from seven different localities. The localities were Kundan Nala near Chinji (two specimens), Chinji (four), Kanatti (one), Parrewali (one) Haritalyanagar (four), Ramnagar (one), and Jammu (four). These finds were described by Gregory, Hellman, and Lewis (1938).

Prior to 1938, the total number of primate fossils from the Siwalik foothills was eighty-two, consisting mostly of maxillae, mandibular rami, molars, and other isolated teeth (Wadia and Aiyengar 1938). No long bones of other postcranial materials had been recovered, so the locomotion of these creatures was unknown. Most of the specimens came from Chinji and Hasnot in the Salt Range (Pakistan) and from Haritalyangar and Ramnagar (India). They were collected by Theobald, Rao, Aiyengar, Lewis, Brown, De Terra (GSI. D. 301), Pilgrim, Lahiri (GSI D. 300), Middlemiss (GSI D. 198), Pascoe, Sen (YPM 13835), and Bose. The largest number of primate fossils was found by Rao and Aiyengar, who held subordinate posts in the Geological Survey of India. Mr. B. K. Bose discovered a specimen of *Sivapithecus* at Dalsar, one mile north of Ramnagar, Jammu. This fossil is now in the collection of the Prince of Wales College Museum at Jammu.

Between 1938 and 1950 there was a lull in research on the Siwalik primate fauna. Meanwhile, Africa, particularly Rusinga Island and the Fort Ternan beds of Kenya, yielded a rich crop of Miocene/Pliocene fauna. Thus the necessity arose for comparative work on the Siwalik and African pre-Pleistocene hominoids in order to establish their exact phylogenetic positions.

In 1951, 1954 and 1962 K. N. Prasad, of the Geological Survey of India, explored the area around Haritalyangar while mapping its geological formations. He discovered eleven specimens (Prasad 1962, 1964). He established the new species *Sivapithecus aiyengari* on the basis of a left mandibular ramus (GSI 18039), naming it in honor of N. K. N. Aiyengar, who had made a substantial addition to the Geological Survey of India primate collection in Calcutta.

In 1959, I explored the Haritalyangar area and found an almost complete primate mandible resembling that of the extant loris, but a little larger (Khatri 1964). In September, 1970, I explored the area around Ramnagar in Jammu for Miocene hominoids, and in May, 1971, I visited Haritalyangar again.

In 1968 the Punjab-Yale University research team explored extensively around Haritalyangar and procured from a peasant an almost complete mandible of a new species, *Gigantopithecus bilaspurensis* (Simons and Chopra 1969a, 1969b). It is presumed to have come from Pliocene Dhok Pathan beds of the Siwaliks.

In addition to this field research, the old material had been re-examined, particularly by Yale University scholars. Tattersall (1968) recognized a fragment of a left mandibular ramus of a large lorisid primate (YPM 19134) containing M3, the roots of M2, and the posterior root of M1. It has been assigned to

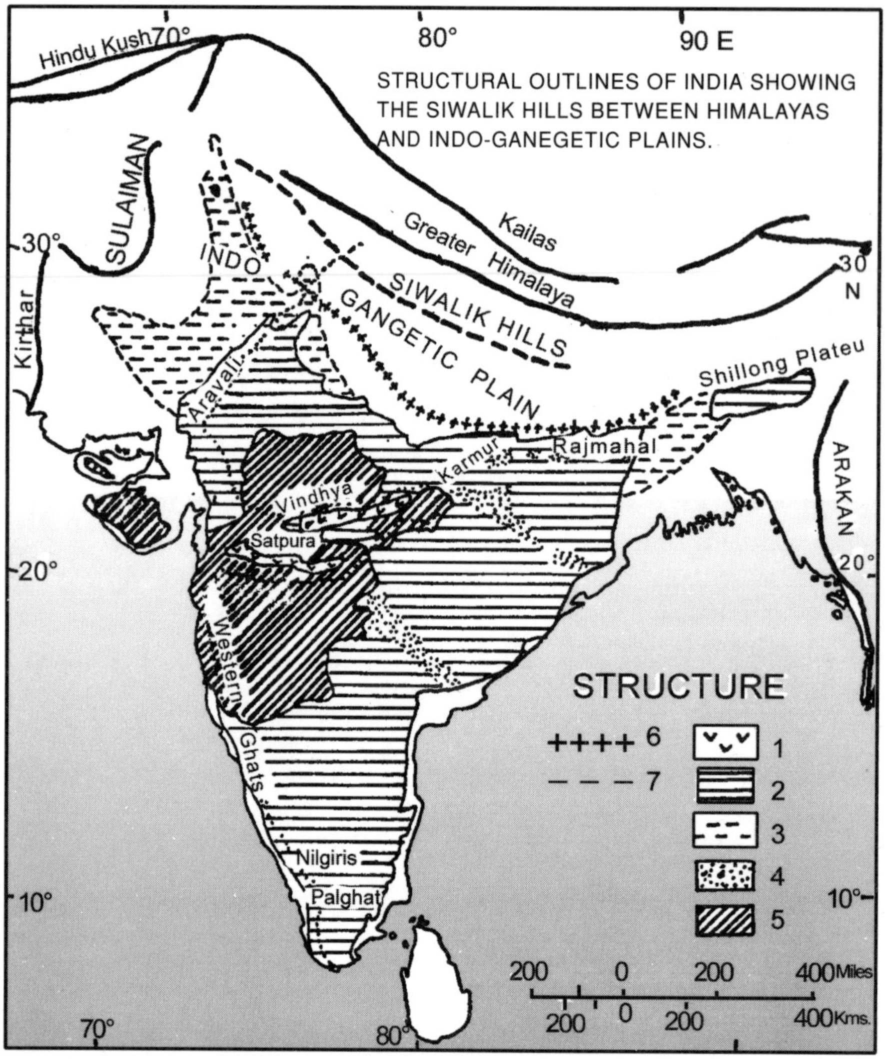

1 Narmada and Tapti troughs 2 Peninsular Block 3 Concealed extensions of 2
4 Gondwana troughs 5 Deccan lavas 6 Boundary of Indo-Gangetic trough 7 Siwalik Hills

Map 1 View of India showing Siwalik Hills vis-à-vis Himalayas and Indo-Gangetic Plain

Indraloris lulli (established by Lewis in 1933). An upper right central insisor of *Dryopithecus* (YPM 16919) was also discovered in the old Siwalik collection at Yale. It fits well in the alveolus of GSI 196 and may actually belong to it.

The Siwalik Hills

The Siwalik foothills extend for more than 1,600 kilometers along the Himalayas from Baluchistan to Assam (Map 1). They are sixteen to fifty-nine kilometers wide[1]. The sand gravels and conglomerates forming the Siwalik sediments are 4,570 to 6,100 meters (15,000 to 20,000 feet) thick and they rise to a height of 1,600 meters. Their strike is in a northwest-southeast direction. The word Siwalik is derived from a hill of the same name near Haridwar

[1]Different authors cite different widths for the Siwalik belt. In Jammu it has been reported as twenty-four miles or thirty-eight kilometers (Wadia 1957: 366). Average width of the Siwaliks according to Colbert (1935: 6) is eight miles or thirteen kilometers.

on a bank of the Ganga where the first mammalian fossils were recovered in the 1830's. Falconer, the first student of the Siwalik fauna, extended this name to the whole range. From Chandigarh, the Siwaliks look like small, pinkish hills at the base of a massive wall formed by the high Himalayas, which provide a dark background to the whole scene. The traverses from Jammu to Uddhampur, Pathankot to Dharamsala, and Chandigarh to Pinjor or Bilaspur give a sufficient idea of the physiography and composition of the Siwaliks. Gigantic escarpments, dipslopes, deep, meandering ravines, and huge gullies are the most common surface features of this area of sand and pebbles.

The Himalayas came into existence during the middle of the Eocene with the upliftment of the Tethyan geosynclinal tract of sea deposits. The Siwaliks were formed during the mid-Miocene, a process that continued until the beginning of the Pleistocene. Thus the outermost Himalayan foothills, the Siwaliks, represent a late buckling of the erosional products of the Himalayas themselves and are not very dissimilar from the ones that are now being formed.

Pascoe (1919) and Pilgrim (1919) independently proposed a very ingenious and detailed hypothesis to explain the occurrence of the Siwalik deposits along the southern fringe of the Himalayas. It envisions Siwalik deposition taking place along a great longitudinal river, Pascoe's Indo-brahm and Pilgrim's Siwalik River- which flowed to the northwest. This great master stream was later disrupted by headward erosion of the left bank tributaries of its own lower course, equivalent to the lower Indus of today, and by the similar action of a proto-Ganga and proto-Brahmaputra. De Terra (1936) and Krishanan and Aiyengar (1940) considered this hypothesis untenable in the light of their own research. De Terra considered the Siwaliks as a foredeep deposition on a littoral of almost continuous lagoons, with recently rejuvenated transverse streams forming the boulder beds.

Lithologically, the Siwalik deposits are subaerial waste from the Himalayas, consisting of alluvial detritus swept down by innumerable streams and rivulets. In the fields, it is not possible to recognize the Lower, Middle, and Upper Siwaliks because they form a continuous deposition without any break. This classification is based on the three-tier evolutionary succession of the vertebrate fauna which Pilgrim established after his extensive paleontological studies, particularly of fauna from Potwar and the Salt Range. Earlier, Falconer considered the Siwaliks to be one continuous unit of Miocene age, and Lydekker divided it into upper and lower groups belonging to the Pliocene. Matthew (1924) considered lower, middle and upper Siwalik faunas equivalent to Pontian, Middle Pliocene, and Lower Pleistocene age, respectively. Based on paleontological grounds, the Siwaliks are classified (Wadia 1957:365) as in Table 1.

For stratigraphy and fauna, the Potwar terrain north of the Salt Range, and the Kangra-Haridwar tract in Himachal and Uttar Pradesh are considered type areas. Different opinions regarding age and correlation of Siwalik beds are summarized in Figure 1.

The most important geotectonic features of the Siwalik system are its reversed overthrust faults, which are traceable for enormous distances (Wadia 1957:388). In the extreme

Table 1 Classification of Siwaliks

Upper Siwalik	Boulder Conglomerate zone Pinjor zone Tatrot zone	Lower Pleistocene to Lower Pliocene
Middle Siwalik	Dhok Pathan zone Nagri zone	Pontian to Middle Miocene Middle Miocene
Lower Siwalik	Chinji stage Kamlial stage	Tortonian Helvetian

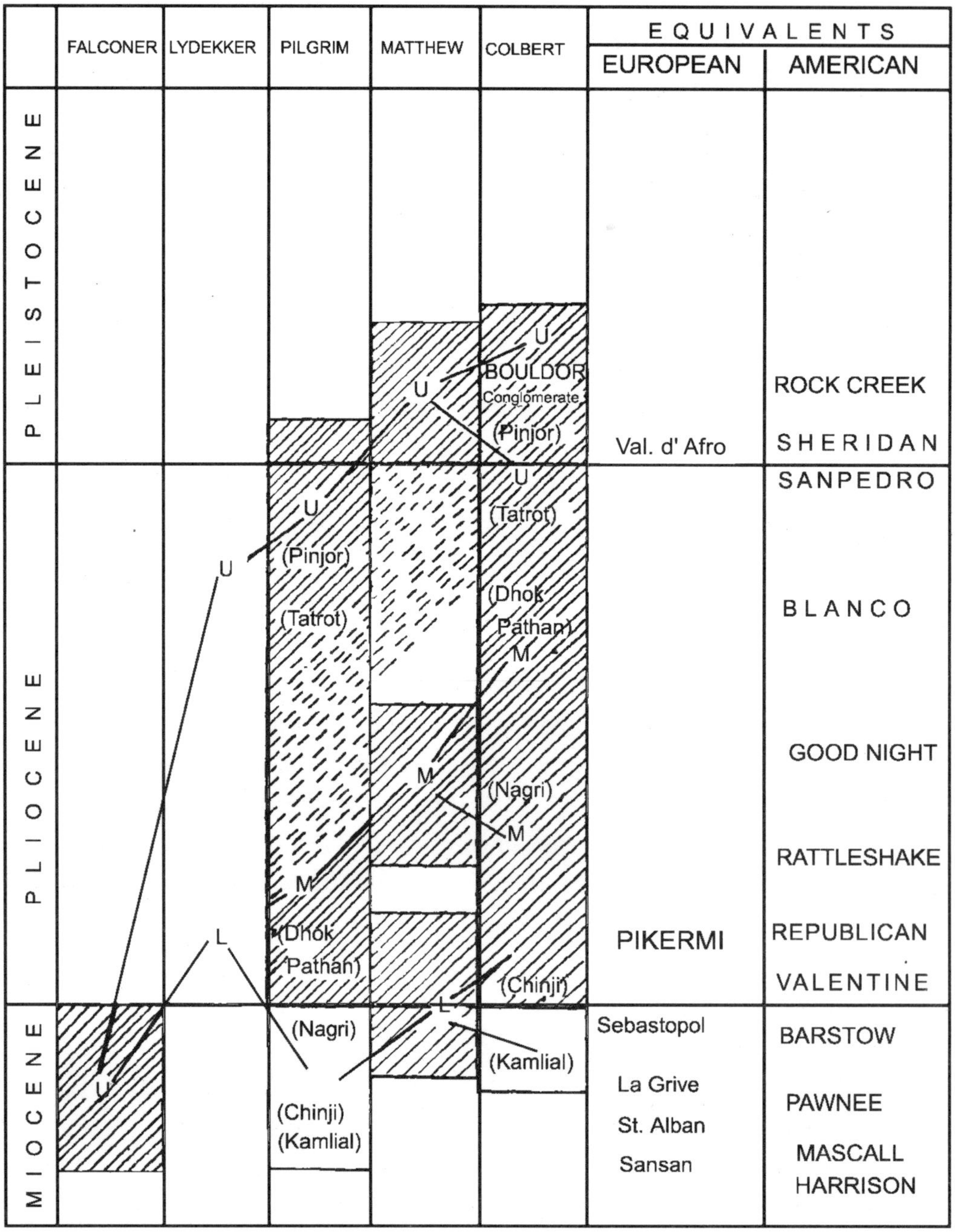

Fig. 1 Comparative views of the correlation of different Siwalik horizons

compression and stresses of tectonic, mountain-building processes, some of the folds became inverted or reversed. In such cases, the middle limb of the fold suffers the severest tension and gets into a highly inclined fracture or Thrust Plane, along which the dislocated portion of the fold slips as an entity over long distances, thus throwing the older pre-Siwalik rocks of the inner Himalayas over the younger ones of the Siwalik outer ranges (Figure 2).

Important Siwalik collections of vertebrate fauna

There are now five notable collections of Siwalik vertebrate fossils. They are located in the British Museum of Natural History, London; the Geological Survey of India Museum, Calcutta; the American Museum of Natural History, New York; Yale University Peabody Museum, New Haven; and the Department of Geology Museum, Punjab University, Chandigarh. The earliest collections, made in the 1830's and later by Falconer and Cautley, are in the British Museum. The collection at Calcutta is the largest and most varied. It was built up mainly through the efforts of Lydekker and Pilgrim and later by several other officers of the Geological Survey of India. The American Museum of Natural History collection was assembled by Brown in 1922. The Siwalik fauna at the Yale Peabody Museum was acquired by the Yale North India Expedition (1931–1933) and by the Yale-Cambridge India Expedition (1935). The Most recent Siwalik collection was developed between 1958 and 1964 at Punjab University, Chandigarh. Most of the fossils have been discovered at locations around Kalka and Pinjor. Table 2 summarizes the names of collectors and expeditions, the year of collection, and the current locations of the

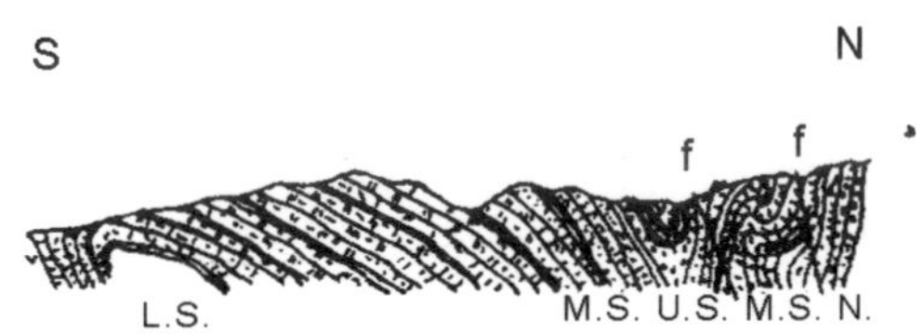

(A) - Section to Illustrate the relations of the outer Himalaya to the older rocks of the mid - Himalaya (Kumaon Himalaya)

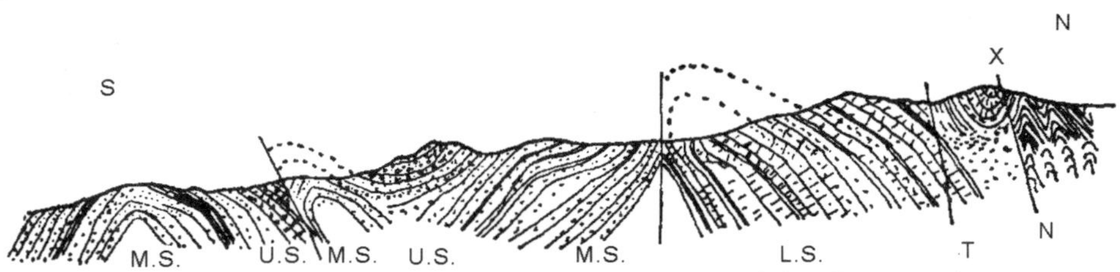

(B) Section across the sub - Himalayan zone east of the Ganges river.

L.S. Lower Siwalik, M.S. Middle Siwalik, T. Tol Series, U.S. Upper Siwalik
N. Older rocks, X. Nummulitic Limestone..

After C.S. MIDDLEMISS

Fig. 2 Sections illustrating the relationship of the outer Himalyas to the older rocks

Table 2 Important Siwalik collections of vertebrate fauna

Series numbers	Collectors	Museums
1.	Falconer and Cautley (1830–1850)	British Museum of Natural History, London, U.K.
2.	Richard Lydekker (1876–1886) and Guy E. Pilgrim (1900–1930)	Geological Survey of India Museum, Kolkata
3.	Barnum Brown (1922–1923) –American Museum of Natural History Siwalik Expedition	American Museum of Natural History, New York
4.	G. Edward Lewis (1931–1933)– Yale North India Expedition	Yale University Peabody Museum, New Haven, U.S.A.
5.	Helmut De Terra (1935)–Yale-Cambridge India Expedition	Yale University Peabody Museum, New Haven, U.S.A. and Cambridge University, Cambridge, England
6.	Exploration for the remains of Early Man in India Research Project (Council of Scientific and Industrial Research, Government of India (1958–1964)	Department of Geology Museum, Punjab University, Chndigarh

fauna.

Hominoid sites of the Siwaliks

Primate specimens have been collected at twelve localities in three main areas (Map 2). The areas are:

1. The much-dissected lower and middle Siwalik belt in the Potwar synclinal basin.
2. The country around Ramnagar, 103 kilometers east-northeast of Jammu.
3. The Haritalyangar area of Bilaspur District, which was once a princely state of the Simla Hills.

The hominoid sites mentioned in the literature are:

1. India

a. Haritalyangar (31°32'N;76° 38'E); thirty kilometers northwest of Bilaspur town, Himachal Pradesh.
b. Chakrana (31° 32'N; 76° 41'E); six kilometers east of Haritalyangar, Bilaspur District, Himachal Pradesh.
c. Ramnagar (32° 49'N; 73° 22'E); at Kirmu and Dal Sar, five kilometers from Ramnagar, a small town, 103 kilometers (by road) east of Jammu.

2. Pakistan (a-d in the Salt Range, Attock District, Punjab; e-i in the Salt Range, Jhelum District, Punjab)

a. Chinji (32° 41'N; 72° 22'E)
b. Kundal Nala (Southwest of Chinji)
c. Kanati (near Chinji)
d. Alipur
e. Hasnot (32° 49'N; 72° 19'30E)
f. Bhandar
g. Jabi
h. Kotal Kund
i. Parrewali

Of these sites, only the first three are now in India. Haritalyangar is the most productive, so it is searched repeatedly by investigators in India.

Haritalyangar (Plates 1–4) is named after the twin villages of Hari and Talyangar, one

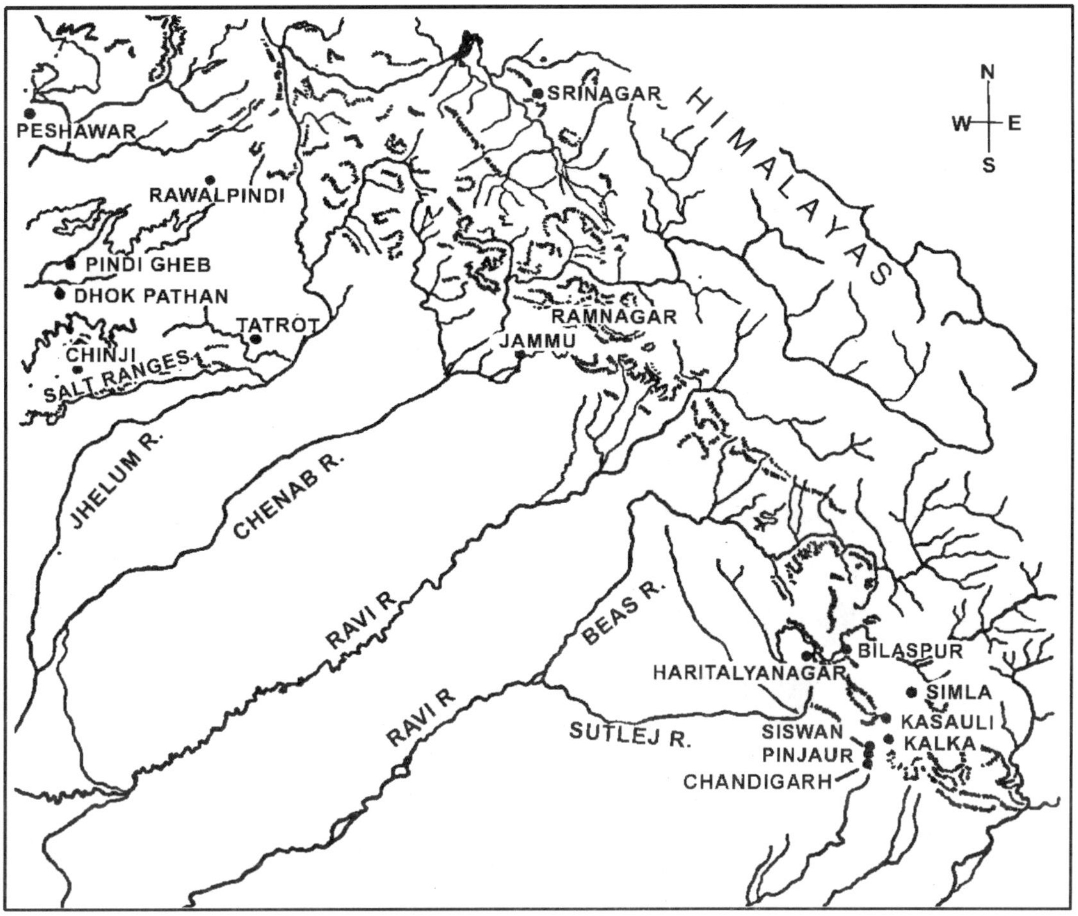

Map 2 Important fossiliferous sites of the Siwaliks

situated at the bottom of the valley and the other at the top. It is about thirty kilometers northwest of Bilaspur and about six kilometers from Dadhol, a bus stop, on the Bilaspur-Ladrol road[2]. On seeing the situation of Talyangar for the first time, one gets the impression that this area might once have been a large lake.

The Hari Temple Cuesta Scarp (Plate 3), locally called *Hari-ka- Tibba,* is a treasure-house of primate fossils. It is only 200 meters north of Hari village and its horizon of red clay is fossiliferous (Plate 4).

The succession of geological horizons (Figure 3) in this area (Prasad 1964) is shown in Table 3.

Nahan Beds: These are the earliest geological horizons exposed in this area. Their hallmark is sandstone interbedded with purple or greenish clay containing fossil wood.

Nagri Beds: These beds consist of massive grey sandstones and pink clays. To the west of Haritalyangar, sandstones are overlaid by variegated clays containing *Hipparion theobaldi* and *Crocuta gigantea.* Four prominent ridges striking east-west, north-south, west-north west-south- southeast, and northwest-southeast are exposed east of Haritalyangar and are rich in fossils.

[2]A new road linking new Bilaspur township with Haritalyangar was constructed after the creation of Govindsagar Lake by the Bakhra dam on the Sutlej River. The old Bilaspur town, with its buildings and radiating roads, is now under this body of water. The road distances cited here are those before the creation of Govindsagar Lake.

Table 3 Succession of geological horizons in Haritalyangar area

	Pinjor Stage: variegated clay and sand-stones	Villafranchian Astian
Upper Siwalik	Tatrot Stage: Hard brown sandstones with clasy	
	Dhok Pathan Stage: brown sandstones, orange clays and dark shades	Pontian
Middle Siwalik	Nagri stage: massive grey sandstones and pink clasy	Sarmtian
Lower Siwalik	Nahan Stage: bright red shales and (Sutlej) sandstones	Upper Tortonian

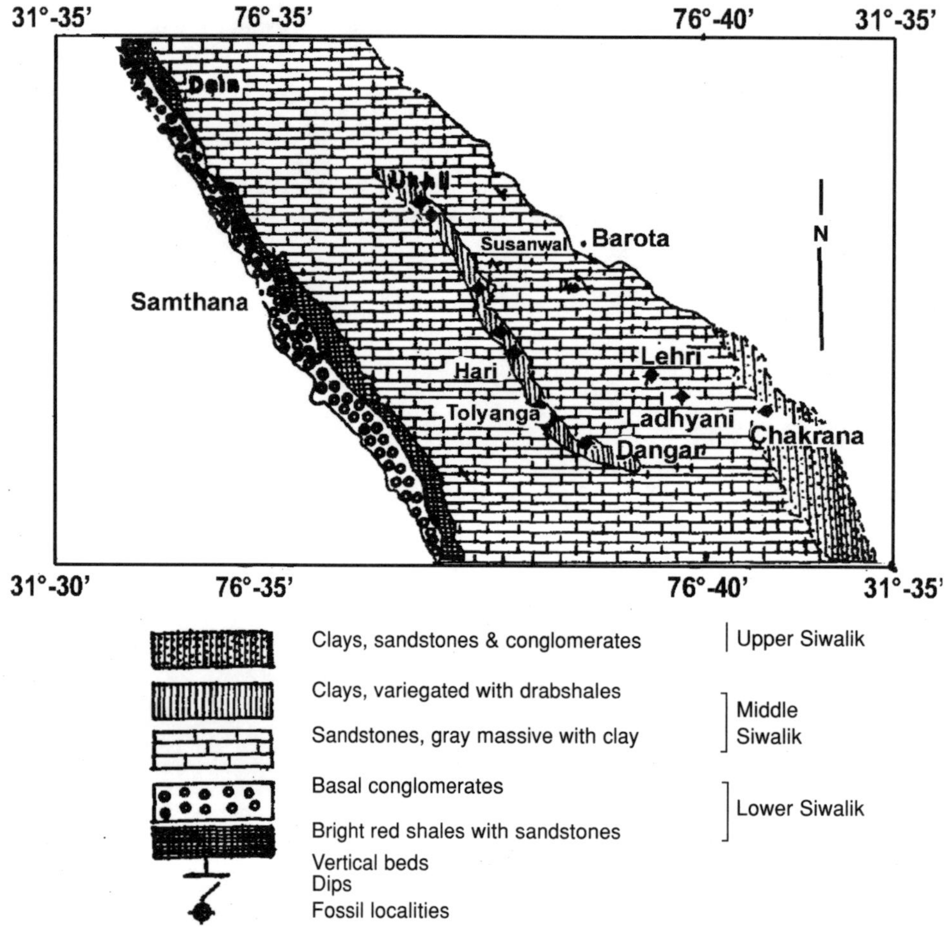

Fig. 3 Geological map of Haritalyangar area in Bilaspur, Himachal Pradesh

Dhok Pathan Beds: These beds are made up of drab clays and sandstones. Two fossiliferous exposures at Ladhyani (31°32'N; 76° 40'E) and Lehri Serail (31°32'N; 76°30'E) yield fauna of Dhok Pathan stage.

Pinjor Beds: These are exposed at Chakrana (31°32'N: 76°42'E), about six kilometers southeast of Haritalyangar, and are comparable to Pinjor. The basal beds at Chakrana are of Tatrot stage (Astian) on paleontological evidence.

The Nagri zone (twelve to eight million years) has yielded the largest number of fossils.

Chakrana is six kilometers southeast of Haritalyangar. The type specimen YPM 13799 of *Ramapithecus brevirostris* was recovered one-fourth mile east of Chakrana.

Ramnagar is a small town 103 kilometers east-northeast of Jammu by road. Lower Siwalik (Chinji) fossiliferous beds are exposed at Kirmu and Dal Sar nearby. At least seven hominoid specimens have been recovered here, GSI D. 198 was collected by Middlemiss; and Pilgrim (1927) based the species *Sivapithecus middlemissi* on it. AMNH 19411 was collected by Brown in 1922, and Brown, Gregory, and Hellman (1924) established the species *Dryopithecus pilgrimi* on it.

Four specimens—numbers 600 (YPM 13822), 601,602, and 603 (Gregory, Hellman, and Lewis 1938: 3–4) — collected by the Yale Cambridge India Expedition of 1935 under De Terra were recovered from the Chinji beds southwest of Ramnagar. Specimen — 600 is now in the Yale Peabody Museum, while the other three are in the Geological Survey of India Museum, Calcutta. All specimens are isolated molars.

The seventh find, which consists of an isolated left lower molar of *Dryopithecus* (previously assigned to *Sivapithecus darwini*), was collected by Bose from Dal Sar, a site two kilometers north of Ramnagar.

Nature of Siwalik Hominoid finds

These finds are generally in the form of isolated teeth and broken maxillary and mandibular fragments. The extreme rarity of upper dentition is difficult to explain. Postcranial material is totally absent. It has been suggested recently that the anthropoid apes of the Siwaliks were victims of hyaenodonts (Prasad 1964: 125). Hyaenodont bones are concentrated in the same localities and horizons in which primates are found. The fragmentary condition of the primate mandibles and maxillae may be due to mastication by hyenas and other carnivorous beasts.

New Hominoid Fossils

Prasad (1962, 1964) collected primate fossils near Haritalyangar. His finds are now in the Geological Survey of India (GSI) Museum at Calcutta. Prasad described the following eleven specimens:

1. GSI 18039. A left mandibular ramus with M_1, M_2, M_3, P_4, alveolus of the canine, and I_1,I_2. The molars and premolars are in position and show an advanced degree of wear. *Sivapithecus aiyengari.*

2. GSI 18040. A fragment of a mandible of an old individual containing M_2 and M_3 with roots firmly in the base of the jaw. *Sivapithecus indicus.*

3. GSI 18041. Single molar, M_1. *Sivapithecus salmontanus.*

4. GSI 18042. Single molar, M_1. *Sivapithecus sivalensis.*

5. GSI 18064 Fragment of a maxilla containing three molars. The M^1 and M^2 are partly worn, therefore details of cusps not clear. The M^3 is well preserved. *Sivapithecus sivalensis.*

6. GSI 18065. An upper right premolar. This is of special importance because most of the other dental material recovered belongs to the lower portion. *Sivapithecus indicus.*

7. GSI 18066. An upper canine from Nagri beds. *Sivapithecus indicus*.

8. GSI 18067. Practically unworn lower right third molar from Nagri beds, east of *Haritalyangar. Sugrivapithecus gregoryi*.

9. GSI 18068. Isolated upper third molar recovered from the Hari escarpment. It is moderately worn but details are clear. *Dryopithecus punjabicus*.

10. GSI 18069. Last lower premolar. *Sivapithecus sivalensis*.

11. GSI 18070. Isolated molar. *Sivapithecus*.

The nearly complete mandible of a loris that I found in 1959 in the Haritalyangar area has not yet been described. The specimen belongs to the Geological Department, Punjab University, Chandigarh.

The almost complete mandible of *Gigantopithecus bilaspurensis* (Chandigarh — Yale Project Register Number 359/68) consists of both horizontal rami of the mandible joined at the symphysis. It contains the left C_1, P_3, and M_{1-3} and the right C_1, P_{3-4}, and M_{1-3}. The horizontal rami are broken off just posterior to the third molars. The specimen belongs to the Department of Anthropology, Punjab University, Chandigarh. It is claimed to be the most complete pre-Pleistocene hominoid mandible ever found in the Indian subcontinent (Simons and Chopra 1969a). It is supposed to have come from the upper levels of the Dhok Pathan beds northwest of Haritalyangar, and thus to be of Middle Pliocene age. But the circumstances of its discovery have not yet been fully described. During my visit to Haritalyangar in May, 1971, I was informed that this specimen had been discovered by a peasant who kept it in an obscure niche in his house and forgot it. When approached by members of the research team, he sold the specimen for a meager amount of money. If this is true, I wonder how one can be sure of its geological horizon.

In summary, there is a published record of thirteen new specimens of hominoid from Haritalyangar discovered between 1951 and 1973. Before that, eighty-two primate specimens were recorded from the Siwalik beds (Wadia and Aiyengar 1938). To these we may add the two primate specimens that were discovered in the old Siwalik collection at the Yale Peabody Museum — YPM 19134 and YPM 16919. Therefore, we have a total of ninety-seven primate specimens from the Siwalik on record.

Revised Classification of Siwalik Finds

Clearly, an excessive amount of splitting of Siwalik genera and species has occurred. The ninety-seven primate finds from the Siwaliks have been categorized into fourteen genera and thirty-one species (Table 4)[3] — one genus and one species of Lorisidae, four genera and five species of Cercopithecidae, and nine genera and twenty-five species of Pongidae. *Dryopithecus* was supposed to contain seven species; *Sivapithecus*, five species; *Ramapithecus*, two species; *Bramapithecus*, three species; and *Sugrivapithecus*, two species. Obviously, something was drastically wrong with the early nomenclature and taxonomy of Siwalik primates. It was long recognized that

[3]Different authors have given different estimates of Siwalik primate genera and species. Colbert (1935) listed thirteen genera and twenty-nine species. Wadia and Aiyangar (1938) counted eleven genera and twenty-one species, and Wadia (1957: 370) mentioned fifteen genera of primates, including anthropoid apes.

Table 4 Fossil primates of the Siwalik Hills (India)

	Lower Siwaliks		Middle Siwaliks		Upper Siwaliks		
	Kamlial	Chinji	Nagri	Dhok Patan	Tatrot	Pinjor	Boulder Conglomerate
LORISIDAE							
1. *Indraloris Lulli* (Lewis), 1933			X				
CERCOPITHECIDAE							
2. *Papio falconeri* (Lydekker), 1886					X		
3. *Papio subhimalayanus* (V. Meyer), 1886					X		
4. *Cercopithecus hasnoti* (Pilgrim), 1910			X				
5. *Semonpithecus palaeindicus* (Lydekker), 1864							
6 *Macacus sivalensis* (Lydekker), 1878			X				
PONGIDAE							
7. *Simla of satyrus*(Linnaeus), 1866					X		
8. *Dryopithecus punjabicus* (Pilgrim), 1910		*X*	X				
9. *Dryopithecus pilgrimi* (Brown, Gregory, and Hellman), 1924		X					
10. *Dryopithecus cautleyi* (Brown, Gregory), 1924							
11. *Dryopithecus frickae* (Brown, Gregory, and Hellman), 1924							
12. *Dryopithecus chinjiensis* (Pilgrim), 1915		X		X			
13. *Dryopithecus giganteus* (Pilgrim), 1915			X				
14. *Dryopithecus sivalensis* (Lewis), 1934			X				
15. *Sivapithecus orientalis* (Pilgrim), 1927			X				
16. *Sivapithecus himalayensis* (Pilgrim), 1927			X				
17. *Sivapithecus aiyengari* (Prasad), 1962		X					
18. *Sivapithecus indicus* (Pilgrim), 1910		X					
19. *Hylopithecus hysudricus* (Pilgrim), 1927			X				
20. *Palaeopithecus(?) sylvaticus* (Pilgrim), 1927			X				
21. *Palaeopithecus sivalensis* (Lydekker), 1879			X				
22. *Palaeopithecus* sp. (Pilgrim), 1913				X			
23. *Palaeosimia rugosidens* (Pilgrim), 1915		X					
24. *Ramapithecus brevirostris* (Lewis), 1934			X				
25. *Ramapithecus hariensis* (Lewis), 1934			*X*				
26. *Sugrivapithecus salmontanus* (Lewis), 1934			X				
27. *Sugrivapithecus gregoryi* (Lewis), 1936			X				
28. *Bramapithecus thorpei* (Lewis), 1934		X					
29. *Bramapithecus sivalensis* (Lewis), 1934				X			
30. *Bramapithecus punjabicus* (Lewis), 1934							
31. *Gigantopithecus bilaspurensis* (Simons and Chopra), 1968							

considerable synonymity exists among the forms, but the problems of correlating specimens and reducing the synonymity were left by earlier workers for a future time when more complete material might be available.

Gregory, Hellman, and Lewis (1938) began this task and reduced the Siwalik pongids to four genera and ten species. In 1965, Simons and Pilbeam suggested a revised classification of the African and Indian material. The African genera and species involved in this new taxonomic assignment were *Proconsul* species, *Sivapithecus africanus*, and *Kenyapithecus wickeri*. Most of the celebrated Siwalik genera and species disappear and are mainly amalgamated with *Dryopithecus*. *Sivapithecus* no longer has generic rank and is no longer considered to be near the line of human descent. It is now only a subgenus of *Dryopithecus*. Similarly, *Sugrivapithecus* is transferred to *Dryopithecus*. The genus Bramapithecus (with its three species — *B. thorpei, B. punjabicus,* and *B. sivalensis)*, the African species *Kenyapithecus wickeri,* and *Dryopithecus punjabicus* are all considered hominid and are classified under *Ramapithecus* (Simons 1961). They are now junior synonyms of Ramapithecus punjabicus (the generic name comes from Lewis's *Ramapithecus brevirostris* and the specific name from Pilgrim's *Dryopithecus punjabicus*). *Sivapithecus aiyengari* (Prasad 1962) is also considered an invalid name.The specimen on which Prasad established this species belonged to an old individual; the canine is absent and the alveolus is filled in with cancellous bone. It belonged to *Dryopithecus aiyengari* (Simons 1967: 330). Thus Simons and Pilbeam (1965) classified all African and Siwalik material into two genera — *Dryopithecus* and *Ramapithecus*. *Dryopithecus* includes *Sugrivapithecus* and *Sivapithecus* and is considered to be an ape in the *Pongidae*. *Bramapithecus* is sunk into *Ramapithecus*, along with the African *Kenyapithecus wickeri*. *Ramapithecus* is considered to be the earliest known hominid, living twelve to eight million years ago in late Miocene or early Pliocene times in Africa and India.

Ramapithecus — The earliest Hominid

Before 1960, Ramapithecus was considered to be the most manlike of the Siwalik pongids, but no more than that. In 1961, Simons began to rehabilitate this genus to its true position. In 1934, Lewis had emphasized its hominid characters, but had classified it under the family Simidae, appending "(Hominidae?)" cautiously. Gregory, Hellman, and Lewis (1938) stated that "while the Siwalik genus *Ramapithecus* and the South African *Australopithecus* are still apes, by definition, they are almost on the human threshold in their known anatomical characters." Hrdlicka (1935), however, thought that *Ramapithecus* was a pongid. His opinion carried weight at that time, so that the importance of *Ramapithecus* was forgotten until Simons (1961) again called attention to its hominid features. Simons also discovered specimens that actually belonged to *Ramapithecus* but were wrongly assigned to other genera.

The specimens which have been said to belong to Ramapithecus are:

1.YPM 13799. A right maxilla and premaxillae with dentition. This was a type specimen on which Lewis established the species *Ramapithecus brevirostris*. It was recovered in 1932 from the Nagri beds at

Chakrana, four miles east of Haritalyangar, northwest of Bilaspur, Himachal Pradesh, India.

2. YPM 13806; YPM 13814; YPM 13833. These three specimens in the Yale collection are mandibular fragments with molars intact. Lewis (1934) established *Bramapithecus* species on this material. They are now regarded as representing the lower jaws of *Ramapithecus*. The genus *Bramapithecus* is not considered valid and, therefore, stands abolished.

3. GSI D. 118, D.119. The right and left mandibular rami of the same mandible recovered from Chinji beds. It was a type specimen on which pilgrim in 1910 established the species *Dryopithecus punjabicus*.

4. GSI D.185. A right maxilla recovered from Haritalyangar, Nagri beds, Bilaspur. It is a co-type of *Dryopithecus punjabicus*, established by Pilgrim in 1910. Simons (1964) diagnosed it as *Ramapithecus*.

5. GSI 18068. Isolated upper third molar from Nagri beds from Haritalyangar. Discovered by Prasad and assigned to *Dryopithecus punjabicus* (Prasad 1962)

6. NMK FT 1272. A left maxilla with canine, roots of P^3, and crown of P^4 to M^2.

NMK FT 1271. A right maxilla with M^1, M^2, and roots of M^3, and a right to M_2.

These two maxillae were made the type specimens of the new genus and species *Kenyapithecus wickeri* established by Leakey (1962).

Based on the above material, particularly after the transfer of the type and co-type specimens of Pilgrim's *Dryopithecus punjabicus*, the new name *Ramapithecus punjabicus* Pilgrim 1910 was coined as a binomen of the new species. The following species are now considered junior synonyms of *R.punjabicus:*

1. *Ramapithecus brevirostris,* Lewis (1934: 162)
2. *Bramapithecus thorpei,* Lewis (1934: 173)
3. *Bramapithecus sivalensis,* Lewis (1934: 173)
4. *Kenyapithecus wickeri, Leakey* (1962: 690)
5. *Dryopithecus punjabicus,* Pilgrim (1910: 63)

The specimens previously assigned to the species *Ramapithecus* but now considered not to belong to it are:

1. YPM 13807. Type specimen of the species *R. hariensis* Lewis (1934). It consists of a distorted maxillary fragment with worn M^1 and fractured and broken M^2. In 1937 lewis transferred this specimen to *Sivapithecus sivalensis,* later regarded as *D.(S.) sivalensis* by Simons and Pilbeam (1965). It is a fragmentary specimen and therefore its exact position is difficult to determine (Pilbeam 1969: 100). Simons (1961) indicated the heteromorphic nature of its lower premolars, more characteristic of pongids than of hominids.

2. GSI D. 168 (YPM 13870 cast). A right horizontal mandibular ramus having crowns of P_3 to P_4 and the canine and incisor alvoeli. Gregory, Hellman, and Lewis (1938) assigned it to *Ramapithecus.* Simons (1964) and Simon and Pilbeam (1965) consider it to be a pongid because of the presence of a simian shelf and heteromorphy in the lower premolars.

Lewis (1934) gave the following diagnostic features of Ramapithecus:

1. Dental arcade of the upper jaw that is parabolic, as in man, rather than U-shaped, as in apes.
2. Face slightly prognathous.
3. Absence of diastema in the dental series.
4. Small canine.
5. Antero-posteriorly compressed dentition.
6. Incisors approximately equal in size.

7. Canine ellipsoid with long axis normal to the curve of the dental arcade.
8. Third premolar and succeeding teeth progressive.

Simons and Pilbeam (1965) gave the following generic diagnosis of *Ramapithecus,* pointing out the main features in which it differs from *Australopithecus* and *Dryopithecus:*

Slightly smaller overall size [except Proconsul africanus, which they renamed *Dryopithecus africanus*], shallower mandible, less complex patterns of tooth crenulation, little or no evidence of cingula or Carabellis'cusps and shorter face. Incisors and canines reduced in relation to cheek-tooth size when compared to *Dryopithecus* but not as markedly as in *Austropithecus*; incisor procumbancy intermediate. Differs from *Dryopithecus* and other apes in showing more widely spaced and much lower molar cusps, so that the central or occlusal fovea of the molars covers more of the crown surface of the tooth (even so these features show some variability in *Ramapithecus* and *Dryopithecus* as well as in modern *Homo* and *Pan*); sides of the upper molars, particularly, are more vertical; also differs from *Dryopithecus* in showing a larger and lower canine fossa, an arched palate, arcuate tooth row and a much shorter rostrum.

Leakey (1967) did not consider this generic definition to be satisfactory because body size, shallower palate, and shorter face are not taxonomically sound characters. He maintained that *Kenyapithecus wickeri* was a separate species and could not be sunk in *Ramapithecus.* He also transferred BMNH M-16649, the type specimen of his *Sivapithecus africanus*, to *Kenyapithecus* as *K. africanus,* a species that he regarded as ancestral to *K. wickeri.* To Leakey, *K. africanus* is the earliest hominid. Pilbeam (1969) considered Leakey's arguments to be "armchair juggling" and therefore dismissed them. Campbell (1966) and LeGros Clark (1964a) accepted the synonymy of *Kenyapithecus wickeri* and *Ramapithecus punjabicus*.

Ramapithecus occurred in Europe, China, Africa, and India. The right M^2 from the Pontian of Melchingen Württemberg in the Swabian Alps of Europe and attributed to *Dryopithecus fontani* by Branco (1898) shows features of *Ramapithecus* (Simons 1964). It occurs in late Miocene deposits. Woo (1958) described the type specimen of *Dryopithecus keiyuanensis* from deposits of uncertain age in Keiyuan, Yunan, China. But Chow (1958) believes that one of the two Chinese finds should be assigned to *Ramapithecus punjabicus*. However, until there is further detailed investigation, the allocation remains uncertain.

In summary, the following points emerge about *Ramapithecus*:

1. It was a *Pan*-sized primate with a short face, arcuate palate, and an *Australopithecus*-like mandible. Dental and facial features resemble very closely those of *Australopithecus africanus*.
2. Circumstantial evidence suggests that *Ramapithecus punjabicus* might have been a tool-using animal and a partial biped.
3. It lived fourteen to fifteen million years ago, in the late Miocene/early Pliocene period.
4. Ramapithecus was a wide-ranging and mobile creature and was present in India, East Africa, Europe, and China.

Gigantopithecus — A new species from Siwalik

The mandible of *Gigantopithecus bilaspurensis* was obtained originally in three pieces. It was identified by G. W. Meyer, co-investigator of the Punjab-Yale University project.[4] Its main diagnostic feature are:

1. Mandible is smaller in absolute size than available mandibles of *G. blacki*.
2. Anterior teeth are relatively smaller than those of *G. blacki*.
3. Teeth preserved (C through M^3) are little worn and do not show the polycuspidation that *G.blacki* teeth do.
4. In this simplicity of teeth, *G. bilaspurensis* resembles some *Dryopithecus* species, e.g. *D. sivalensis* and *D. indicus*.
5. Lower molar protoconids are smaller than metaconids and apexes of lower molar cusps are placed laterally. In this feature the molars are unlike those of *G. blacki* and *D. indicus* but resemble those of Ramapithecus.
6. Cheek-tooth occlusal faces show lingual and labial expansion, so that the sides of the teeth are oriented almost vertically. In this feature too, they resemble Ramapithecus. In *Dryopithecus* and *G.blacki* the sides of the teeth are rounded.
7. Unlike *G. blacki molars*, those of *G. bilaspurensis* are not clearly divided into trigonid and talonid portions by a lingual indentation between the metaconid and entoconid.

There have been two main opinions regarding the phyletic relationship of *Gigantopithecus*. One school considers this genus to be an aberrant pongid with some changes in dental morphology as a result of either (1) adaptation to a new manner of feeding or (2) allometric changes to its large absolute size. According to the second school, the correct placement of the genus is in Hominidae as (1) ancestral to later hominids or (2) an extinct side branch of the Hominidae that lived in Southeast Asia contemporaneously with *Australopithecus* and/or *Homo*. Weidenreich (1946), von Koenigswald (1949, 1952, 1958), Heberer (1959), Dart (1960), and Woo (1962) advocated the placement of *Gigantopithecus* in Hominidae, while Pei and Woo (1956), Pei and Li (1959), Remane (1950, 1960), Ti-Cheng (1962), and Simons and Pilbeam (1965) thought that it belonged to the Pongidae.

Gigantopithecus bilaspurensis was undoubtedly a very large primate. It is smaller than the Chinese Pleistocene species of *Gigantopithecus*, but it has larger premolars and molars than most other hominoids. In many characters this specimen bears more similarity to *Australopithecus, Ramapithecus*, and *Dryopithecus* than to *Gigantopithecus blacki*. It has been suggested (Simons and Chopra 1969b: 1) that although *Gigantopithecus* is far from the line of human ancestry, and that this feature might have arisen in parallel with the similar mandibular and dental mechanics of *Ramapithecus*. Thus, *Gigantopithecus bilaspurensis* is thought to represent a side branch of Asian apes which achieved a dental mechanism closely approximating that of hominids. This ape lived in open country and

[4]The program has ceased to operate. I regret that this promising international collaboration has come to such a sorry end and that the jaw of an ape should have become a bone of contention, leading to acrimony and mistrust between two parties of rational men.

its ancestor might have been a gorilla-like forest dweller similar to *Dryopithecus indicus* (Simons and Chopra 1969b).

Summary

1. To date, ninety-seven primate specimens from the Siwalik foothills of the Himalayas have been discovered.
2. In age they extend from Lower Siwalik to Upper Siwalik, i.e., from middle Miocene to early Pliocene.
3. In the literature these specimens have been classified in fourteen genera and thirty-one species.
4. The Siwalik primate fossils generally consist of mandibular and maxillary fragments, isolated teeth, and molars. Upper dentition is very rare. No cranial or limb bones have been recovered.
5. The family Pongidae includes such genera as *Dryopithecus, Sivapithecus, Bramapithecus, Ramapithecus,* and *Sugrivapithecus.*
6. In a revised classification (Simnons and Pilbeam 1965), only two Siwalik genera are considered valid. viz., *Dryopithecus* and *Ramapithecus.*
7. *Sivapithecus* was once thought to be nearest to the line of human descent (Pilgrim 1910, 1915, 1927), and it held separate generic rank. Now it is reduced to a subgenus of *Dryopithecus* in the family Pongidae.
8. *Ramapithecus* is considered to be the only known late Miocene/early Pliocene hominid and the forerunner of man. It is a separate genus in the Hominidae. *Ramapithecus punjabicus* lived in India fourteen to eight million years ago, from upper Miocene to early Pliocene.
9. *Bramapithecus* (Lewis 1934), *Dryopithecus sivalensis* (Pilgrim 1910), and *Kenyapithecus wickeri* (Leakey 1962) are now considered to be synonyms of *Ramapithecus punjabicus* in the Simons and Pilbeam classification.
10. An almost complete mandible representing a new species, *Gigantopithecus bilaspurensis,* was discovered in 1968. It is thought to resemble species of *Australapithecus, Ramapithecus,* and *Dryopithecus* more than it does the Chinese Pleistocene species *Gigantopithecus blacki.*
11. A future problem for investigators in the Siwalik Hillis is to find cranial and postcranial bones of *Ramapithecus.* This will help to elucidate the evolution of erect posture, locomotion, behaviour, and most important, the capacity to make tools.
12. An attempt should be made to fix age of different Siwalik beds by radiometric method so that their correlation could be done more confidently. Faunal correlations between mammals of Africa and India would then be more meaningful.*

REFERENCES

Branco, W., 1898, Die menschenänlichen Zähne aus dem Bohnerz der Schwäbischen Alp. *Jahreshefte des Vereins für Vaterländische Naturkunde in Württemberg* 54:1–144.

Brown, Barnum, W.K. Gregory, Milo Hellman, 1924, On three incomplete anthropoid jaws from the Siwaliks, India. *American Museum Novitates* 130.

Campbell, B., 1966, *Human Evolution.* Chicago: Aldine.

Cautley, P.T., H. Falconer, 1868, "Notice on the remains of a fossil monkey from the Tertiary state of the Siwalik Hills," in *Palaeontological memoirs and notes of H. Falconer* 1. *Edited by C. Murchison, 292–297.* London: Hardwicke.

Chow, M.C., 1958, Mammalian faunas and

correlations of Tertiary and early Pleistocene of South China. *Journal of the Paleontological Society of India* 3:123–130.

Colbert, Edwin H., 1935, Siwalik mammals in the American Museum of Natural History. *Transactions of the American Philosophical Society*, n.s. 26: 1–69, 378–398.

Dart, R., 1960, The status of *Gigantopithecus, anthropologischer Anzeiger* 24: 139–145.

De Terra, H., 1936, Geological factors determining higher anthropoid evolution in India. *American Journal of Physical Anthropology* 21:8.

Falconer, H., 1837, Note on the occurrence of fossil bones in the Siwalik range, eastward of Hardwar. *Journal of the Asiatic Society of Bengal* 6:233–234.

———, 1859, *Descriptive catalogue of the fossil remains of vertebrates from the Siwalik Hills, the Nerbudda, Perim Island, etc. in the Museum of the Asiatic Society of Bengal.* Calcutta.

———, 1868, *Palaeontological memoirs and notes of H. Falconer,* volumes one and two, Edited by C. Murchison, London: Hardwicke.

Falconer, H., P.T. Cautley, 1836a, *Sivatherium giganteum:* a new fossil ruminant genus from the valley of the Markanda in the Siwalik branch of the sub-Himalayan mountains. *Asiatic Researches* 19:1–24.

———, 1836a, *Sivatherium giganteum:* a new fossil ruminant genus from the valley of the Markanda in the Siwalik branch of the sub-Himalyan mountains. *Asiatic Researches* 19:1–24.

———, 1836b, Note on the fossil hippopotamus of the Siwalik Hills. *Asiatic Researches* 19:39–53.

———, 1846–1849, *Fauna antique sivalensis,* parts one through nine. London: Smith and Elder.

Gaudry, A., 1890, Le Dryopithèque. *Société Géologique de France. Memoranda* 1:5–11.

Gregory, W.K., Milo Hellman, 1926, The dentition of *Dryopithecus* and the origin of man. *Anrthropological Papers of the American Museum of Natural History* 28:1–23.

Gregory, W.K., Milo Helman, G.E. Lewis, 1938, *Fossil anthropoids of the Yale-Cambridge India Expedition of 1935.* Carnegie Institution of Washington Publication 495:1–27.

Heberer, G., 1959, The descent of man and the present fossil record. *Cold Spring Harbor Symposium on Quantitative Biology* 24:235–244.

Hoouer, D.A., 1951, Questions relating to a new large anthropoid ape from the Mio-Pliocene of the Siwaliks. *American Journal of Physical Anthropology* 9:79–95.

Hopwood, A.T., 1933a, Miocene primates from Kenya. *Journal of the Proceedings of the Linnaean Society of London* 38:437–464.

———, 1933b, Miocene primates from British East Africa. *Annals and Magazine of Natural History,* series 10, 11:96–98.

Hrdlicka, A., 1935, Yale fossils of anthropoid apes. *American Journal of Science, series* 5, 29:34–40.

Khatri, A.P., 1964, Recent exploration of the remains of early man in India. *Asian Perspectives* 7:160–182.

Krishanan, M.S., N.K.N. Aiyengar, 1940, Did the Indobrahm or Siwalik River exist? *Records of the Geological Survey of India* 75:1–24.

Leakey, L.S.B., 1943, A Miocene anthropoid mandible from Rusinga, Kenya. *Nature* 152:319–320.

———, 1959, A new fossil skull from Olduvai. *Nature* 194:491–493.

———, 1960, *Adam's ancestors* (fourth edition). New York: Harper and Row.

———, 1962, A new Lower Pliocene fossil primate from Kenya. *Annals and Magazine of Natural History,* series 13, 4:689–969.

———, 1963, "East African fossil Hominoidea and the classification within this super-family," in *Classification and human evolution.* Edited by S.L. Washburn, 32–49. Chicago: Aldine.

———, 1966, Homo habilis, Homo erectus and the australopithecines. *Nature* 209:1279–1281.

———, 1967, An early Miocene member of Hominidae. *Nature* 213:155–163.

———, 1972, "*Homo sapiens* in the Middle Pleistocene and the evidence of *Homo sapiens* evolution," in *The origin of Homo sapiens.* United Nations Educational. Scientific and Cultural Organization, Ecology and Conservation Series 3:25–29. Paris.

Leakey, L.S.B., J.F. Evernden, G.H. Curtis, 1961, Age of Bed I, Olduvai Gorge, Tanganyika. *Nature* 191:478–479.

Leakey, L.S.B., M.D. Leakey, 1964, Recent discoveries of fossil hominids in Tanganyika at Olduvai and near Lake Natron. *Nature 202:5–7.*

Leakey, L.S.B., P.V. Tobias, J.R. Napier, 1964, A new species of genus *Homo* from Olduvai. *Nature* 202:7–9.

Leakey, M.D., 1971, *Olduvai Gorge: excavations in Beds I and II (1960–1963).* London: Cambridge University Press.

Le Gros Clark, W.E., 1964a, *The fossil evidence for human evolution.* Second edition. Chicago: University of Chicago Press.

———, 1964b, The evolution of man. *Discovery* (London) 25:49.

———, 1967, *Man-apes or ape-men? The story of discoveries in Africa.* New York: Holt, Rinehart and Winston.

Le Gros clark, W.E., L.S.B. Leakey, 1951, The Miocene Hominoidea of East Africa. *Fossil Mammals of Africa* 1:1–117. London: British Museum (Natural History).

Lewis, G.E., 1933, Preliminary notice of a new genus of lemuroid from the Siwaliks. *American Journal of Science,* series 5, 27:134–138.

———, 1934, Preliminary notice of new man-like apes from India. *American Journal of Science,* series 5, 27:161–179.

———, 1936, A new species of *Sugrivapithecus. American Journal of Science,* series 5, 31:450–452.

———, 1937, Taxonomic syllabus of Siwalik fossil anthropoids. *American Journal of Science,* series 5, 35:139–147.

Lydekker, R., 1880, Siwalik and Narbada Probscidia. *Palaeontologia Indica,* series 10, 1(5):182–292, plates 29–46.

———, 1882, Siwalik and Narbada Equidae. *Palaeontologia Indica,* Series 10, 2(3):67–98, plates 11–15.

———, 1884a, Siwalik and Narbada Carnivora, *Palaeontologia Indica,* series 10, 2(6):179–363, plates 26–45.

———, 1884b, Siwalik and Narbada Bunodont Suina. *Palaeontologia Indica,* series 10, 3(2):35–104, plates 6–12.

———, 1886, The fauna of the Karnul caves. *Palaeontologia Indica,* series 10, 4(2): volumes 1–4 *passim.*

Macinnes, D.G., 1943, Notes on the East African Miocene primates. *East Africa and Uganda Natural History Society Journal* 17:141–181.

Mathew, W.D., 1924., Fossil animals of India. *Natural History, 208–214.*

Napier, J.R., 1963a, Brachiation and brachiators. *Zoological Society of London Symposium* 10:183–195.

———, 1963b, "The locomotor function of hominids," in *Classification and human evolution.* Edited by S.L. Washburn, 178–189. Chicago: Aldine.

———, 1967, Evolutionary aspects of primate locomotion. *American Journal of Physical Anthropology,* n.s. 27:333–343.

Napier, J.R., A.C. Walker, 1967, Vertical clinging and leaping — a newly recognized category of locomotor behaviour of primates. *Folia Primatologica* 6:204–219.

Pascoe, E.H., 1919, The early history of the Indus, Brahmaputra, and Ganges. *Quarterly Journal of the Geological Society of London 75:138–155.*

Pei, W.C., Y.H. Lt., 1959, Discovery of a third mandible of *Gigantopithecus* in Liu-Cheng, Kwangsi, South China. *Vertebrata Palasiatica* 2:193–200.

Pei, W.C., J.K. Woo, 1956, New materials of *Gigantopithecus* teeth from South China. *Acta Palaeontologica* 4:477–490.

Pilbeam, D.R., 1966, Notes on *Ramapithecus,* the earliest known hominid, and *Dryopithecus. American Journal of Physical Anthropology* 25:1–25.

———, 1967, Man's earliest ancestors. *Science Journal* 3(2): 47–53.

———, 1968, The earliest hominids. *Nature* 219:1335–1338.

———, 1969, Teritiary Pongidae of East Africa: evolutionary relationship and taxonomy. *Bulletin of the Peabody Museum* 31:1–185. New Haven: Yale University.

Pilbeam, D.R., E.L. Simons, 1965, Some problems of hominid classification. *American Scientist* 53(2):237–259.

Pilgrim, G.E., 1910, Notices of new mammalian genera and species from the Tertiaries of India. *Records of the Geological Survey of India* 40: 53–71.

———, 1915, New Siwalik primates and their bearing on the question of evolution of man and Anthropoidea. *Records of the Geological Survey of India* 45:1–74.

———, 1919, The Siwalik River. *Journal of the Asiatic Society of Bengal,* n.s. 15:81–99.

———, 1927, A *sivapithecus* palate and other primate

fossils from India. *Palaeontologia Indica,* n.s. 14:1–25.

Prasad, K.N., 1962, Fossil primates from the Siwalik beds of Haritalyangar, Himachal Pradesh, India. *Journal of the Geological Society of India* 3:86–96.

———, 1964, Upper Miocene anthropoids from the Siwalik beds of Haritalyangar, Himachal Pradesh, India. *Palaeontology* 7:124–134. London.

Remane, A., 1950, "Bemerkungen über *Gigantopithecus blacki,*" *in Über die neun Vor- und Frühmenschenfunde aus Afrika, Java, China, and Frankreich.* Edited by H. Weinert, 113–148. *Zeitschrift für Morphologie und Anthropologie* 42.

———, 1960, Die Stellung von *Gigantopithecus. Anthropologischer Anzeiger* 24(2–3):146–159.

Robinson, J.T., 1963a, "Adaptive radiation in the australopithecines and the origin of man." in *African ecology and human evolution.* Edited by F.C. Howell and F. Bourlière, 385–416. Chicago: Aldine.

———, 1963b, Australopithecines, culture and phylogeny, *American Journal of Physical Anthropology,* 21:595–605.

Simons, E.L., 1961, The phyletic position of *Ramapithecus. Postilla* 51:1–9.

———, 1963, Some fallacies in the study of hominid phylogeny. *Science* 141:879–889.

———, 1964, On the mandible of *Ramapithecus. National Academy of Science Proceedings* 51; 528–535.

———, 1965, New fossil apes from Egypt and the initial differentiation of Hominoidea. *Nature* 205:135–139.

———, 1967, The earliest apes. *Scientific American* 217:28–35.

———, 1968, A source of dental comparison of *Ramapithecus* with *Australopithecus* and *Homo. South African Journal of Science* 64:92–112.

Simons, E.L., S.R.K. Chopra, 1969a, A preliminary announcement of a new *gigantopithecus* species from India. *Proceedings of the Second International Congress of Primatology, Atlanta, Gerogia, 1968* 2:135–142. Basel: Karger.

———, 1969b, *Gigantopithecus* (Pongidae, Hominoidea): a new species from North India. *Postilla* 138:1–8.

Simons, E.L., D.R. Pilbeam, 1965, Preliminary revision of the Dryopithecinae (Pongidae, Anthropoidea). *Folia Primatologica* 3:81–152.

Tattersali, I.M., 1968, A mandible of Indraloris (Primates, Lorisidae) from the Miocene of India. *Postilla* 123:1–10.

Tattersali, I.M., E.L. Simons, 1969, Notes on some little-known primate fossils from India. *Folia Primatologica* 10:146–153.

Ti-cheng, T., 1962, The taxonomic position of *Gigantopithecus* in Primates. *Vertebrata Palasiatica* 6:375–383.

Von Koenigswald, G.H.R., 1949, Bemerkungen über *"Dryopithecus" giganteus* Pilgrim. *Eclogae Geologicae Helvetiae* 42:515–519.

———, 1952, *Gigantopithecus blacki* von Koenigswald, a giant fossil hominoid from the Pleistocene of southern China, *Anthropological Papers of the American Museum of Natural History* 43:292–325.

———, 1957, Remarks on *Gigantopithecus* and other hominoid remains from southern China. *Proceedings of the Koninklijke Akademie van Wetenschappen, Amsterdam,* series B., 60(3): 153–159.

———, 1958, *Gigantopithecus* and *Australopithecus. The Leech* 28:101–105.

Wadia, D.N., 1957, *Geology of India. London:* Macmillan.

Wadia, D.N., N.K.N. Aiyengar, 1938, Fossil anthropoids of India: A list of the fossil material hitherto discovered from the Teritiary deposits of India. *Records of the Geological Survey of India* 72(4):467–494.

Weidenreich, F., 1946, *Apes, giants and men, Chicago*: University of Chicago Press.

Woo, J.K., 1958, New materials of *Dryopithecus* from Keiyuan, Yunan, *Vertebrata Palasiatica* 2(1):38–42.

———, 1962, The manidibles and dentition of *Gigantopithecus, Palaeontologia Sinica* 146:1–94.

**First published in Palaeo-Anthropology, Morphology, and Palaeo-Ecology, (Ed.) Russel H. Tuttle,* (Mouton Publishers, Hague)

— A.P. KHATRI

Hominid Fossils
(Stages of Human Evolution)

MAN, LIKE ALL OTHER BIOLOGICAL BEINGS, is a product of evolution. The story of his evolution is best documented in the form of fossilized bones. Since for the greater part of his history man was not burying his dead kins, the bones of dead humans were scavenged by carnivores and insects and destroyed by natural elements. Only occasionally when the bones got incorporated into alluvial, lacustrine, aeolian or cave sediments which were chemically suitable for their preservation did they get fossilized. For this reason the fossils of early humans are rare and they are found only in the form of individual bones and teeth and often in a damaged and fragmentary condition. Complete skeletons become available only after the practice of intentional burial came into existence around fifty thousand years ago. Further, in most cases the presence of fossils is known only when the sediments containing them have been exposed by natural erosion. Thus, discoveries of early fossils are rare and very valuable. Each find, therefore, constitutes an important link in the long chain of evolution.

Zoologically, man belongs to the Primate Order, which also includes apes and monkeys, to the Hominoidea Superfamily, which comprises apes and man, and to the Family Hominidae (hominids in popular English) which includes both living and extinct forms of man. Anatomically and genetically he is closer to the apes and among them closest to chimpanzee which along with gorilla is found only in Africa. Because of this closeness there is little doubt that the apes and man had a common ancestor. Apes flourished extensively in the warm tropical regions of Asia, Europe and Africa during the Miocene period which lasted from about 20 million to 5 million years ago. The better known ape forms of this period are Sivapithecus and Ramapithecus.

On the basis of the anatomical closeness of the apes and man, Charles Darwin, who propounded the theory of evolution, nearly one-and-a-half century ago, had predicted that the earliest ancestors of man are likely to be found in Africa, though the initial discoveries of human fossils were made in Europe and Asia. For several decades the cradle of mankind kept swinging between these two continents. But from the twenties of the twentieth century more and more early fossil finds have been made in Africa, starting from the Pliocene period which lasted from five million to two million years ago.

While other zoological families have several or many genera and species, the hominid family is represented only by two genera– *Australopithecus* and *Homo,* and only a few species in each genus. The *Australopithecus* genus became extinct about a million years ago. Similarly, two species of the genus *Homo* - *Homo habilis* and *Homo erectus*–became extinct in the past and today only one species– *Homo sapiens sapiens* survives. All the living humans belong to this species.

Man differs from other biological forms by his possession of culture. Biologically, he differs from other primates on account of his ability to stand and walk upright, his prehensile hands and larger brain. His earliest appearance in the fossil record can be detected on the basis of the presence of these attributes in the bones. Culturally, he can be identified in the archaeological record by the presence of tools, i.e., objects fashioned by man by modifying natural materials like stone, bone and wood for serving certain functions. In our present state of knowledge man as a biological creature appeared considerably earlier than man as a cultural being.

The earliest known hominid fossils belong to the genus *Australopithecus* and they date back to around four-and-a-half million years ago. Some six species of this genus are known. These are: *A. ramidus, A. afarensis, A. aethiopicus, A. africanus, A. boisei* and *A. robustus.* However, because of the limited quantity and fragmentary nature of fossil evidence there is no agreement among the anthropologists about the status of certain species. For example, many anthropologists consider *A. boisei* as a form of *A. roubustus* and not as an independent species.

At present *A. ramidus* is the oldest known hominid dating back to 4.4 million years. It is represented only by a few teeth and other fragmentary bones. The fossils were found in 1992 and 1993 by Gen Suwa of Tokyo University and Tim White of the University of California, Berkeley near a place called Aramis on the river Awash in northeastern Ethiopia. While little is known of the brain size and stature of the creature there are sufficient indications that it was more evolved than the apes and less evolved than *A. afarensis* or Lucy which until now was the oldest known ancestor. The discoverers claim that *ramidus* was the ancestor of *afarensis*. The fossil remains of Lucy were found by Donald Johanson in 1974 at Hadar, also on the Awash river in Ethiopia, and included pieces of the cranium, jaw, arm and leg bones and a part of the pelvis. These fossils are dated to around 3.5 million years. *Afarensis* fossils have also been found in Tanzania. The *afarensis* was ape-like in the form of the head and size of the brain but it walked on two legs like man. The anatomical evidence of bipedal gait is substantiated by the discovery by Mary Leakey of foot-prints at Laetoli in Tanzania.

The next stage is represented by *A. africanus* whose fossil remains, including complete skulls and jaws and other bones, have been found at a number of sites in south and east Africa, Its brain-size has been estimated at about 485 cc which is just a little more than that of a chimpanzee. In the structure of its face and teeth the africanus is more evolved than the *afarensis*. *A. africanus* lived between 3 and 2 million years ago. Another Australopithecus species, also found in south and east Africa, was *A. robustus* which is so named because it was more massively built and had powerful jaws and a much wider face. It had huge molars, some an inch across, adapted to chewing coarse plant matter. To support its powerful jaw muscles it sported a gorilla-like bony crest on the skull. *A. robustus* lived between 2.2 and 1.4 million years ago and eventually became extinct, perhaps due to competition by *A. africanus. A. boisei* found by L.S.B. and Mary Leakey at Olduvai in Tanzania is generally thought to be a variant of *A. robustus.* Gen Suwa and Tim White have recently suggested that both *A. robustus* and *A. boisei* were branches of another Australopithecus species *A. aethiopicus*, which branched off from *A. afarensis* around 3 million years ago.

A. afarensis led to the evolution of the genus Homo which is Latin for man and to which all living humans belong. *H. habilis* had a larger brain, ranging from 500 to 800 cc, and its hand bones show that it had the same manual dexterity as modern humans. However, the major claim of this species to the true human status is that it was the first hominid to make tools. These tools are small stone choppers made by removing a few flakes from cobbles. *H. habilis'* physical remains and tools have so far been found only in east Africa and they date between 2.2 and 1.6 million years.

H. habilis eventually evolved into *H. erectus* which is the first hominid to have migrated out of Africa and colonised large tracts of Europe and Asia. It had a much larger brain ranging from 900 to 1200 cc, very close to modern human. Other anatomical features distinguishing it from earlier hominid forms are considerably flattened face and prominent brow ridges. *H. erectus* made larger and more complex tools like handaxes and cleavers, was able to hunt large animals and controlled fire. It lived between 1.6 and 0.4 million years ago.

H. erectus led to the emergence of our own species, *H. sapiens* around 400,000 years ago. Its brain size was not appreciably larger than that of *H. erectus* but most of the skulls are nearer to the maximum of *H. erectus.* Other features distinguishing it from *H. erectus* are a more bulging forehead, less massive brow ridges and more angular eye sockets. *H. sapiens* enlarged its habitat and made significant advances in stone tool technology. The tools became smaller and thinner and show more economical use of the raw material. The archaic *H. sapiens* lived between 400,000 and 40,000 years ago.

Two sub-species are known in *H. sapiens,* namely *H. sapiens neanderthalensis* and *H. sapiens sapiens*. The Neanderthal species, for long thought to be representing a brutish form of humanity, appeared around 130,000 years ago and became extinct around 35,000 years ago. The Neanderthals had the same brain size as the modern humans, ranging between 1400 and 1800 cc but they differ from us in having more robustly built bones, prominent prognathism or forward projection of the face, more prominent brow ridges and more elongated skulls on the back.

They were the first hominids to have started burying their dead in graves, accompanied by rituals and grave goods, thus showing the emergence of belief in life after death and consciousness of 'spirituality'. A skeleton from Shanidar cave in lraq belongs to a man who suffered from arthritis from young age but lived up to the age of 45 years. This shows that by this stage humans had learnt to care for their disabled kins. Neanderthal burials have been found over a wide region, comprising southern Europe, northern Africa, the Near and Middle East, and Central Asia.

Homo sapien sapiens or the modern man, almost indistinguishable from us, appeared around 40,000 years ago. His skulls are characterized by the loss of prognathism and prominent brow-ridges and high-domed brain case. This species colonized islands in the Indian and Pacific oceans, including New Guinea and Australia as also the New World. It produced spectacular art in the form of sculpture, painting and engraving, and eventually learnt agriculture (cultivation of plants and domestication of animals) which led to many subsequent inventions and the establishment of civilization.

— V.N. MISRA

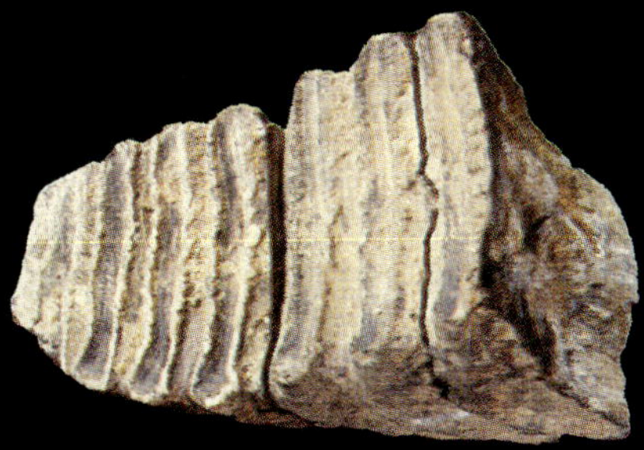

Narmada Valley : Molar segment of Elephus Namadicus, Mid-Pleistocene Period

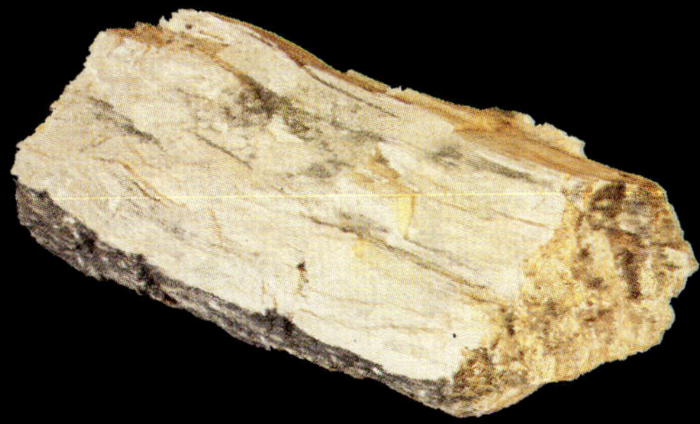

Akal, near Jaisalmer (Rajasthan) : Wood Fossil, 170 million years old

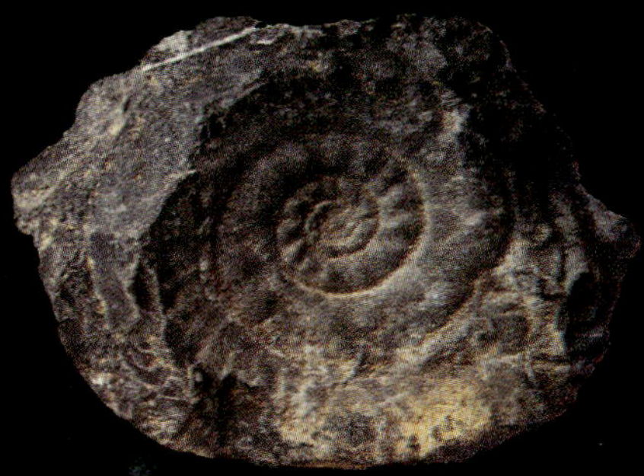

Amonite (Shell Fossil)

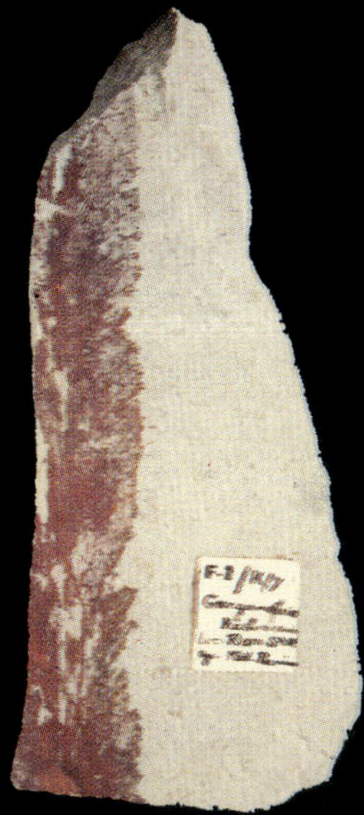

Kashmir, Risin Spur : Leaf Fossil (Gangamopteris Kashmirensis), Mid - Permian

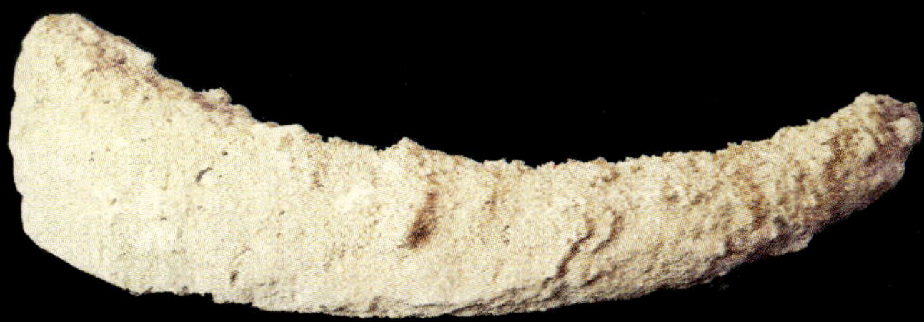

Narmada Valley: Tusk of Elephus Namadicus, Mid-Pleistocene Period

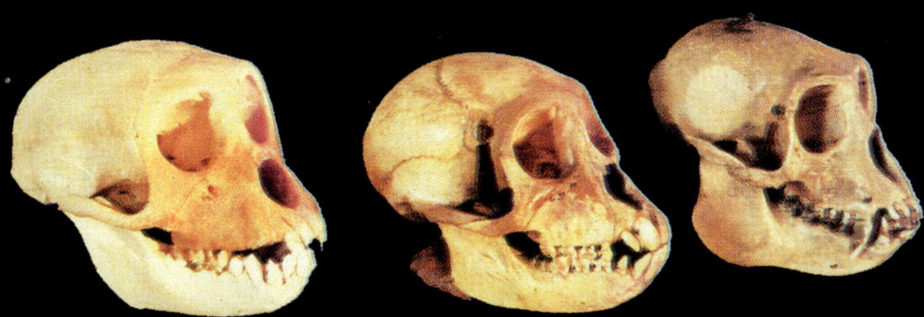

South East Asian Monkeys

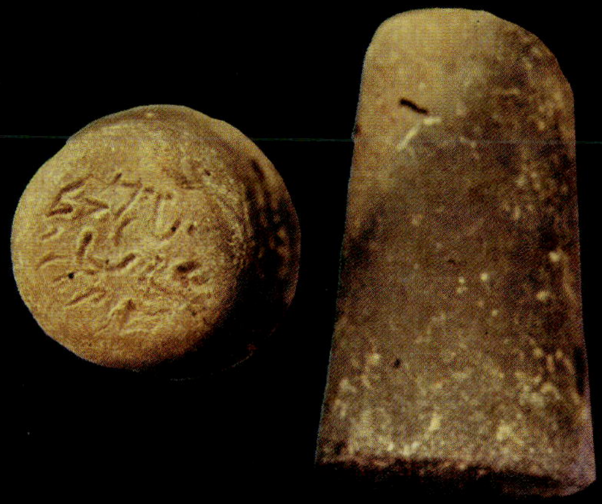

Kamrej: Terracotta inscribed seal, 1st-3rd century A.D.

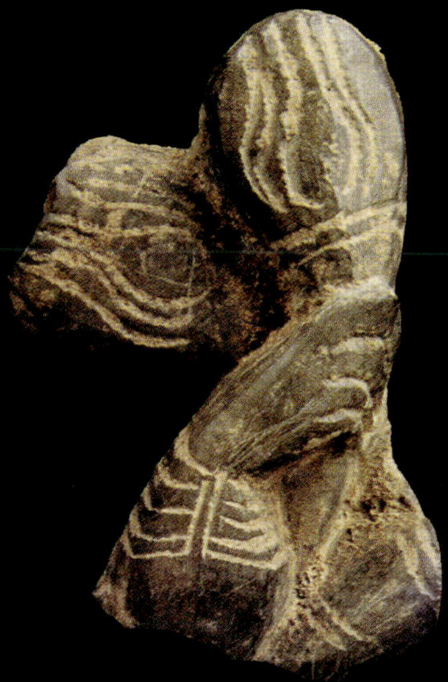

Kamrej: Stone sculpture, 1st-3rd century A.D.

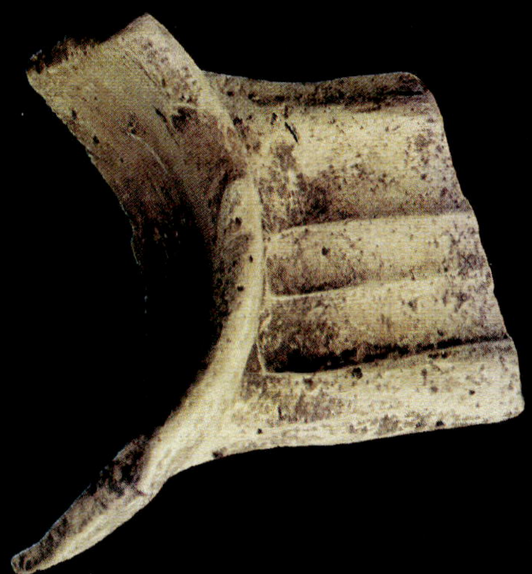

Kamrej: Handle of an amphora, 1st-3rd century A.D.

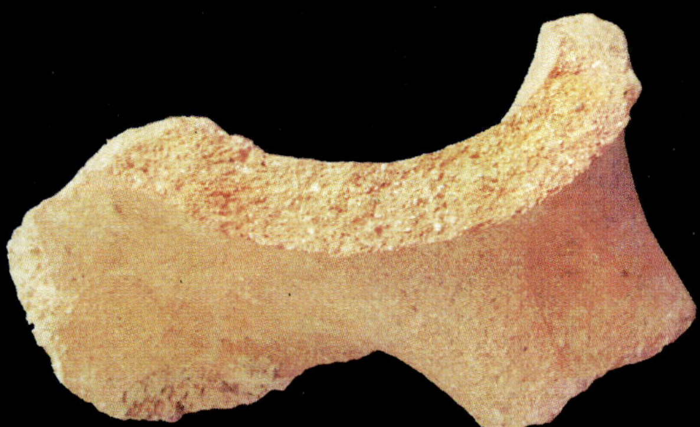

Kamrej: Amphora sherd, 1st-3rd century A.D.

The Pleistocene Mammalian Fossils of the Narmada River Valley and their Horizons

THIS WRITE-UP IS A PRELIMINARY ACCOUNT OF the Pleistocene mammalian fauna of the Narmada, based on the writer's collection accumulated since 1958. This study also attempts to work out the stratigraphy of the ancient alluvium to place the fossil beds in their proper sequence. The study has revealed that the Narmada fossils cannot be lumped together, placed under a single label of 'Narmada group' and called Middle Pleistocene, as is being done.

Similarly, the fossils from several horizons cannot be equated with those of the Boulder Conglomerate Zone(Colbert 1935)of the Shiwalik foothills of the Himalayas. In fact, the Narmada's richest fossiliferous bed, the yellowish or pinkish cross-bedded sand as exposed at Devakachhar (P1. IIa), is Upper Pleistocene (Khatri 1961), and is associated with the Late Acheulian stage (Khatri 1963a) of the Hand Axe culture. It appears that the Narmada acted as a backwater sanctuary for animals whose survival was threatened in other areas of the subcontinent by such factors as climatic fluctuation. A thorough study of the collection may reveal the exact stratigraphic ranges of the various species within the sequence of deposits, due to good stratigraphical control of

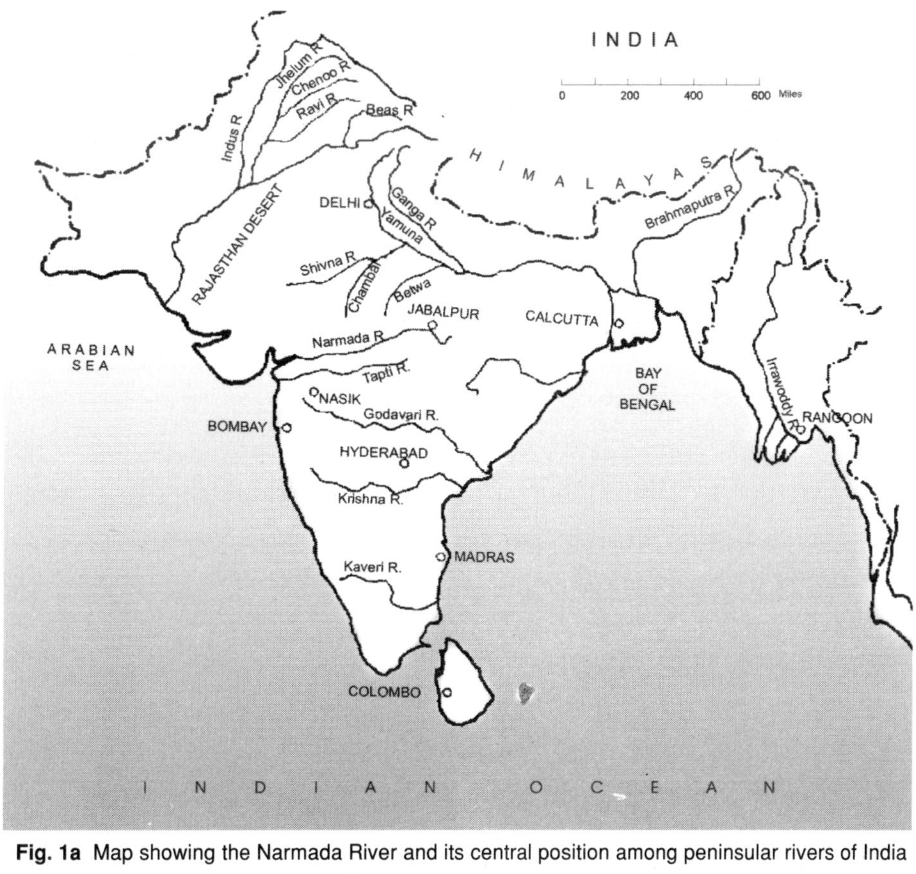

Fig. 1a Map showing the Narmada River and its central position among peninsular rivers of India

the data while collecting.

Historical Note

The first discovery of mammalian fossils in the Narmada Valley was made at Jabalpur by a Captain Sleeman in 1830. The credit for bringing this discovery to light goes to Dr. G.G. Spilsbury of the Bengal Medical Establishment, then stationed at Jabalpur. He conveyed this news to James Prinsep, the Secretary of the Asiatic Society of Bengal, who in turn published it (Prinsep 1832). Dr. Spilsbury also published the first drawing of a vertebrate fossil from India. It was that of an elephant jaw from the Umar Nadi (Omar Nadi), a sub-tributary of the Narmada (Spilsbury 1833). Spilsbury continued to make collections (1833-41) and published reports of them in the Journal of the Asiatic Society of Bengal. He was repeatedly encouraged in this endeavor by James Prinsep. That very decade, Dr. Hugh Falconer, an assistant surgeon of the East India Company, announced his find of vertebrate fossils-tortoise shells-in the Shiwaliks (Siwaliks) of Dehra Dun.

W. Theobald (1860) published the first account of the stratigraphy of the Narmada's ancient alluvium. He collected many fossils and listed several fossiliferous sites. Mr. C. A. Hacket's name is associated with the discovery of the first prehistoric tool from the Narmada, a beautiful hand axe made of quartzite from Bhatera (Bhutra) on the Narmada near Gadarwara. An account of this implement was published by H.B. Medlicott (1873). From the

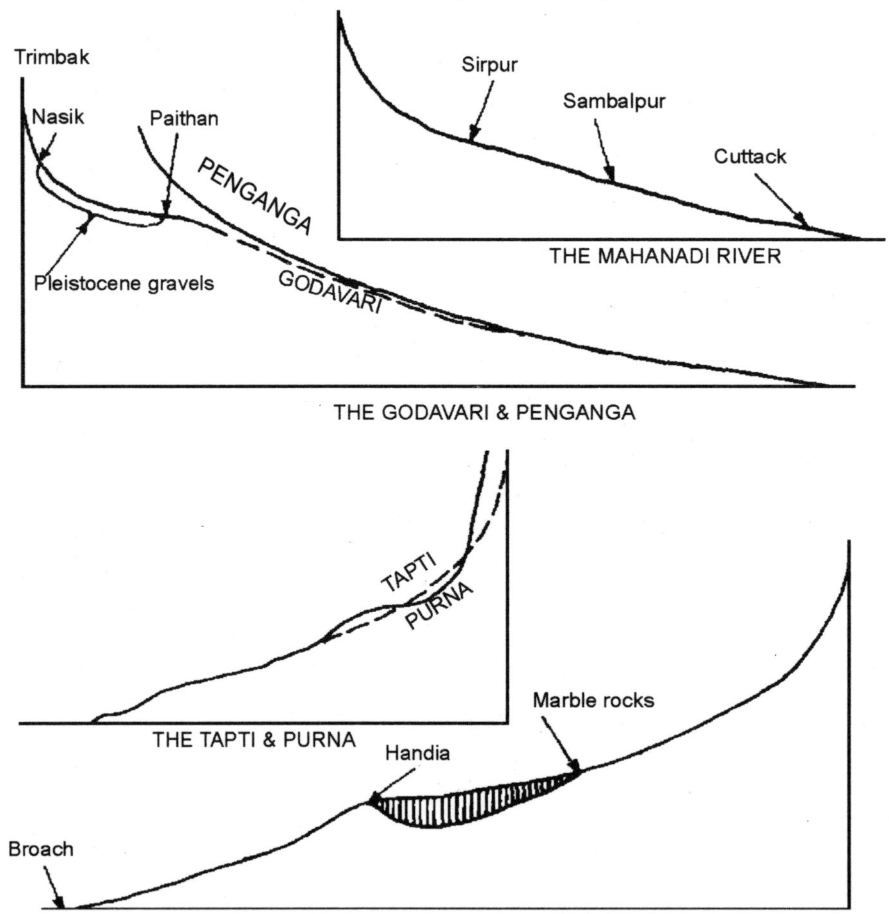

Fig. 1b River profiles of the Narmada, Godavari, Penganga,Tapti and Purna and Mahanadi Rivers of peninsular India

valley, Hacket discovered many fossils which can be seen in the Palaeontological Gallery of the Indian Museum at Kolkata. Medlicott maintained (1873) that they date from the Upper Pleistocene; Falconer thought them to be of the Pleiocene. Vredenburg (1906) studied the irregularities of the gradient of the Narmada, Tapi, Godavari, Purna and Mahanadi, and suggested that they are the products of Pleistocene movements which occurred in peninsular India.

R. Lydekker (1880, 1882, 1884 a-b) and G. E. Pilgrim (1905) published an account of the Narmada fossils along with the Shiwalik fossils, but no other work is extant. The Yale-Cambridge expedition, under the leadership of Helmut De Terra, visited the valley for a fortnight in 1935 and explored the fossiliferous localities already mentioned by Theobald. They attempted to correlate the deposits of the Narmada with the Shiwaliks and interpreted the Stone Age evidence from the Narmada in terms of Sohanian culture (De Terra and Paterson 1939). There ensued a lull in research until 1958, when the writer started exploring this valley and published several papers regarding stratigraphy and prehistory (Khatri 1961, 1962, 1963 a-b, 1964). An Oldowan pebble-tool horizon called 'Mahadevian' was discovered *in situ*. Discoveries of several stages of the Chelles-Acheul culture established the evolution of the Early Stone Age in the valley.

The Narmada River

The Narmada(Fig.1) or Narbada (the Namadas of Ptolemy; Nammadios of the Periplus) is one of the holy rivers of Hindustan. Flowing across the middle of the Indian subcontinent, it forms the traditional dividing line between the north and the south. Originating on the summit of the plateau of Amarkantak at about 22^0 40':81^0 45' on the Maikala Range in eastern Madhya Pradesh, it runs a total course of 80 miles to join the Gulf of Cambay in the Arabian Sea near Broach in the Gujarat state. Its source in the Maikala hills has provided a name by which it is often referred in ancient scriptures, Maikala Kanya, or 'daughter of Maikala.' It is also known as *rewa* (Sanskrit root 'ray', 'to hop'), owing to the leaping nature of the stream down its rocky bed.

Geology of the Narmada

From its source on the Amarkantak up to the Marble Rocks at Bheraghat, the Narmada flows through lava country underlain by gneissic Archean rocks (Fig. 2).These thick sheets of lava were laid down towards the end of the Cretaceous period when a vast area of peninsular India experienced a stupendous outburst of volcanic activity. The liquid lava welled out from the fissures and cracks and was deposited in horizontal bedded sheets of basalt.

At the Marble Rocks near Bheraghat, the Narmada makes a fall of nearly 40 ft. before leaping into an area of crystalline dolomitic limestone belonging to the Dharwar system. At the end of the gorge a fertile plain stretches to Handia, 200 miles downstream, and is flanked by massive sandstone and quartzite formations of the Vindhyas and Satpuras in the north and south, respectively. It is said that this extensive plain is not a valley which the river has eroded for itself, but is a two-fault plane which the stream has usurped for its channel. This alluvium filled rift in the rocks runs parallel to the Vindhyas, and is more than 500 ft. deep, as proved by recent tube-well borings

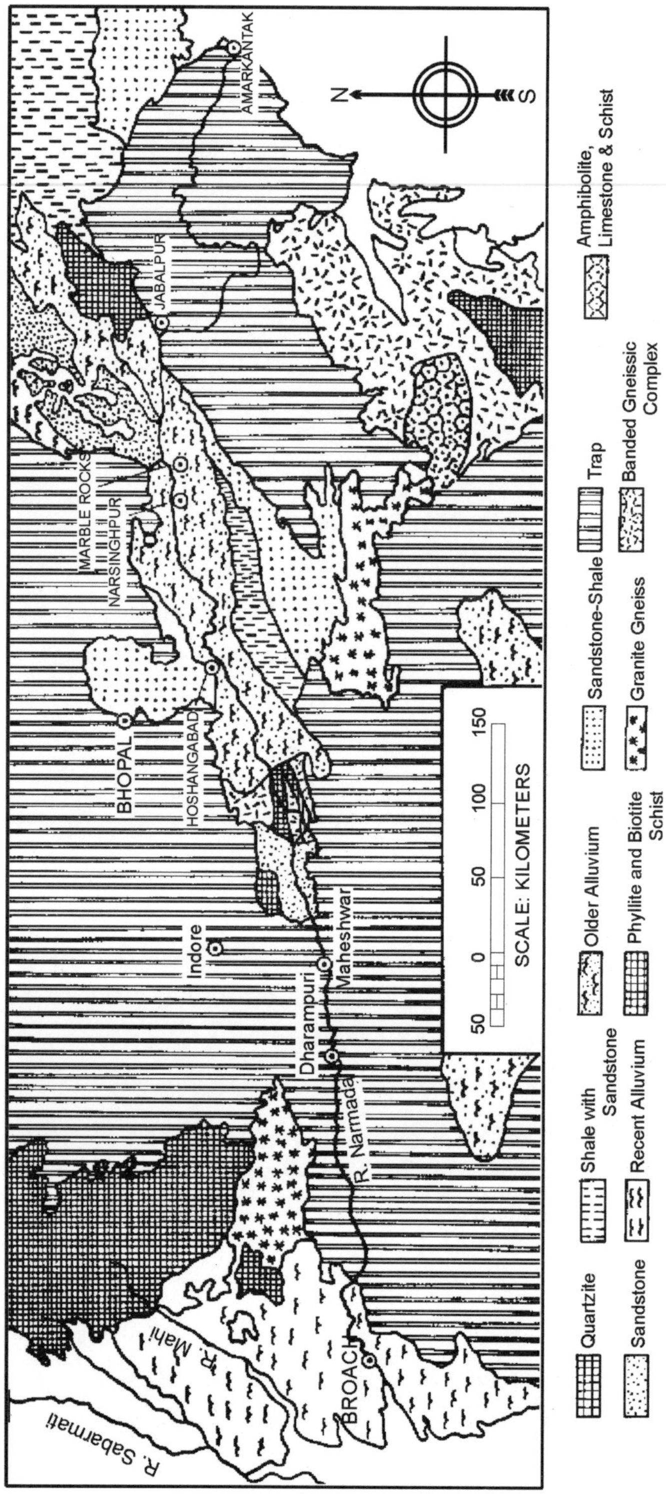

Fig. 2 Geological map of the Narmada Valley

at several places. It is assumed to have originated as a result of the bending or 'sagging' of the northern rim of the peninsula sometime during the upheaval of the Himalayas. The massive sandstone escarpments of the upper Vindhyas to the north of the Narmada are of the Torridonian age. These are in contrast to the thick-bedded, massive, red and yellow sandstone of the Mahadeva and Pachmarhi hills south of Piparia, which belong to the middle Gondwana series of the Triassic epoch.

From Handia, the Narmada flows again through basalt country for some distance until it is caught up in mountainous terrain of sandstone and quartzite which continues up to Mandhata. Thence for nearly 100 miles, with an exception in the Dhar forest area where the lower Vindhyan rocks are exposed, extends another fertile plain eroded in trap rock country. On the last lap of its journey, the Narmada flows through alluvial country and forms a 17-mile-wide estuary before emptying into the Arabian Sea.

Stratigraphy of the 'Ancient' Alluvium

The following are the main horizons which the present investigation has been able to delineate. They are depicted in a generalized section of the valley (Fig. 3).

Red Clay

The undermost stratum in the Narmada stratigraphical sequence is composed of deep red clay exposed at Hoshangabad (Kharra ghat), Bhatgaon, Ajhera, Serra Bhopali (or Serragaon) in the Hoshangabad district (Figs. 4-9) and in the Narsinghpur district at Barmhanghat (Khurd), Gararu, Murgakhera, Kharaiya, Mahadeo Piparia, and at another score of places (Fig. 10). In the Shukkar River this was seen at Gadarwara in the vicinity of the railway bridge and on the Sher at Devakachhar, Ratikarar and on the Umar at Umaria and Tindni (Fig. 11), in numerous khads and ravines. The thickness of the exposed bed varies between four and twelve ft. and seems to have undergone much erosion before the next deposit was laid over it. This

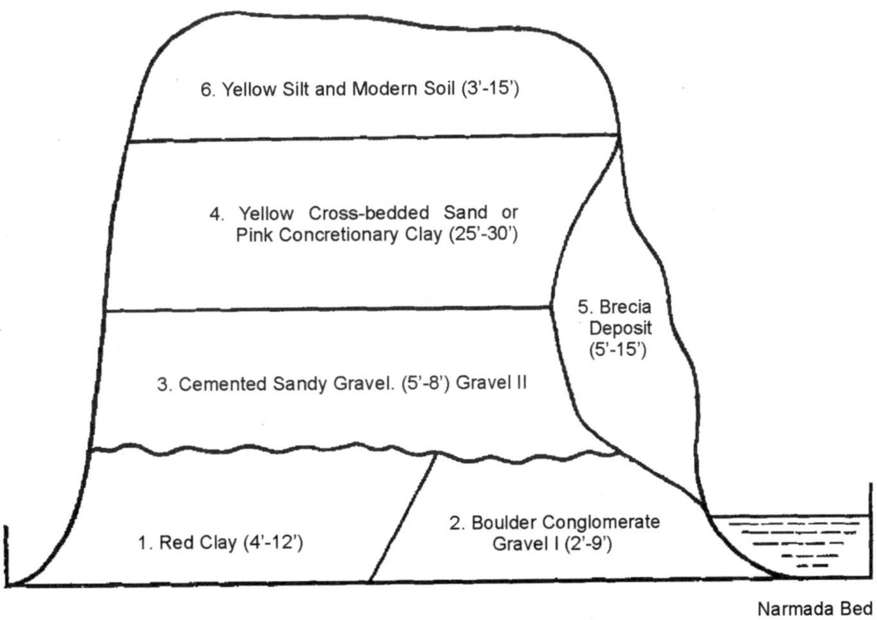

Fig. 3 Generalized section of the Narmada Valley

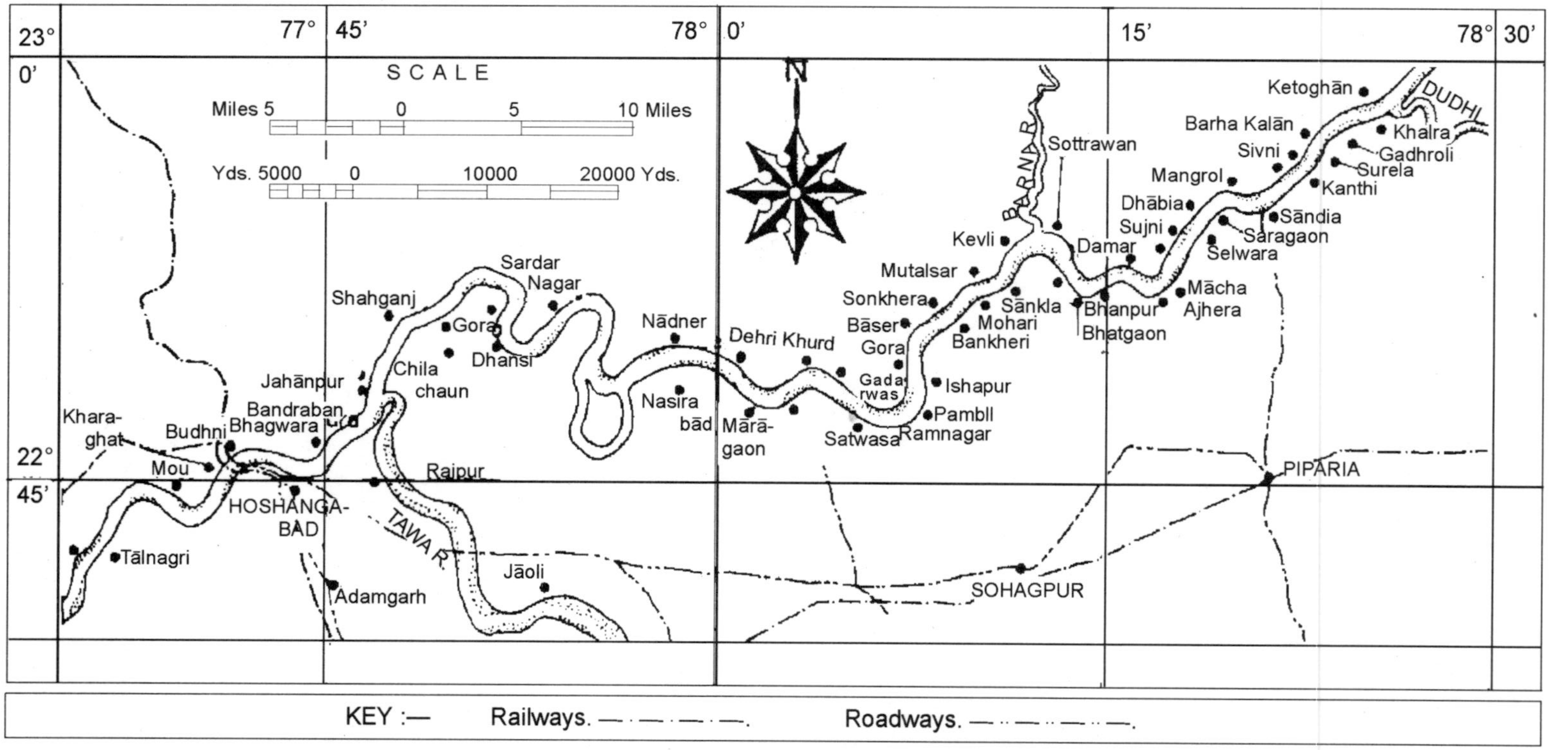

Fig. 4 The Narmada River in Hoshangabad district. The localities noted on the map were visited and were found either implementiferous or fossil-yeilding or both

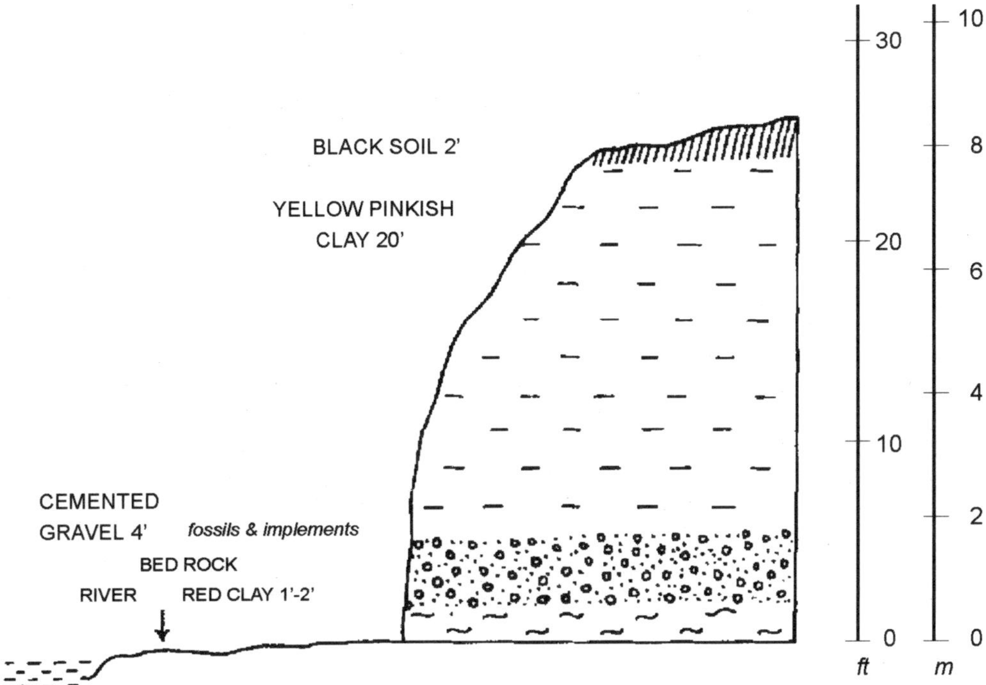

Fig. 5 Section of the right bank of the Nramada River near the railway bridge, Hoshangabad

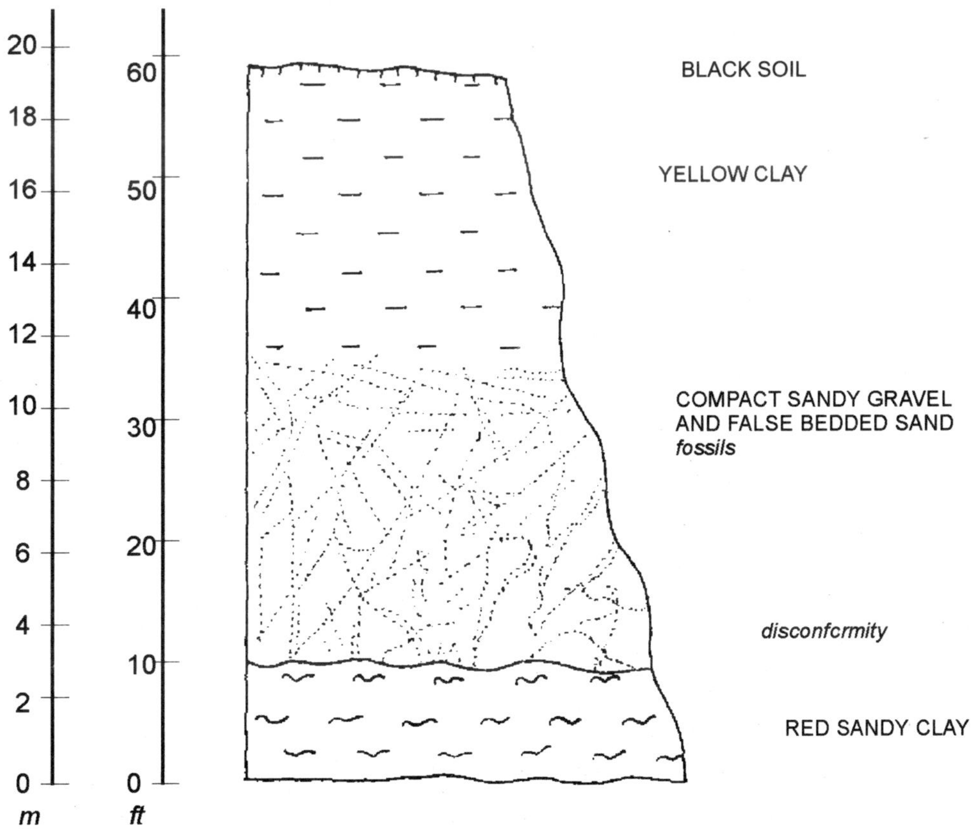

Fig. 6 Cliff section between Galchi and Bhatgaon, Hoshangabad district

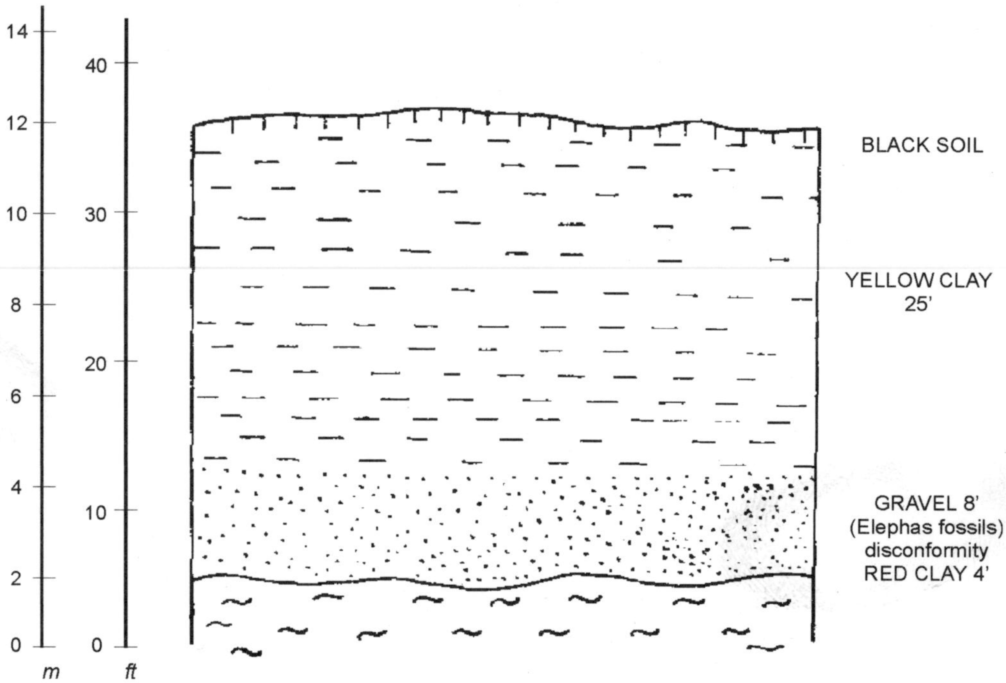

Fig. 7 Cliff section at Ajhera, Hoshangabad district

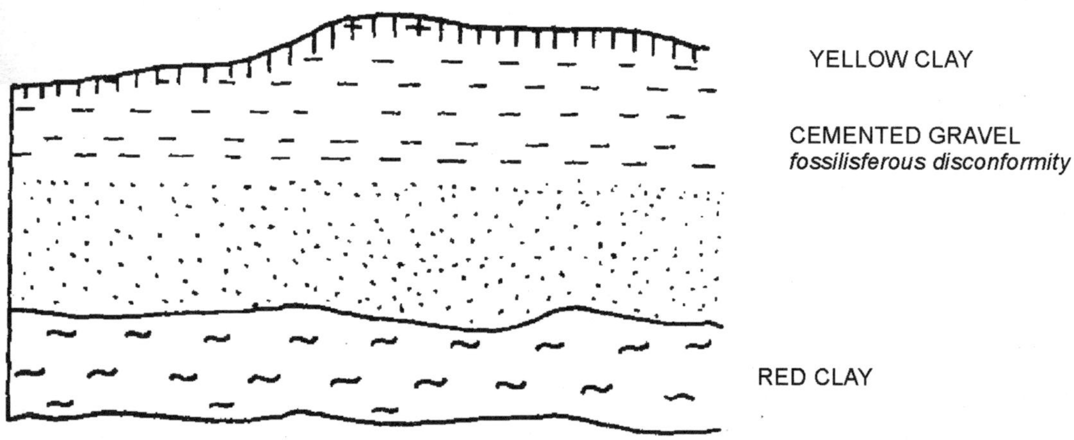

Fig. 8 Section of the right bank of the Narmada River at Sarra(Bhopali), Hoshangabad district

unconformity is most conspicuous at the above-mentioned sites.

Boulder Conglomerate (Gravel I)

Although this deposit occurs rarely in the valley, it is found well developed at Hasalpur (Fig. 12), a village about 5 mile downstream from Hoshangabad, and at Kankar Ghat below the Public Works Department office in the town of Hoshangabad. At Mahadeo Piparia (Narsinghpur district), huge broken blocks of this deposit are lying near the edge of the stream.

Its exact stratigraphical position is a matter of controversy. De Terra has put it below the Red Clay. The author, following Dr. M.R. Sahni, has shown it lying against the Red Clay. Further observations, however, incline the author

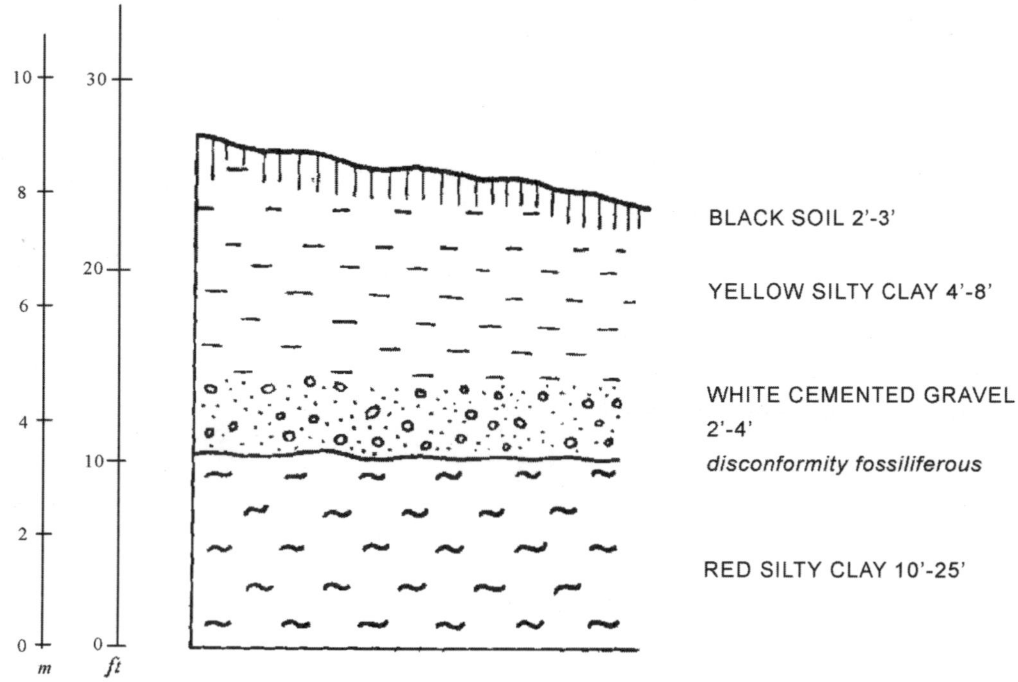

Fig. 9 Cliff section at Dhansi

toward the viewpoint that the deposit now called Gravel I may be nothing but the earlier facies of the deposit now called Gravel II. In any event, we can say definitely that because of the 'Mahadevian' type of tools found in it, the deposit is a near contemporary of the Red Clay in its erosional phase.

Cemented Sandy Gravel (Gravel II)-(Pls. IIIb, IVb and Figs. 13-14)

As alluded to above, this bed rests unevenly on the Red Clay stratum and is generally found to occur 15-20 ft. above the present water level. It is frequently encountered in the valley in the form of huge blocks eroded from their actual level by the river in flood. Sometimes the deposition is so broad that it extends for furlongs inside the banks at Sandia, 12 miles north of Piparia (Fig. 4), and appears during the digging of wells, sometimes with fossils *in situ*, in villages nearby. Blocks of this gravel are used as building material, like laterite slabs, in the southern states of India; the author has extracted many valuable fossils from the walls of many houses so built in villages perched on either side of the Narmada.

The Gravel II stratum is richly fossiliferous, but sometimes bones exhibit their limy whiteness, revealing a state of partial petrifaction. The tools have been chiselled out of this deposit at Sagun Ghat on the Narmada, near its junction with the Sher Nadi (Figs. 4 and 10) and represent an inferior Acheulian variety. The presumption of intervening stages between these tools and those recovered from earlier deposits is confirmed by typological study of loose material gathered from the river bed. Good examples of this cemented deposit can be seen at Bhagwara (P1. IIIb), Bandraban, Bhatgaon, Dhabla, Saragaon and Sandia in the Hoshangabad district (Fig. 4); and at Barmhan, Sagun Ghat, Pithera and other upstream locations in the Narsinghpur district (Figs. 10-11). In the Sher Valley, the localities most

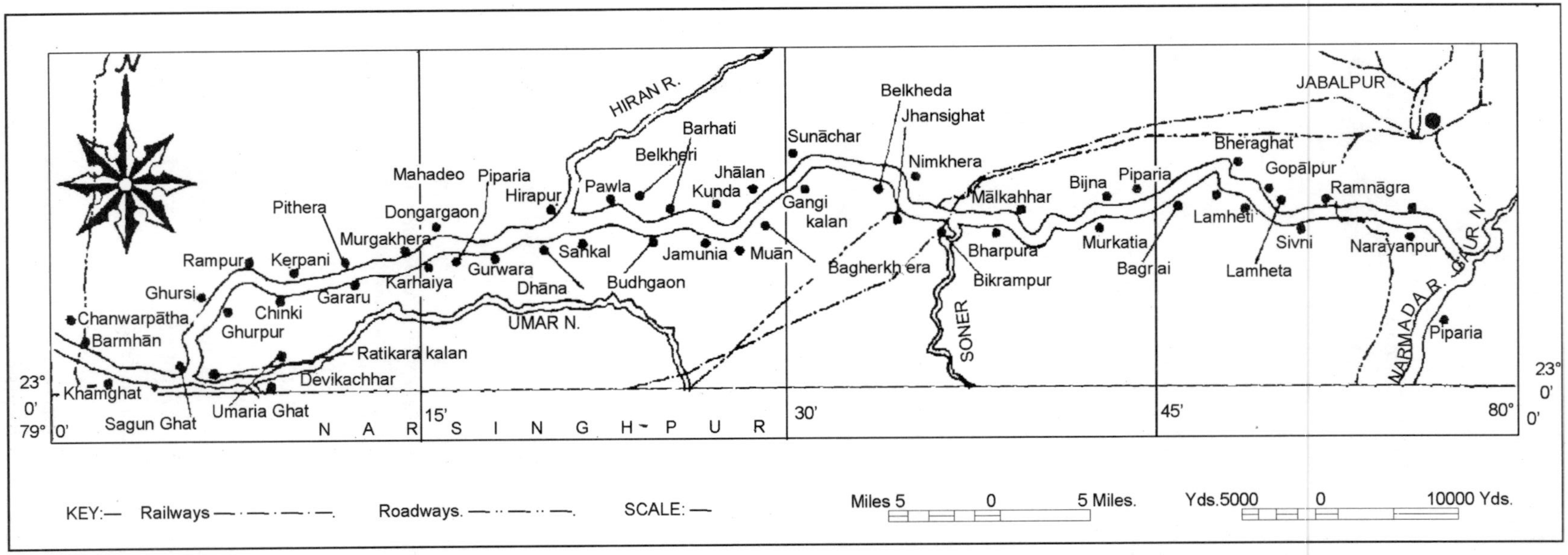

Fig. 10 The Narmada from Barmhan to Jabalpur with important fossil or tool yeilding localities, Narsinghpur and Jabalpur districts, MadhyaPradesh

conspicuously exhibiting this horizon are Manoria, Devakachhar and Ratikarar; Umaria Ghat and its surroundings on the Umar Nadi are also noteworthy.

Yellow Cross-bedded Sand (Fig. 15)

Continuing conformably over the cemented sand of Gravel II is a massively thick layer of silt and sand varying between 25 and 30 ft. It shows cross-bedding and is a product of a sluggish river, unable to carry its load farther down. This sandy deposit is the richest stratum in fossils and Late Acheulian tools of high workmanship. In addition to this stage of Chelles-Acheul culture, Nevasian or Series II appears in the upper layers of this horizon which gradually merge with modern black soil. At certain places the colour of the sand changes from yellow to pinkish, also becoming concretionary as at Hoshangabad. According to the present investigation, this deposit and the Cemented Sandy Gravel (Gravel II), are products of the late Pleistocene, as are the animal remains found fossilized in these strata.

Breccini Deposit (Gravel III)-(P1. Ib and Fig. 16)

This deposit is extensively exposed at several places in ancient hollows of the denuded banks. It contains bones which are minimally fossilized and show remains of recent fauna. The localities noteworthy for this deposit are Bhatgaon and Ajhera in the Hoshangabad district (Fig. 4), where three complete, semi-fossilized Elephas skulls of the present living species, Elephas indicus, were found. The same phenomenon is repeated at Barmhanghat, near the bus stand adjacent to the temple, farther upstream (P1. IIIb, Fig. 13). In addition to recent fauna was found the rolled material of Nevasian or Series II tools (Middle Stone Age)and rolled hand axes, flakes and cleavers of earlier periods showing the redeposition of earlier displaced material. The breccial deposit is of some antiquity; it is indicated to be earlier than modern soil by the presence of bones that have fossilized, however minimally. But let it be remembered that this does not form a part of the third cycle of deposition as indicated by De Terra. It is encountered only infrequently.

Yellow Silt and Modern Soil

The yellow cross-bedded sand gradually ends up in silt, capped by a small layer of humus or black soil. No fossils but Series II tools and microliths are found on the surface.

The occurrence of laterite in the Narmada Valley has a significant bearing on the stratigraphy of the ancient alluvium. R.D. Oldham (1893) mentioned that the laterite in the Narmada Valley occurs below the Boulder Conglomerate (Gravel I) level. On Oldham's authority, De Terra suggested that since the Boulder Conglomerate is of the Middle Pleistocene, as indicated by the fauna it contained, and because the laterite is lying immediately below it, the laterite dates from pre-Middle Pleistocene or Lower Pleistocene. The present investigation does not support this. The laterite has not been noticed lying immediately underneath the Boulder Conglomerate. Moreover, the investigation at Adamgarh hillock and at Chidgaon (Fig. 17) shows that the lateritization process might have taken place in the Upper Pleistocene at a time when early man in the Narmada Valley was manufacturing tools of the Early Acheulian type. The sections showing the best stratigraphical position of the laterite

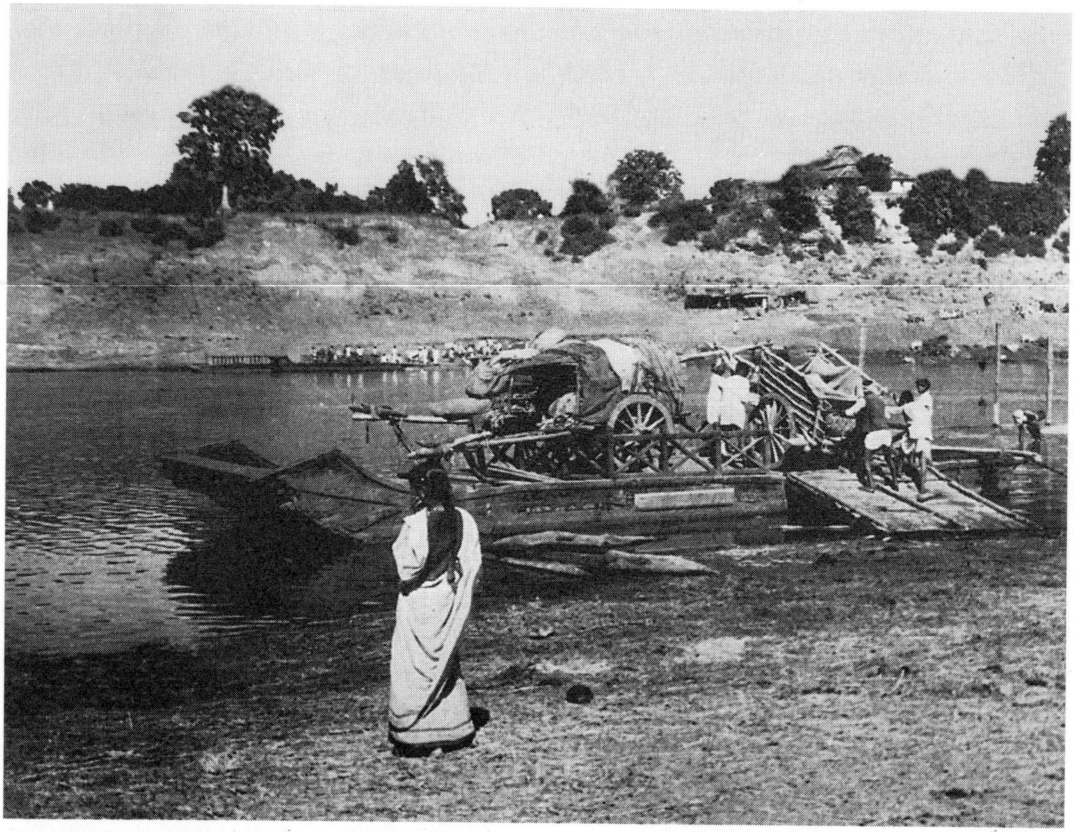

Plate Ia River Narmada at Barmhan ghat, Narsinghpur district. M.P. The opposite banks is of yellow brownish silt and sometimes yields bones of animals of present times though fossilized to some extent

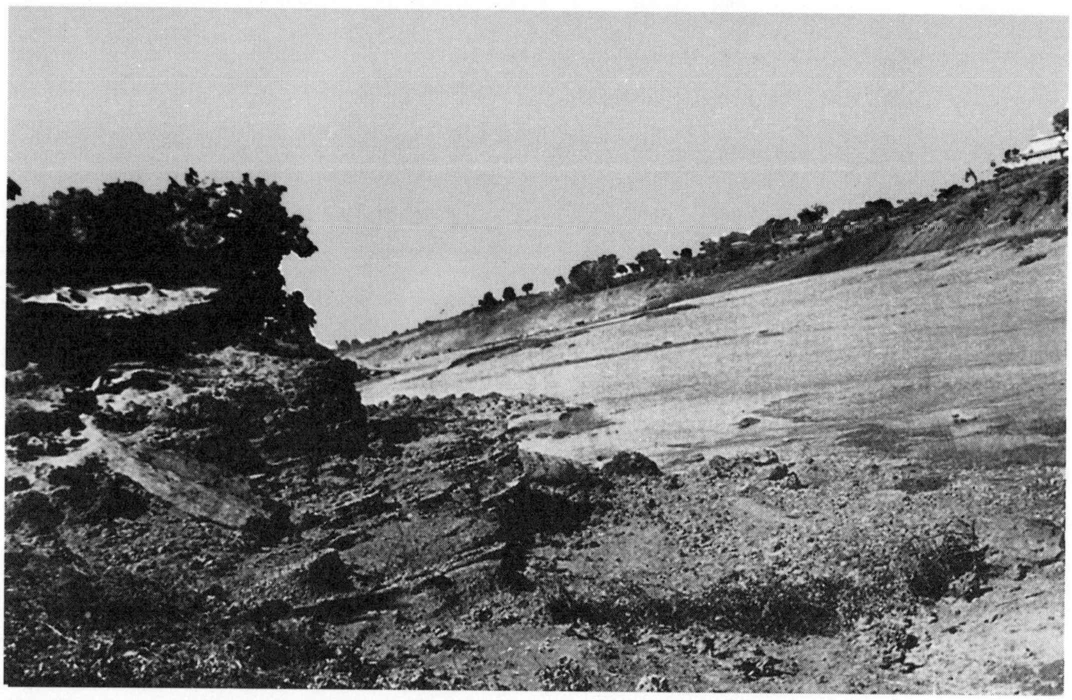

Plate Ib Gravel III exposed on the bank of the Narmada at Barmhan ghat, Narsinghpur district. M.P. Middle stone age tools and rolled quartzite palaeoliths were found *in situ* in the deposit

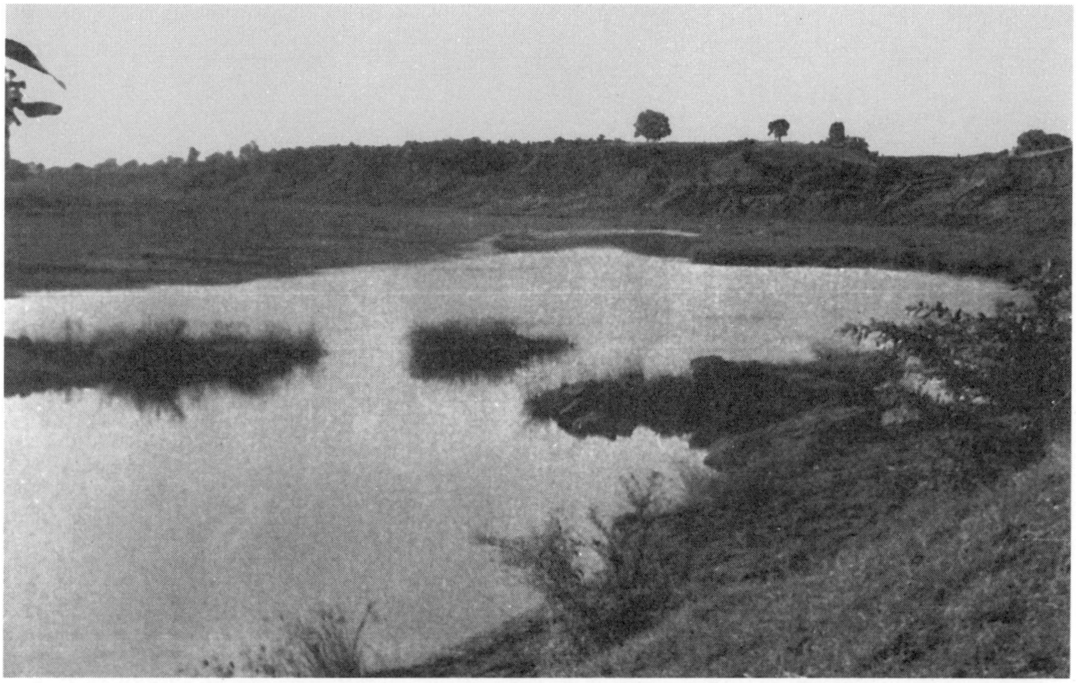

Plate IIa River Sher at Devakachhar, Narsinghpur district. M.P. The horse-shoe meander above is one of the richest fossil-yielding sites in the Narmada Valley

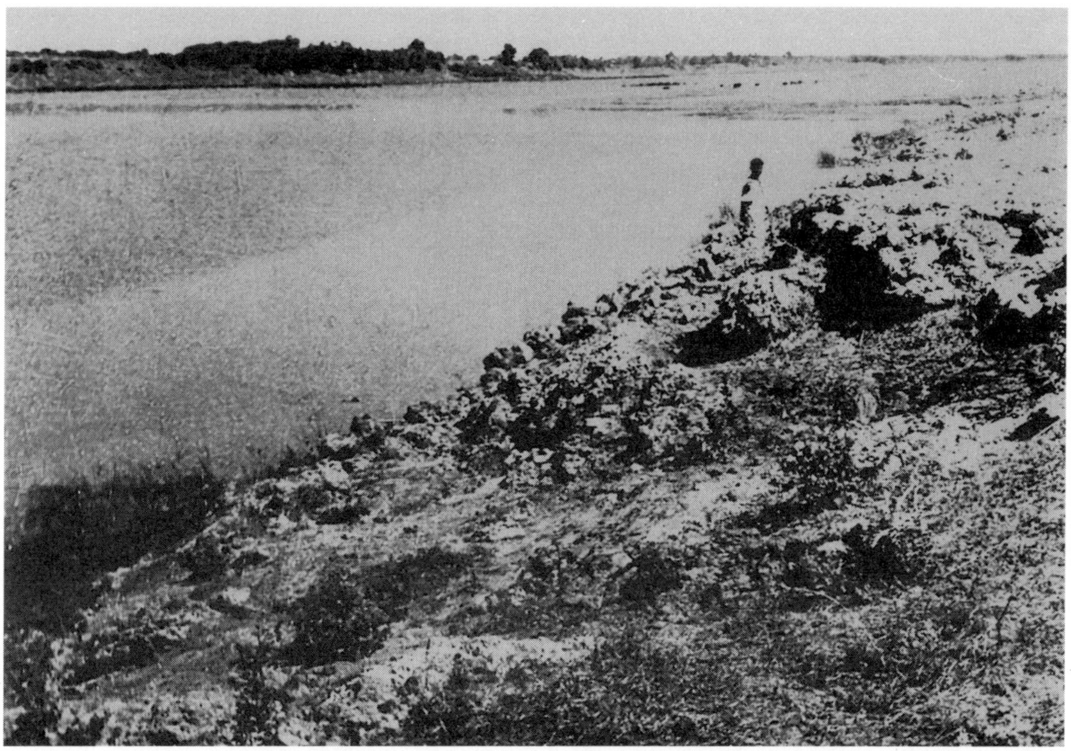

Plate II b A fossiliferous deposit on the left bank of the Narmada near Bandraban, five miles upstream from Hoshangabad town, M.P. advanced acheulian handaxes and cleavers were also recovered along with fossils

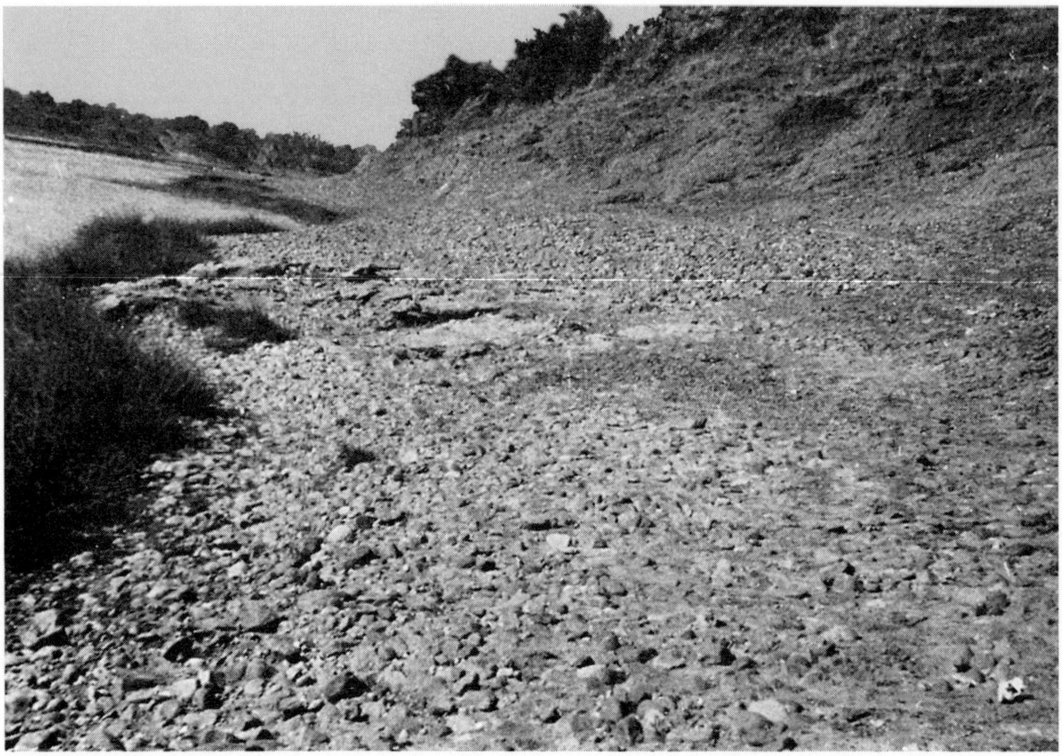

Plate III a Bhagwara gravel on the right bank of the Narmada at Hoshangabad. Richly implementiferous. Fossils also found

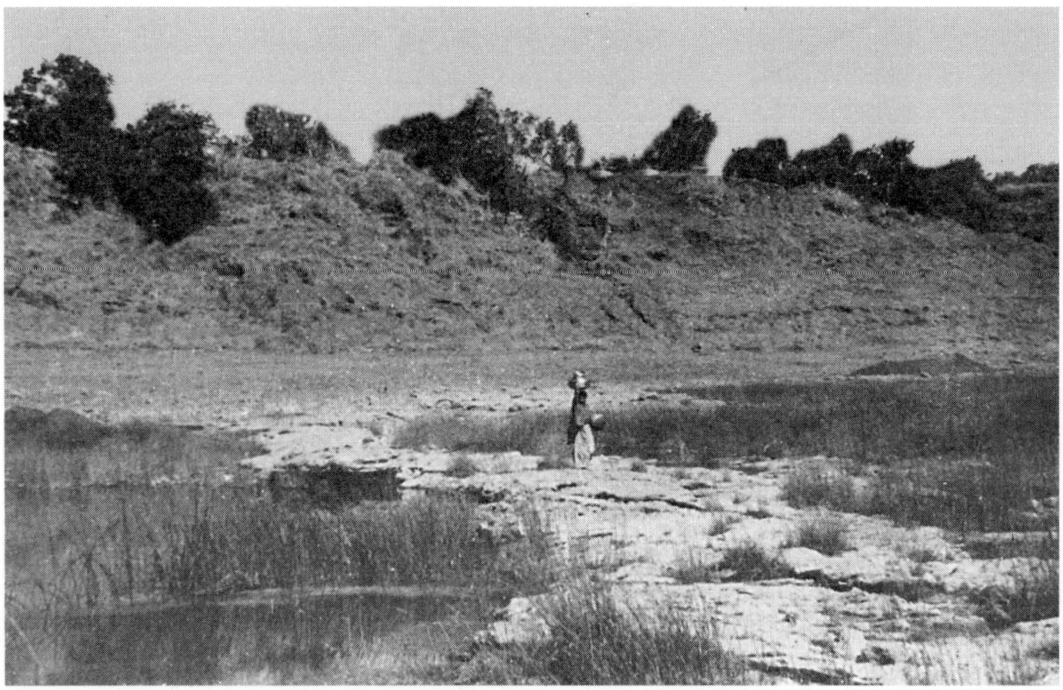

Plate III b Gravel II on the right bank of the Narmada at Bhagwara, Hoshangabad, M.P.

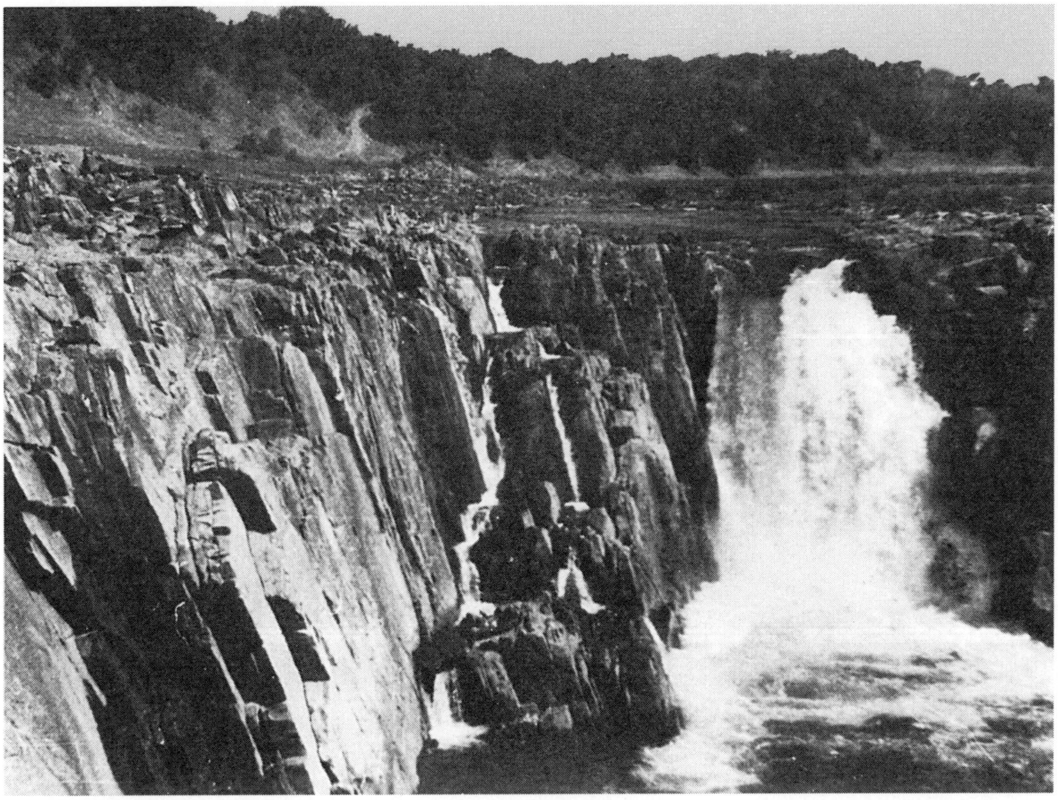

Plate IV a Dhuandhar fall of the Narmada at Bheraghat. Near this place one can see the ancient course of the river

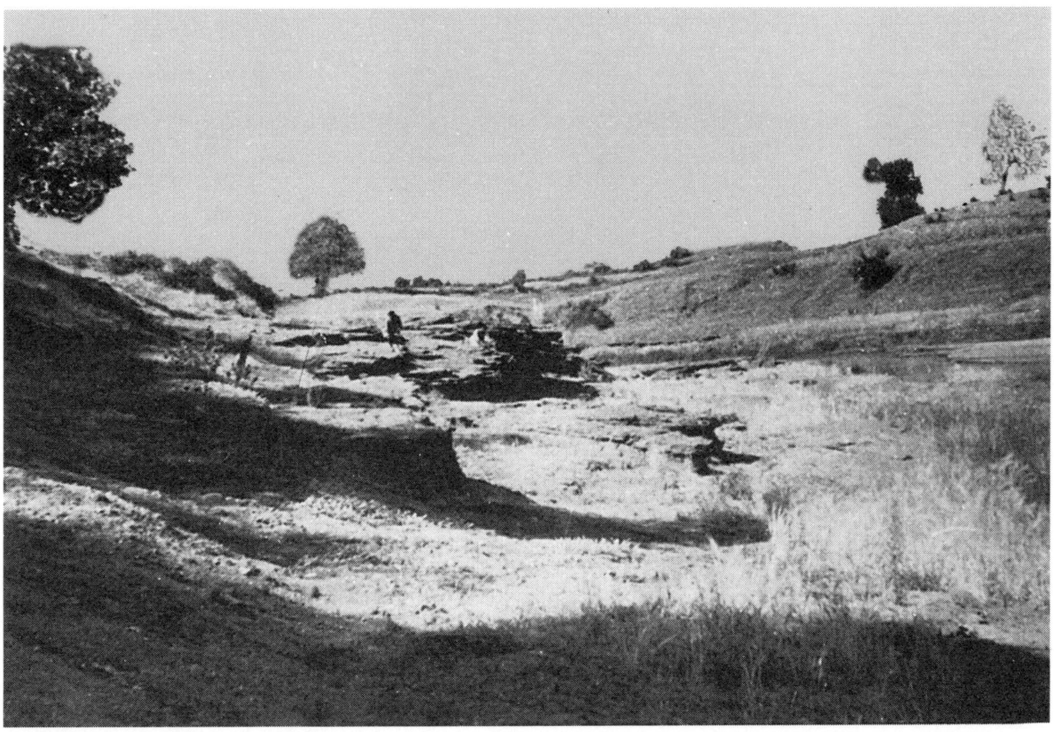

Plate IV b Fossiliferous deposit at Sagun Ghat, on the Narmada in Narsinghpur district. Gravel II is exposed extensively

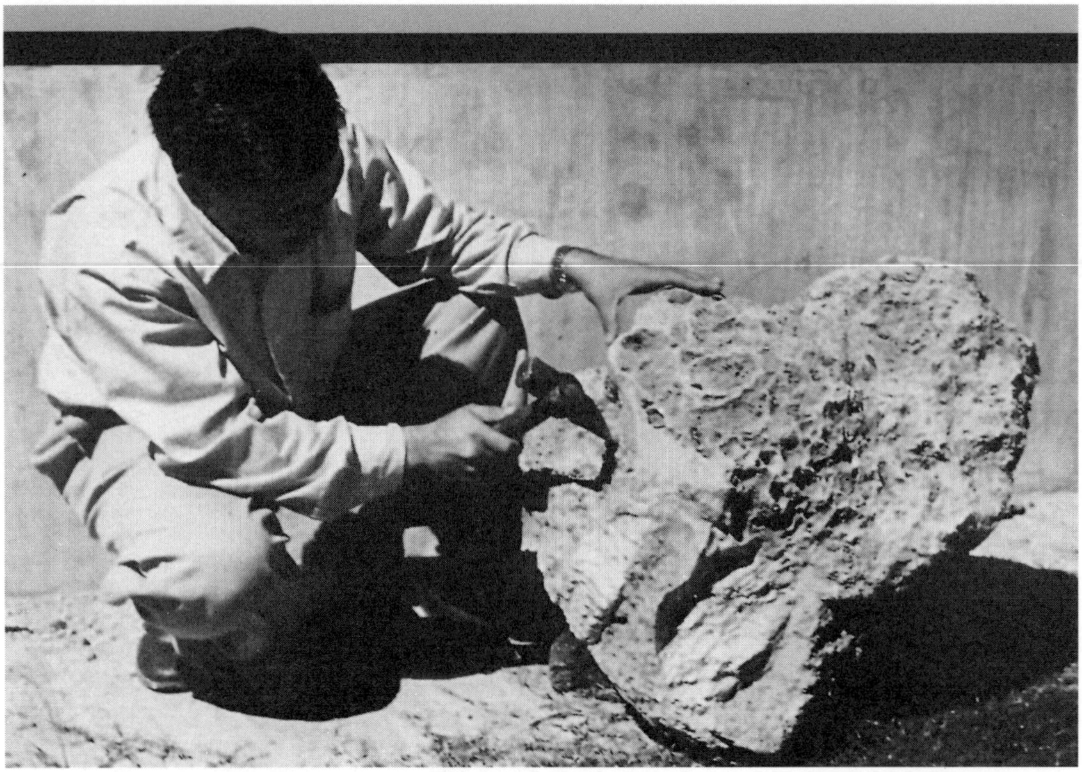

Plate V a Skull of *Elephas indicus* found *in situ* at Ajhera, on the left bank of the Narmada. Hoshangabad disrict

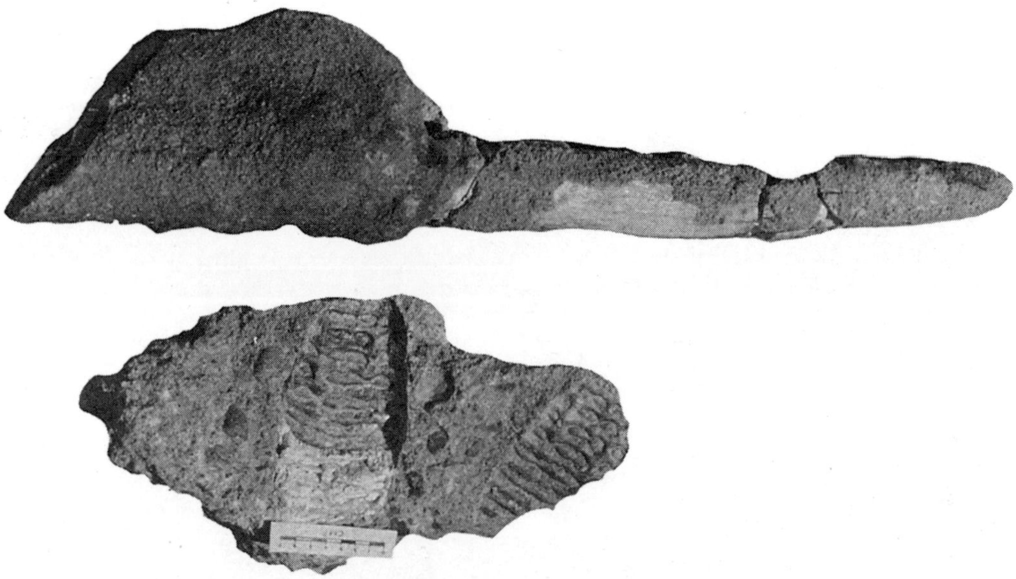

Plate V b Tusk and molars of the same individual

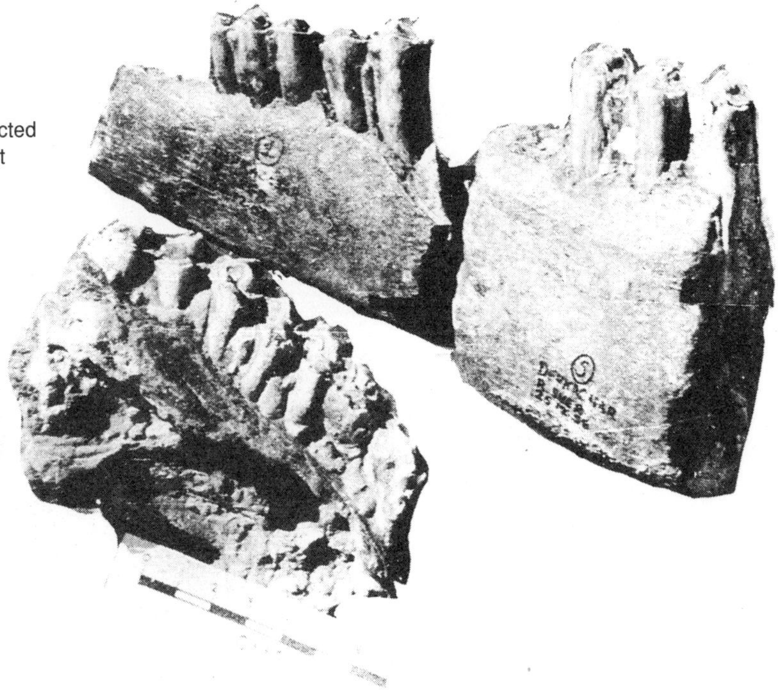

Plate VI a Fossilized bovine ramii collected from the bed of River Sher at Devakachhar, Narsinghpur district, M.P.

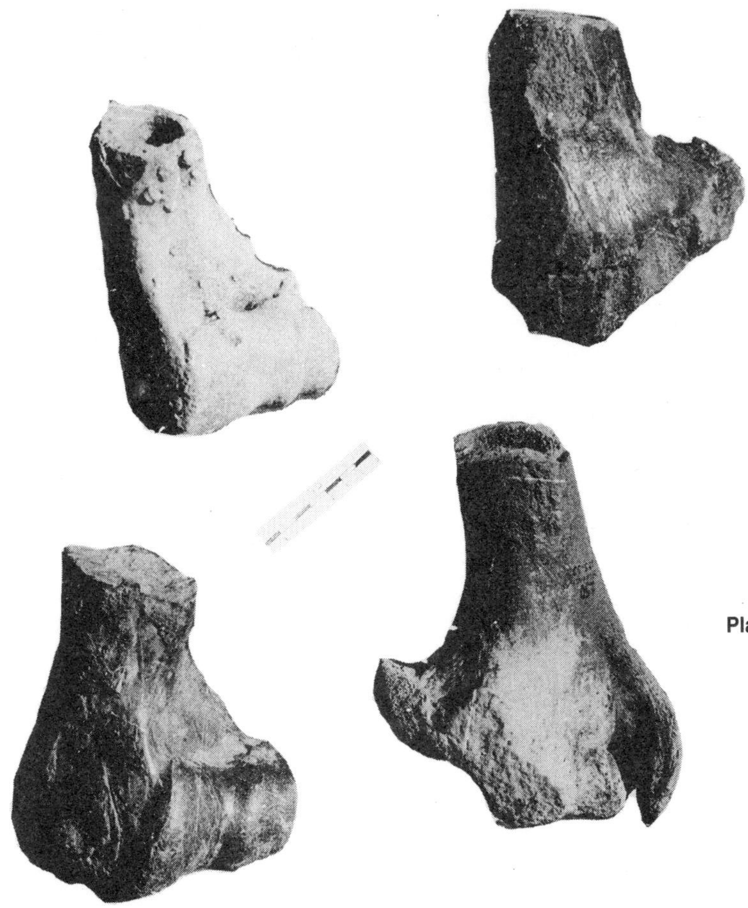

Plate VI b Fossil specimens of the 'ends' of long bones of extinct mammals. Devakachhar, R. Sher, Narsinghpur district, M.P.

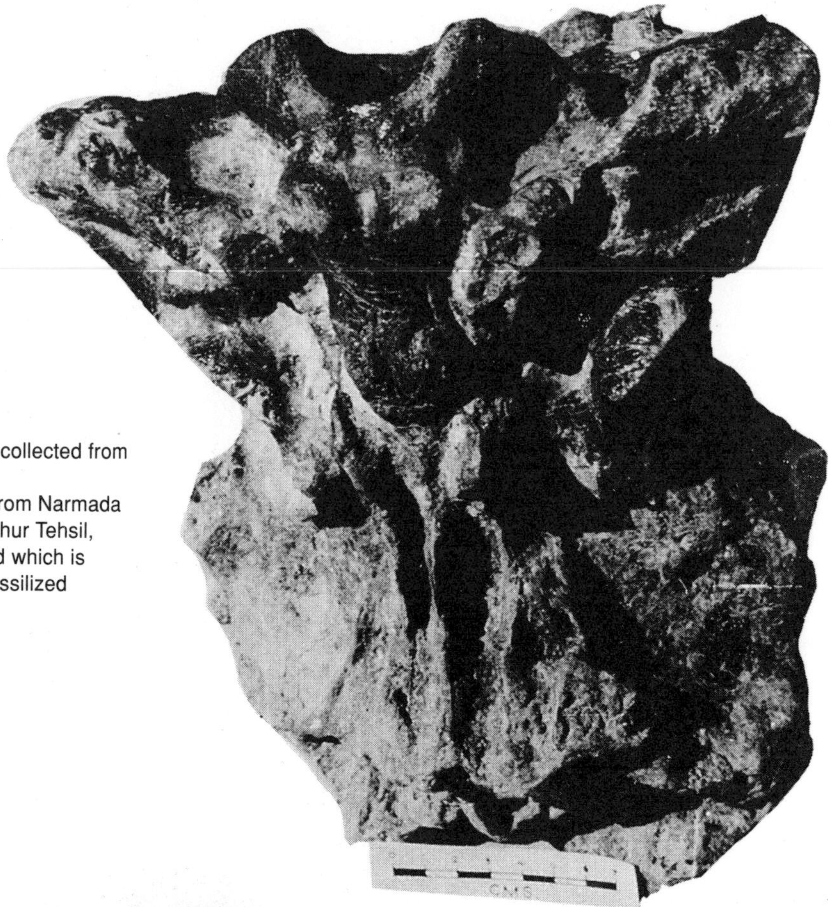

Plate VII a Bovine skull, collected from the district. A specimen from Narmada bed in Sohaghur Tehsil, Hoshangabad which is completely fossilized

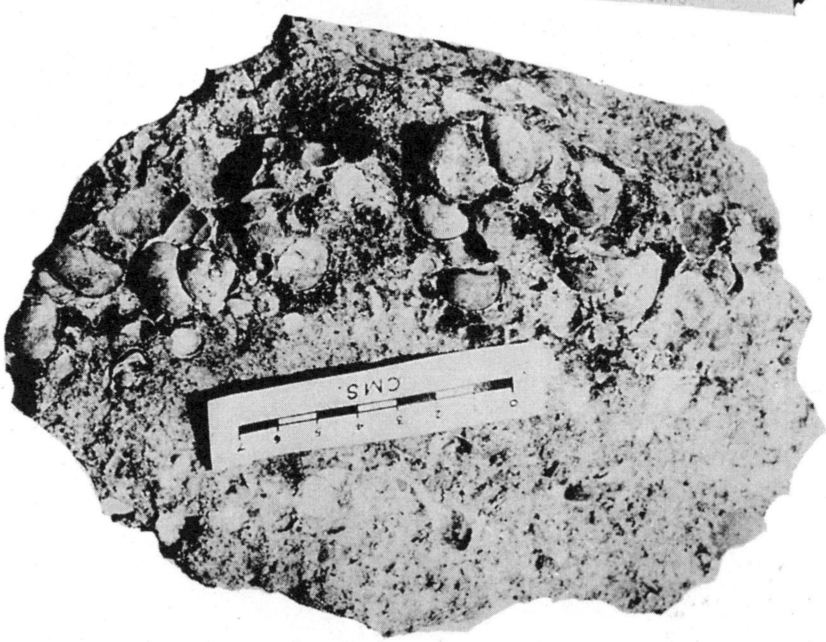

Plate VII b A block of gravel II showing fossilized gastropods and clams. Loc: Devakacchar, River Sher, Narsinghpur district, Madhya Pradesh

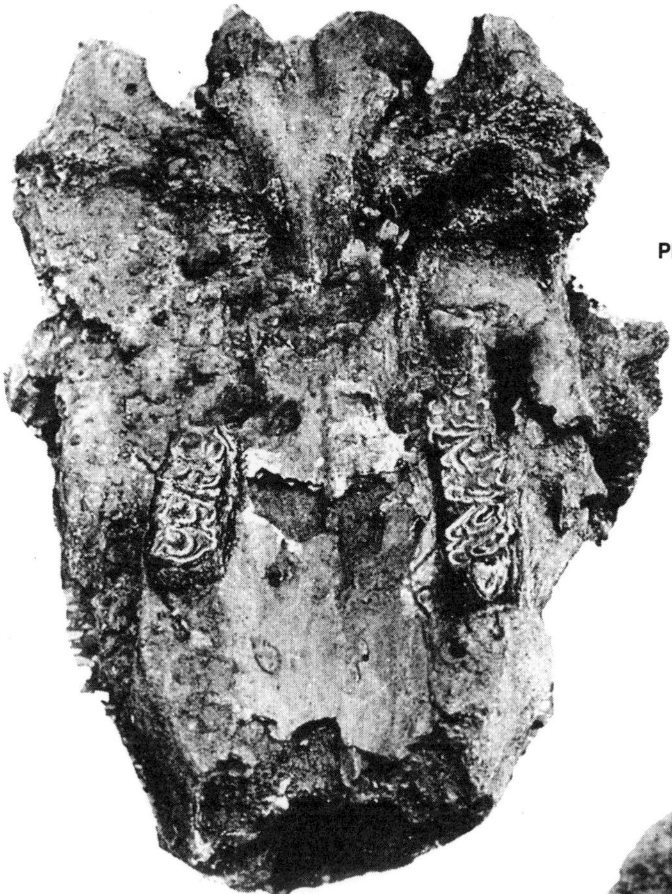

Plate VIII a A fossilized skull of *Bubalus palaeindicus* found on the right bank of the Umar Nadi at Umarghat near Devakachhar. Narsinghpur district, M.P.

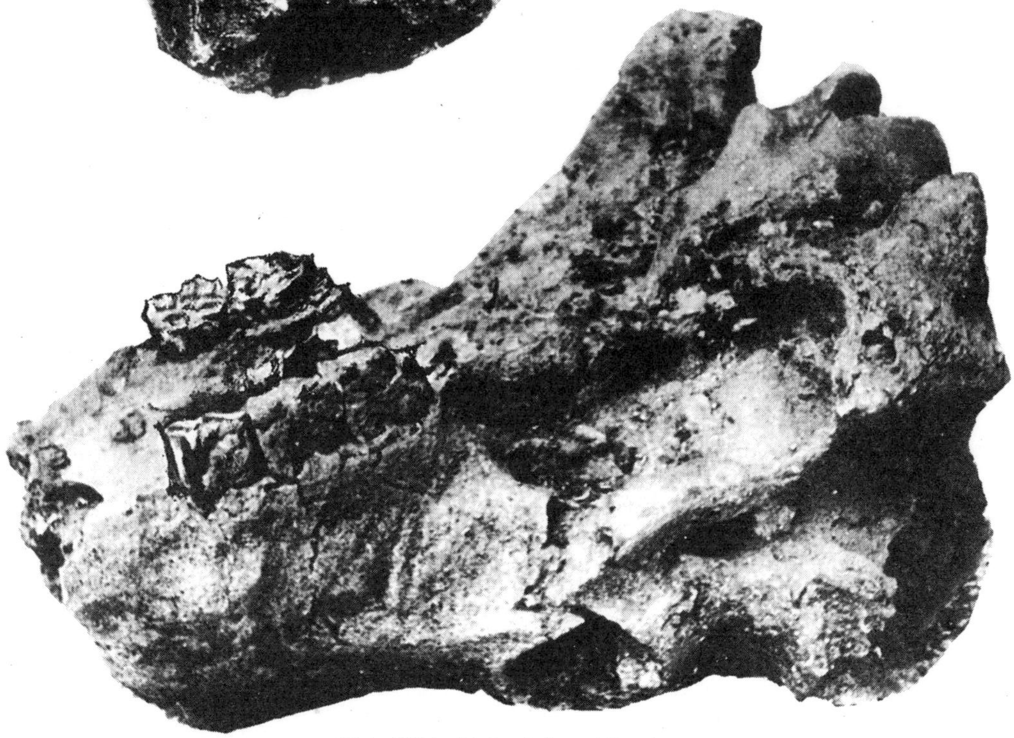

Plate VIII b A lateral view of the above

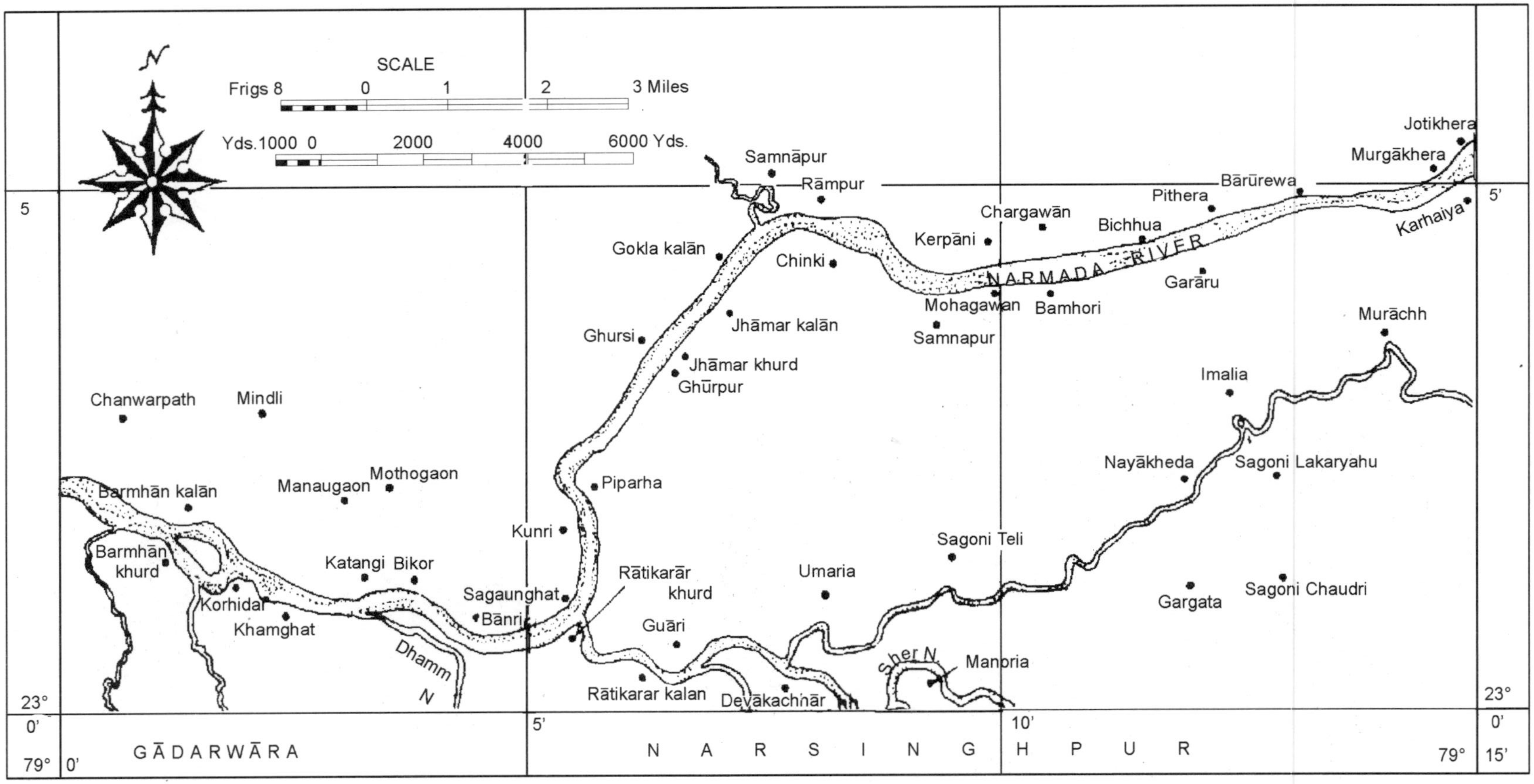

Fig. 11 The Narmada with its tributaries, the Umar and Sher Rivers, with implementiferous and fossiliferous sites, Narsinghpur district, Madhya Pradesh

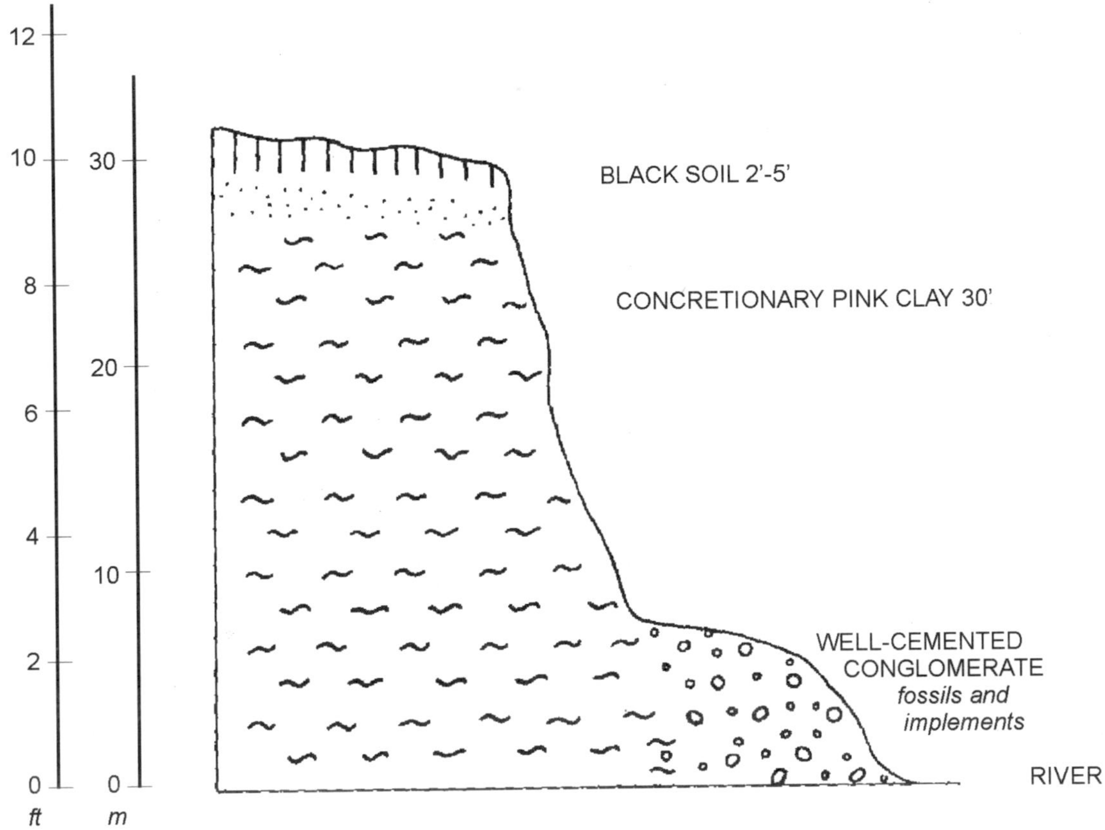

Fig. 12 Left bank of the Narmada River near Hasalpur

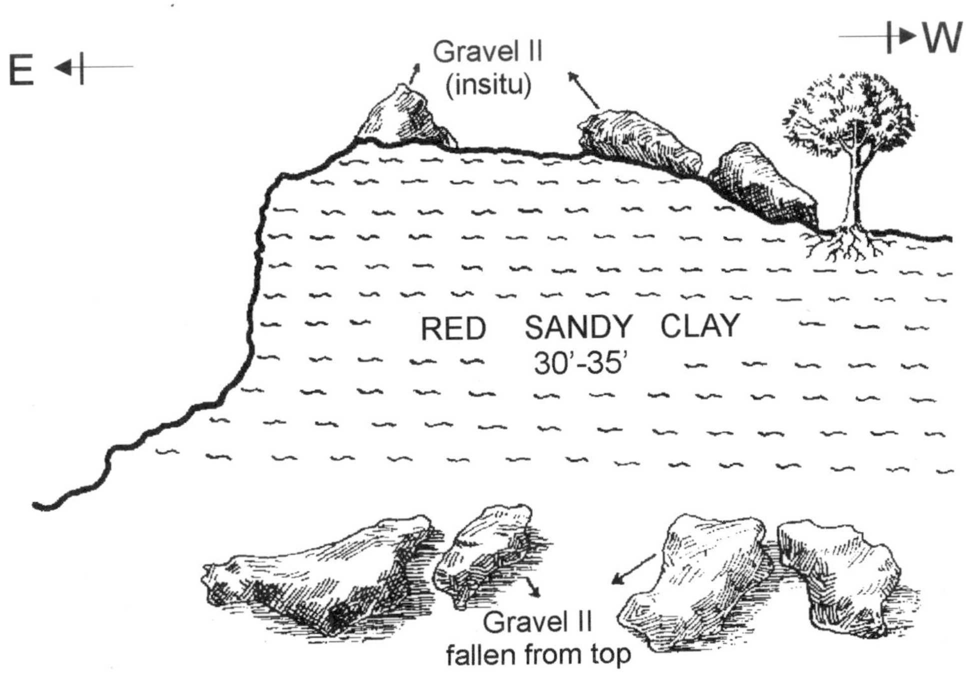

Fig. 13 Section of the southern bank of the Narmada River at Barmhan Ghat, Narsinghpur district

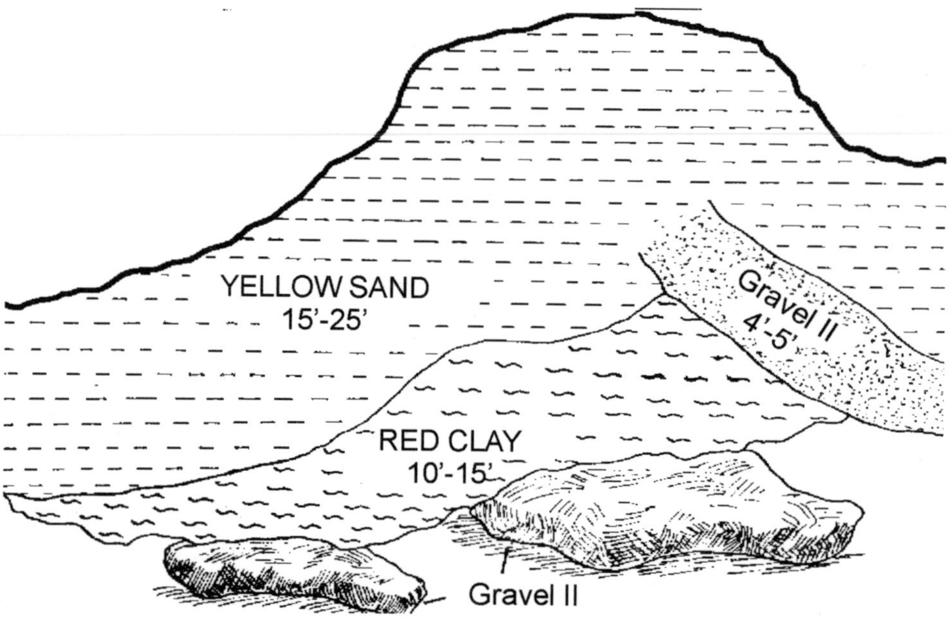

Fig. 14 Section of the Bela Ghat on the Sher River, a mile and a half upstream from Devakachhar, Narsinghpur district

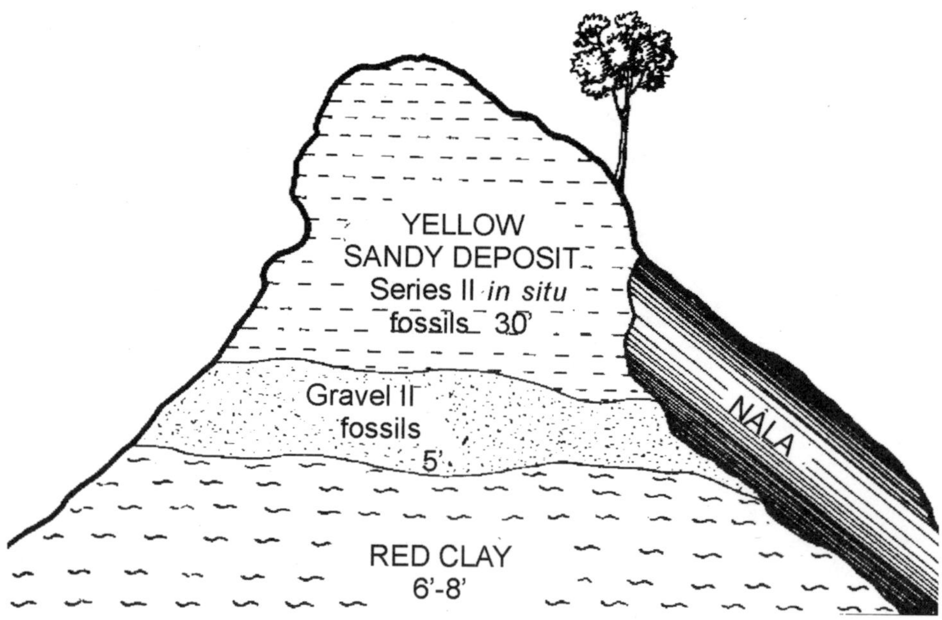

Fig. 15 Section near Umaria Ghat on the Umar River, near Devakachhar, Narsinghpur district

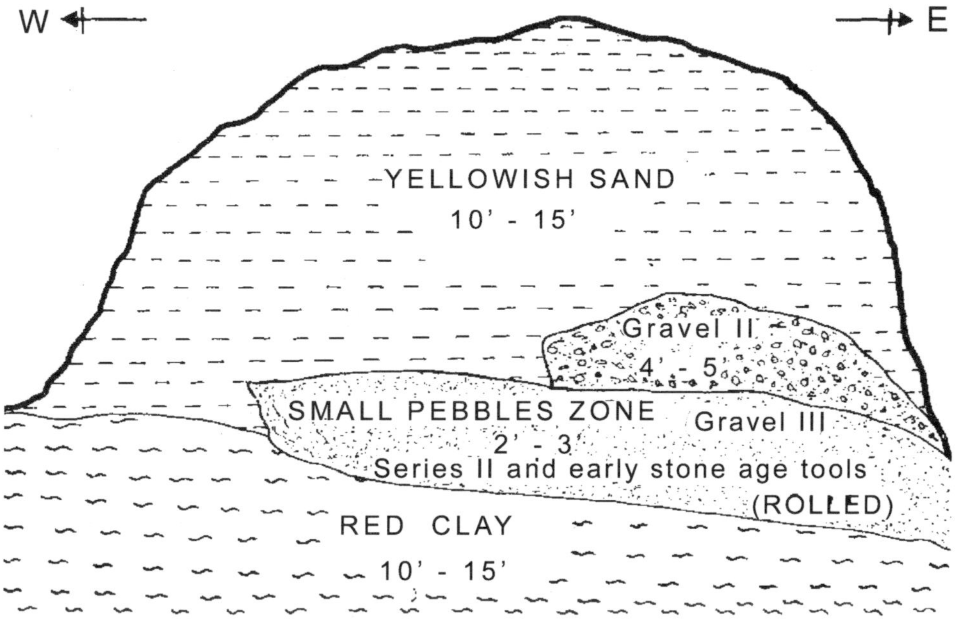

Fig. 16 Section of the southern bank of the Narmada River, at Barhman Ghat, Narsinghpur district

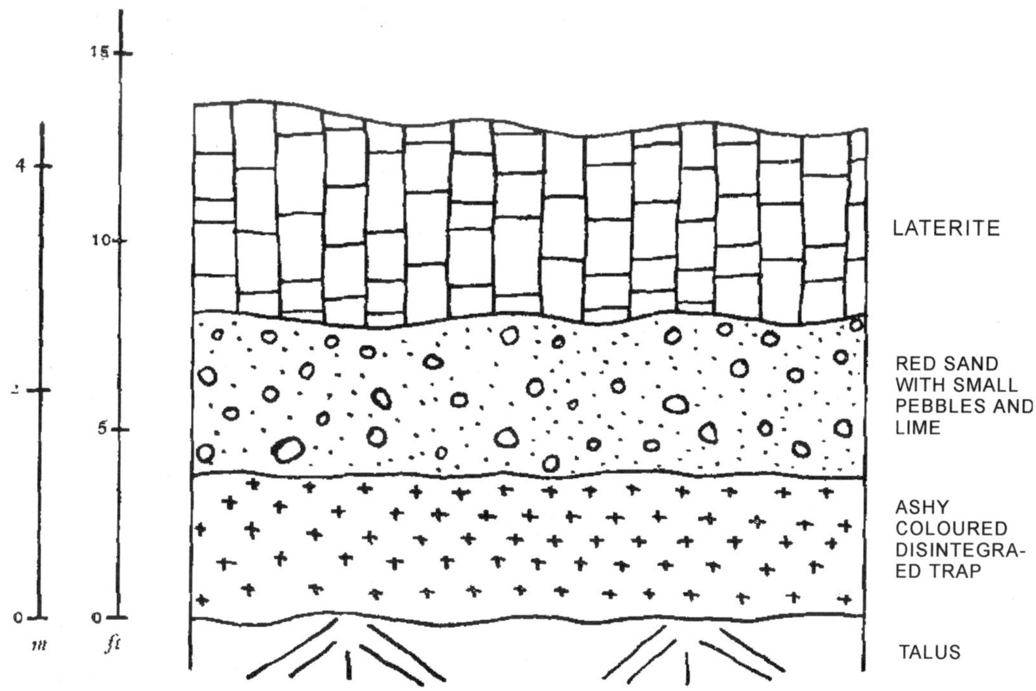

Fig. 17 Section exposed in a gully near Chidgaon

were seen in a gully near Chidgaon, a village on the Hoshangabad-Harda bus line, and at Tugaria, near Adamgarh hillock, about one and a half mile south of the town of Hoshangabad. The Early Acheulian tools *in situ* were found at Adamgarh hillock in the slopes where the laterite has been deposited in pockets.

Fossiliferous Horizons

Mammalian fauna has been collected *in situ* from four horizons: the Boulder Conglomerate (Gravel b), the Cemented Sandy Gravel (Gravel II), the yellow or pinkish Cross-bedded Sand, and the Breccia and gravel (Gravel III) deposited in the hollows of the banks made of earlier deposits. Earlier investigators, particularly William Theobald (1860:291), mentioned having extracted a big Elephas tusk, similar to one discovered at Hoshangabad by this writer, from the Red Clay horizon of the Narmada at Bilthari, 12 miles from Barmhanghat downstream on the Narmada in Narsinghpur district. But the Hoshangabad tusk came from the base of the yellowish or pinkish clay which, at Kharra Ghat, the site of discovery, rests on the Vindhyan quartzite. It seems that the early forms of Pleistocene fauna persisted until the beginning of the Holocene and then perished under the stress of climatic and human onslaught. It is not without significance that the teak forests of the Narmada still teem with wild life, including some ancient species, particularly those of the Cervus family,whose fossils have also been found in the Shiwalik foothills of the Himalayas. Elephants were a common sight in the jungles of central India as recently as the 16th century; it is recorded history that Akbar, the great Moghul emperor, used to hunt them enroute to Deccan on journeys to conquer or to chastise. The great Indian bison still roams the jungles of central India, though now restricted to the limited area of Chindwara and neighbouring tracts, and is also represented in the fossil record of the Narmada beds.

The fossils from four horizons also illustrate the various degrees of fossilization. Boulder Conglomerate fossils are thoroughly fossilized and are dated to Middle Pleistocene by previous investigators. In the current investigations, only the Hoshangabad conglomerate yielded fossils, although very few. What it contained were fragments of long bones, except for one or two complete specimens, and a bovid horn. Among surface finds, however, there are specimens with 100 per cent fossilization, such as the bovid skull from Sohagpur Tehsil, Hoshangabad (Pl. VIIa), which might belong to that phase. The Cemented Sandy Gravel (Gravel II) fossil material is very difficult to extract because of the hard matrix in which it is imbedded. Fossils are plentiful, but the fossilization is imperfect. The white calcium of embedded bones shines when they accidentally break during the extraction process.

The richest source of mammalian fossils in the Narmada is the Yellow Cross-bedded Sand, which also yields Late Acheulian and Nevasian tools. The area encompassed by the Narmada, the Sher and the Umar near Devakachhar, is the next best collecting-ground for Pleistocene fossils in the whole of India outside the Shiwalik zone. Complete skulls, ramii, molars, long bones of Elephas namadicus, Hippopotamus, Bos and Equus have been recovered from this locality, *in situ* and in the loose sand of the present bed. Fossilization of fauna is also remarkably complete in this bed. The specimens are generally stained red or yellow because of iron in the sand, particularly at Barurewa, Sher and the Umar, all in Narsinghpur district.

The deposits formed in the hollows of the river banks (Gravel III) also show fossilization. These bones generally belong to present-day fauna. In one such deposit, occurring at Bhatgaon and Ajhera, Hoshangabad district (Fig. 4), the writer recovered three large skulls of Elephas indicus (P1. V, a-b), the present-day species of Indian elephant, and many other bones of large animals.

Fossils from the Fields

The fields along the bank of Barurewa Nadi, a tributary of the Sher, yield an extraordinary wealth of bones mixed with kankar and show slight fossilization. They are found on the surface. These fields are only a few miles away from the village of Devakachhar and can be visited with the help of the local guide. These slightly fossilized bones belong to present-day fauna and represent the youngest stage among the Narmada fossils. Gravel III fossils and those found in the fields belong to the same category.

Fossil Fauna

From a collection of more than a thousand fossils, the species which can be assuredly identified are as follows:

A. Probascidae

1. Elephas namadicus (antiquus): Tusks, molars, mandibles, ramii, anterior and posterior ends of long bones

2. Elephas indicus: Skulls with teeth and tusks intact (P1. V, a-b)

B. Hippopotamoidae

Hexaprotodon namadicus: Skulls, molars and canines

C. Bovoidae

1.Bos namadicus (Pls. VI a; VII a; VIII a-b)

Bubalus palaeindicus: Skulls, maxillary fragments, ramii, upper and lower dentition, parts of long bones, etc.

D. Equidae

Equus namadicus: Ramii, dentition, fragments of long bones

E. Suidae

Sus species: ma

F. Cervoidae

Cervus species: horn

No remains of the Rhinoceros, Ursus, Leptobos or Stegodon listed by Pilgrim (1905) from the Geological Survey of India collection have been found. The confusion probably arises from the incorrect placement of Leptobos and Stegodon, which characterize the Pinjor fauna of the Shiwalik series, under the Narmada label. Moreover, Dr. Teilhard de Chardin of the Yale-Cambridge expedition, who critically examined the collection in Kolkata, reported that the skull claimed to be of the Leptobos may very well be a damaged Bos skull. He further noted that the fragments of tusks assigned to Stegodon are so fragmentary and imperfect that not even a generic identification is possible, much less a specific identification (De Terra and Paterson 1939: 318).

Among the invertebrate fossils which occur in large numbers, the following can be mentioned with certainty: (T) Gastropoda: Melania, Pludina, Bithynia; Lamellibranchia: Unio n-arginalis, Unio Vorrugatus.

Fossilized Ivory Tusk of *Elephas Antiquas* (*Namadicus*)

This is a rare and important find made by the present writer in the Narmada Valley. The tusk measures 2.14 m in length along the outer curve and is 51 cm in maximum circumference near the root end. The tip end, which should have been at about 70-75 cm, was not found intact. It was probably swept away in the flood. The break was not found to be recent, as proved by a study of a section of the anterior end. At its root end pebbles adhere to the tusk; a cement of sand and lime preserves the original break from the cranium. It appears on reconstruction that the tusk would have extended a few centimeters more on the root end side. At the time of the elephant's fatal accident, the total length of this tusk should have been approximately 3 m, taking into account its missing portions.

The writer found the tusk *in situ* on 12 December 1960, at the base of the yellow-brownish sandy clay belonging to the upper group of the Narmada alluvial stratigraphy at a place called Kharraghat, near the Hoshangabad railway bridge. The spot of discovery is about a furlong downstream from the bridge, along the northern bank uhich is 4 to 6 m high at this place. The discovery location was at that time about 3 m above the water level and 5.6 m from the water's edge. Before this find, three instances of such a discovery had been recorded; all of them are compared with the present find in the table below. It is clear from the measurements that the present tusk belongs to Elephas namadicus (a variety of Elephas antiquus), like the earlier three discoveries. Moreover, the writer saw a very similar tusk in the fossil gallery of the Musee National d'Histoire Naturelle, Paris. It was recovered in 1895 by a railway engineer, M. Le Blane, from the quaternary alluvium at Tilloux near Gensac-laPallue (Charante). That tusk also measures 3 m in length and was found in association with a man-made stone implement. The resemblance between the French specimen and the present find impresses one that their owners must have belonged to the same species, though separated by thousands of miles of land and sea barriers.

In 1805, Major General Tremlow (Pilgrim1905: 200) was the first to discover such a tusk, at Paithan, south of Aurangabad on the Godavari River. After being taken to London, however, the tusk disappeared. It was believed to have a maximum circumference of 72.5 cm.

In 1859, William Theobald, of the Geological Survey of India, made a second discovery, this time from the Narmada at Bilthari, 12 miles from Barmhanghat downstream on the Narmada in the Narsinghpur district (Theobald 1860: 291). According to Theobald, the tusk was found embedded in the Red Clay. It is now kept in the Indian Museum at Kolkata. Its length along the outer curve is 2.31 m and it has a maximum circumference of 63.5 cm. Theobald notes that a few years before his arrival, a similar tusk was known to have been found at that very place and taken to Sagar. It probably belonged to the same individual as his. It was believed to be over 3.5 m long.

In 1904, G.E. Pilgrim made the third discovery of this coveted object in the alluvial deposit of the Godavari at Nandur. He excavated a complete skull of Elephas namadicus with a portion of the tusk having a maximum circumference of 62.5 cm. He published an excellent paper describing the find and its implications, with comments on the age and distribution of the species (Pilgrim 1905).

The present discovery of the Elephas antiquus (namadicus) tusk is the second discovery of its kind from the Narmada and the fourth discovery, including the two Godavari finds, during the last 100 years. This fact itself speaks for the rarity and invaluability of the grand tusk. Its value is further enhanced by its perfect preservation and the proper recording of the stratigraphical horizon of its embedment. Data recently collected from the valley help determine the age of the tusk. The present investigation places the yellow sandy clay in the Upper Pleistocene. The clay is richly fossiliferous, at many places yielding Late Acheulian tools along with fossilized mammals. Accordingly, this ivory tusk may also date back to the Upper Pleistocene.

COMPARISON OF THE *ELEPHAS ANTIQUUS (NAMADICUS)*
TUSKS RECOVERED FROM THE NARMADA AND GODAVARI RIVERS

LOCALITY: RIVER: DISCOVERER: YEAR:	HOSHANGABAD NARMADA A. P. KHATRI 1960	BILTHARI NARMADA W. THEOBALD 1859	NANDUR GODAVARI G. PILGRIM 1904	PAITHAN GODAVARI MAJOR GEN. TREMLOW (1850s)
1. Actual length of tusk or portion obtained	2.14 m (7.05 ft.)	2-31 (7-7 ft)	—	—
2. Probable total length of tusk	3.00 m (9.IO ft.)	3.66 (I2 ft.)	—	—
3. Maximum circumference	51 cm (20.7 in.)	63.50 (25 in.)	63-50 (25 in.)	72-5 (29.0 in)
4. Minimum circumference	40 cm (15-7 in)	45-72 (I8 in.)	20.32 (8.o in.)	—
5. Maximum diameter	20 cm (7.87 in.)	—	—	—
6. Minimum diameter	14 cm (5.51 in.)	—	—	—

Summary and Conclusion

The area between Bhera Ghat and Handia is a rock basin 200 miles long and nearly 500 ft. deep, which the Narmada filled with its deposits in Pleistocene times. Six strata are distinguished in this alluvium; four of them are fossiliferous. Nearly seventy such sites — either fossiliferous or implementiferous or both — were discovered.

In the Narmada collection of fossils is represented Elephas namadicus, Bos namadicus, Equus namadicus, Hippopotamus, Bison, Buhalus, Sus and Cerrus. These fossils range in time from Middle Pleistocene to Holocene. The degree of fossilization varies from horizon to horizon. The earliest, but not all of the mammalian fossils, can be compared with those from the Boulder Conglomerate Zone of the Shiwalik foothills of the Himalayas. The Narmada Valley is unique in all of India in the coexistence of fossil fauna with different stages of Chelles-Acheul culture.*

REFERENCES

Colbert, E.H., 1935, Siwalik mammals in the American Museum of Natural History. *Transactions of the American Philosophical Society* (n.s.) xxvi, 1-10: 1-401.

De Terra, H. and T.T. Paterson, 1939, *Studies on the Ice Age in India and Associated Human Cultures.* Carnegie Institute Publication No. 493. Washington. pp. I-354.

Falconer, Hugh, 1859, *Descriptive Catalogue of the Fossil Remains of Vertebrata from the Siwalik Hills, the Nerbudda, Perim Island, etc., in the Museum of the Asiatic Society of Bengal.* Calcutta.

——, 1961, Stone Age and Pleistocene chronology of the Narmada Valley. *Anthropos* lvi: 519-30.

——, 1962, Origin and development of Series II Culture in India. *Proceedings of the Prehistoric Society of Great Britain* xxviii: 191-208.

——, 1963a, 'Mahadevian': an Oldowan pebble culture of India. *AP* vi: 186-97.

——, 1963b, A century of prehistoric research in India. *AP* vi: 169-85.

——, 1964, Recent exploration for the remains of Early Man in India. *AP* vii: 160-82.

——, 1966, Origin and development of the handaxe in the Narmada Valley. *Centenary Volume of Prehistoric Research in India.* Calcutta University.

Lydekker, R., 1880, Siwalik and Narbada Probosidia. *Pal Indica* (x) 1, 5: 18--292.

——, 1882, Siwalik and Narbada Equidae. *Pal Indica* (x) ii, 3: 67~8.

——, 1884a, Siwalik and Narbada Carnivora. *Pal Indica*(x) ii, 6: 179-363.

——, 1884b, Siwalik and Narbada Bunodont Suina. *Pal Indica* (x) iii, 35-104.

Medlicott, H.B., 1873, Note on a celt found by Mr. Hacket in the ossiferous deposit of Narbada valley (Pliocene of Falconer): On the age of the deposits. *Records of the Geological Survey of India* ii, 4: 49-57.

Oldham, R.D., 1893, *A Manual of the Geology of India.* ist edition. Calcutta.

Pilgrim, G.E., 1905, On the occurrence of *Elephas Antiquus* (*Namadicus*) in the Godavari alluvium, with remarks on the species, its distribution and the age of the associated Indian deposits. *Records of the Geological Survey of India* XXXI;I, 3: 199-218.

Prinsep, J., 1832, Note on the Jabalpur fossil bones. *Journal of the Asiatic Society of Bengal.* I: 456-58.

——, 1833, Note on the fossil bones discovered near Jabalpur. *Journal of the Asiatic Society of Bengal* I1: 583-88

——, 1834, Note on the fossil bones on the Nerbudda valley discovered by Dr. G.G. Spilsbury near Narsinghpur *Journal of the Asiatic Society of Bengal* I11: 39~403.

Spilsbury, G.G., 1833, Account of the fossil bones discovered in the bed of the Omar Nadi near Narsinghpur on Garawarda in the valley of the Nerbudda. *Journal of the Asiatic Society of Bengal* ii: 388-95.

——, 1834, Geological section across the valley of the Nerbudda from Tendukheri to Bittoul. *Journal of the Asiatic Society of Bengal* iii: 388-95.

——, 1837, Notice of new sites of fossil deposits in the Nerbudda valley. *Journal of the Asiatic Society of Bengal* vi: 487 - 89.

——, 1840a, Notes of a march from Birmhan Ghat on the Nerbudda to Umurkuntuk, the source of that river. *Journal of the Asiatic Society of Bengal* ix: 889-903.

——, 1840b, Notes on various fossil sites on the Nerbudda illustrated by specimens and drawings. *Journal of the Asiatic Society of Bengal* viii: 95~52.

Theobald, W.,1860, On the tertiary and alluvial deposits of the central portion of the Nerbudda valley. *Mem. Geological Survey of India* ii: 279-98.

Vredenburg, E., 1906, Pleistocene movement as indicated by irregularities of gradient of Narbada and other rivers in the Indian peninsula. *Records of the Geological Survey of India* xxxiii: 33-45.

**First Published in Asian Perspectives, Vol. IX, 1966.*

— A.P. KHATRI

Looking at Indian Art History – A Model

Art has no autonomous status. This applies to art of all countries, including India. It is because art is a product of the culture which is practiced by a group of people in a particular time and space. Art is, therefore, 'Culture-specific' and not universal. We have 'Greek Art', 'Chinese Art', 'Indian Art', 'Iranian Art' each one of these has been the product of its unique culture. Religion has been a major component of early culture, hence there are religion specific art nomenclature, such as the 'Buddhist Art', 'Islamic Art', 'Christian Art', but these terms related more to the 'themes' of the works of art than the 'styles, forms and symbolism' which constitute an 'Art'. This is so inspite of the fact that all cultures are pluralistic in development. They imbibe various elements from various sources, at various points of time. It gives them forms which have been changing but not ending unless completely uprooted due to politico-religious reasons as in Egypt, Iran, and Greece where old religions and cultures have been completely replaced by Islam and Christianity without leaving any trace in their current cultures.

'Culture' is, however, not easy to define since it is not an object and it has no shape. Culture can only be understood or realized through the pattern of living of the particular people. The pattern of living is determined by belief-systems embodied in their classics and folk literature, written down and oral, both.

Indian Scenario

When seen within this framework, the Indian culture, hence Indian art, has a long history of multiple dimensions. It had, like many other arts, its roots into the individual beliefs of a variety of kinds but floating, interacting and changing. These were greatly influenced by the pattern of living — to begin with, hunting and gathering, then herding of animals, then marginal farming, followed by agriculture and finally by urbanization. From this point onwards the journey took towards abstract thinking and imagining. All these are recorded in prehistoric paintings, sculptures and engraving, neolithic images, urban art and philosophical thoughts and experiences. However, like the Chinese, Indian Culture and Indian art witnessed remarkable phenomenon of 'change-in-continuity'.

Pre-Vedic, Vedic and Non-Vedic: Symbiotic Relationship between Human and Nature

In the Vedic Tradition, however, we see different trends emerging on the scene although here also we have the folk-elite interaction situation since the Vedic iconography and imagery is the outcome of the pre-Vedic beliefs some of which were picked up by the Vedic seers for their philosophical thoughts.

A great sense of symbiotic relationship between Humans and the Natural Environment in which he lives, after all man is also a part of nature, dawned upon the Indian people in the Vedic tradition itself, that man cannot survive on this planet unless nature is also preserved. Imposing divinity on the elements of nature and thereby preserving them was the mechanism developed by the

Vedic people. Hunting of animals and indiscriminate cutting of all kinds of trees were given up in favour of agricultural production and animal husbandry. All this is reflected in Indian art. Art, it may be mentioned here, is not visual alone; art is present in mental forms and pictures also and are the images described in words. The Vedic imagery is verbal; Indra, Mitra, Varuna are described in human forms with their individualistic characteristics but their images in bones, stone or clay are generally wanting. However, during the Vedic Age not every one and not every group of people was changed to Vedic belief-system, rituals and idealism; masses beyond the influence of the Vedic mode of thinking still had a large gamut of beliefs and belief-systems which were either village specific or region specific; only rarely did these beliefs or belief-systems were seen cutting across their geographical regions even though similarities may be discernible.

Two Streams of a Single Process: Folk and Elite

We have, therefore, two parallel streams of approaches to beliefs-systems, hence imagery and art — the Folk and the Elite, so to say. But we find both of them interacting with each other and not operating in exclusiveness.

It was bound to happen the way it happened since the Vedic thought-process, sometimes called 'Higher Tradition', kept on accommodating the non-Vedic or Folk beliefs, sometimes called 'Lower Tradition', or even 'Little Tradition', since the Vedic thoughts started not only growing and changing organically upwards but also 'expanding' in time and space in those very areas where the so-called 'Lower Tradition' had their own forms settled over centuries, i.e.,. villages and forest areas.

Why the Upward Mobility of Lower Traditions takes Place?

It may, however, be noted that while the Lower or Folk traditions were accommodated by the practitioners of the Higher traditions of the organized religions in order to make themselves acceptable by the people of the non-Vedic traditions, the belief-systems of the Lower traditions were also getting effected by the belief-systems of the Higher Traditions. For example, the snake or serpent worship tradition, of apparently the Lower traditions, was fully accommodated in Vaishnava, Shaiva, Buddhist and Jain belief-systems of Higher Tradition. Similarly, the snake or serpent worshipers took to Naga Worship in the Naga-Panchami festivals all over the country which was a product of Higher Tradition.

However, as will be explained later, the visual art of the 2nd century B.C.-2nd century A.D. bracket had some other historical situations in which certain icons developed, or else became more popular than earlier.

Indian Art is, therefore, a very complex phenomenon with various strands coexisting and intertwining. It may, however, be noted that religion and rituals played a very important role in this phenomenon. But all religions born in India were inclusive, sharing a host of things and a host of ideas, thoughts, philosophies, symbols, motifs, signs, and even pattern of rituals whether it is the concept of divinity in human beings or the rituals of circumambulation, *Pradikshina*.

To begin with, I will deal with one of the

basics of the human existence, the male and the female of the *Maithuni Sansar*. It is broadly termed as 'Purusha' and 'Prakriti' in the Higher Tradition of the Vedic origin. The reason for doing so is the fact that all concepts emerge out of it.

Purusha and Prakriti: The Basic Concept Underlying all Creation

Purusha (male) and *Prakriti* (female) are considered as the two major principles behind all creation. *Purusha* is the Supreme Being. It is the 'soul', or the original source of the Universe. It is the real 'force' but it remains passive. Without it nothing can be created, but on its own, it cannot create any thing. When personified, it becomes a male god, like Brahma, Vishnu and Mahesh.

Prakriti, on the other hand, is spirit or the Creative Force. It is active but it also remains dormant. In it lies the origin of all things. It is the original producer of the entire material world. It is the Primary Energy or *Shakti*. When personified, it assumes the form of spouse of a male god. It is thus, Durga, Lakshmi. Parvati, and the like.

Purusha and *Prakriti* are, therefore, complementary to each other. However, there is no causal relationship between them. To begin with, both are passive. Both remain inactive. But their togetherness results in 'creation' of the universe. After the *Pralaya* or Deluge every thing merges into *Prakriti* and remains there in the dormant stage.

Divinity in Nature and Protection of Environment

The manifested world, of which we all are parts, both visual and non-visual, and living and non-living, is called 'nature'. Like *Purusha* and *Prakriti*, all things natural are interdependent for their fulfillment. Preservation of environment is a new slogan but its awareness was always there in ancient Indian traditions, both folk and elite. Attributing 'divinity' to each item of nature was the most clever and effective method through which the environment was preserved. What is divine is not hurt, if hurt it will curse you and destroy you. Thus, Respect and Fear for the elements of nature protect the nature from every harmful act of the human beings. However, 'fear' is not emphasized, it is dormant, generally only 'respect' is emphasised.

We, therefore, call trees as *Vriksha Devatas* and do not cut them, for example Pipal, Kadamba, Amalaka, etc. are not cut. Similarly, we imposed divinity on many other life-giving items of nature such as the rivers, mountains, air, sun, moon, etc. and protect them against pollution and destruction. Terms like Ganga Maiya, Gau Mata, Vayu Devata, Surya Devata, Chandra Devata, etc. eloquently exemplify it. For the Hindu mind, the 'Mother' concept and the 'Devata' concept are, it may be noted, interchangeable.

'Folk-Elite and Elite-Folk' Model

To our mind, the 'Folk-Elite and Elite-Folk' model presented here takes care of the emerging trend in Indian art history since it is based upon the holistic approach. It is as follows:

Before the birth of the Vedic culture and Vedic *Devavada* or Divinity, India had floating beliefs emerging out of Folk traditions. The Vedic traditions picked up a few of these pre-Vedic beliefs, gave them philosophic thoughts

A MODEL FOR UNDERSTANDING THE
EVOLUTIONARY PROCESS OF INDIAN ART

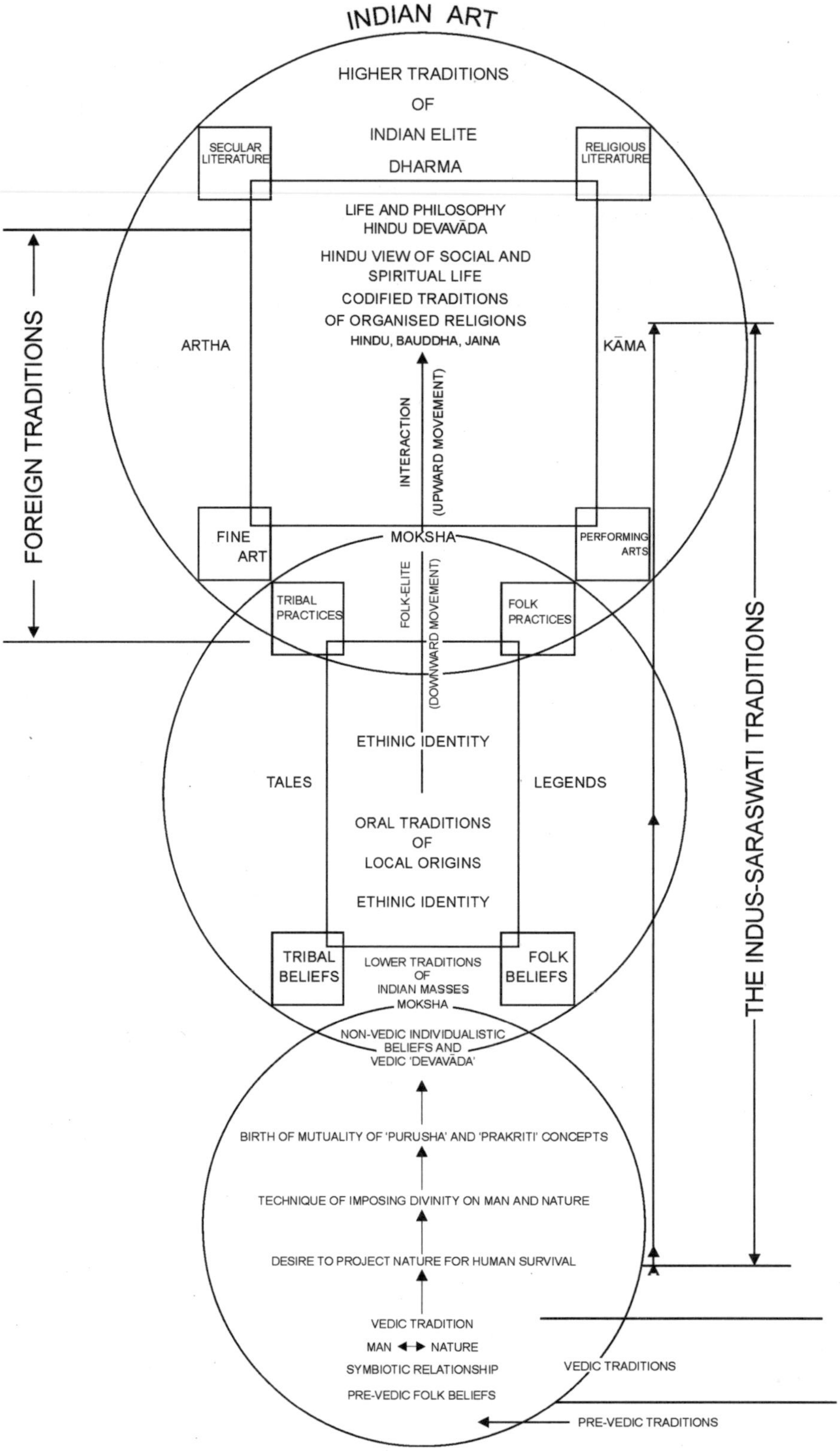

FOLK-ELITE AND ELITE-FOLK INTERACTION MODEL

and imposed on them divinity since these were the givers of life-sustaining elements, such as the water, the tree, the fire, etc., and required to be protected. During this period the Indus-Saraswati Civilization developed (4th–3rd millennium B.C.) some of whose traditions have continued till today. From the 4th century B.C. through the early centuries of the Christian era Greeks, Sakas, Kushanas, Hunas, etc. came through NW India and contributed their own elements in the field of costume and coiffure, in the field of 'ideals of kingship', and in the field of language, literature and icons. The resultant form is called 'Hinduism', including Buddhism and Jainism, since both of them belonged to one and the same *Sanatana* stream, which was vastly different from the Vedic cycle but deeply rooted in that.

While all this was happening in the realm of Higher Tradition, a section of the Hindu sages laid down the principle of *Chatura Purusharthas*, or Four Principles of Good Human Life—*Dharma, Artha, Kama* and *Moksha*, keeping *Dharma* on the top of all since it alone governed the rest, afterall *'Dharma'* is primarily the 'Code of Conduct' which the Hindus developed over a long period of time for the creation of a 'Conflictless Society'.

On the Folk and Tribal levels many belief-systems remained floating in the society. Some of them were very popular with the masses at the folk level, and the organised religions picked them up and integrated them in their own folds through various stories they created round their divinities Shaiva, Vaishnava, Shakta, Buddhist and, Jaina alike, for example Serpent Worship. This so-called Folk-Elite Interaction was the continuous process but for the sake of convenience we can say that there are two cycles — Protohistorical (the PreVedic-Vedic) and Historical (Hindu, Buddhist and Jain). But both were continuous, one leading to the other in an unbroken chain.

— **S.P. GUPTA**

1 Palaeolithic Period or Old Stone Age

HUMAN CULTURAL EVOLUTION BEGAN during the Quaternary Period, of the geological timescale, which is conveniently subdivided into Pleistocene, with a timespan of 2.5 million years and the Holocene, the present starting from about 12000 B.C. The Pleistocene is further subdivided into Ice Ages or Glacials, when Continental ice sheets covered much of the temperate latitudes in Europe and America. There were alternating periods of Cold and Warm temperatures, called Glacial and Interglacial phases of Global climate. Evidences for such changes are seen on the ground in regions affected by advance and retreat of ice sheets. Early man's culture during Pleistocene is classified into Lower, Middle and Upper, the last finishing at the end of the Last Glaciation. From the archaeological perspective, they are stages of man's technological devolopment rather than mere chronological periods. The Pleistocene period is marked by the Palaeolithic or Old Stone Age Culture, divided into Lower, Middle and Late Stone Ages. Man dwelled in camp sites and had no permanent habitation. Tools were made on the availability of raw materials and also in accordance with man's adaptation to changing face of environment. They were shaped by the process of flaking. Subsistence was based on hunting, gathering and fishing.

The Lower Palaeolithic is dominated by the chopper-chopping tools made on pebbles and handaxe industry. The handaxe made of stone is a bifacial stone implement well adapted for the use in the hand. With handaxes are found cleavers, also bifacial tools made on cores, like the handaxes, but instead of the end being pointed in handaxes, cleavers have axe like edge. The Lower Palaeolithic provides the earliest known traces of stone tool manufacture. The Middle Palaeolithic, on the other hand, includes a wide range of flakes, which are detached from a block of stone. Tools were made out of these flakes. Blade industry predominates the Upper Palaeolithic as well as Mesolithic. Blades are long parallel sided flakes taken out of long cores. They are also made into other tools such as scrapers, points and burins. During this period man also started breaking and chipping bones and converting them into tools. Technically, flakes and blades are same, but distinguished by their length/ breadth ratio.

Now, in Upper Palaeolithic man's aesthetic sense developed as is evident from petroglyphs and rock paintings as well as shell objects during this period.

Stone and bone tools were used for hunting, butchering, breaking and pulverizing bones for marrow extraction, scraping of tree barks, crushing and processing tubers and plant food, as well as crafting wooden tools and weapons. During this period caves and rock- shelters were man's main habitational sites.

The Mesolithic is marked by the hunting and gathering economy and early transition to community life. During this period man's main habitation remained in caves and rock-shelters. Settlements had plastered floors with storage facilities. Crude hand-made pottery was manufactured. Unlike free flaking technology of the Palaeolithic Period, stone tools were now shaped by the process of pressure-flaking.

The dead were disposed of in single, double and multiple burials. Such a transition stimulated the beginning of community life, agriculture and the transition to Neolithic or New Stone Age.

Lower Palaeolithic

The Indian Lower Palaeolithic represents two techno-cultural traditions, the Sohanian and the Acheulian (Fig I.1). The Sohanian culture emerged in the Mindel-Riss Interglacial (300

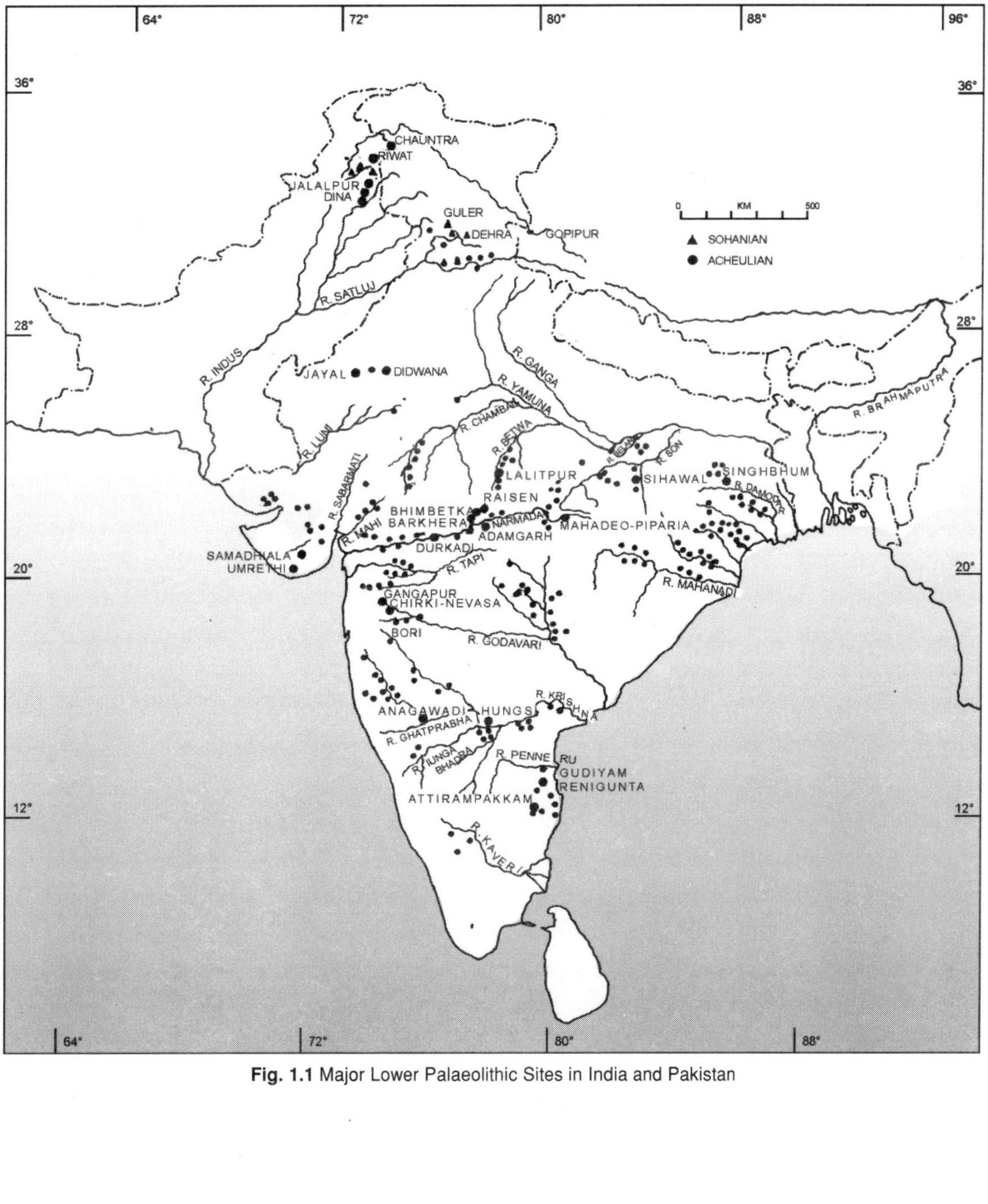

Fig. 1.1 Major Lower Palaeolithic Sites in India and Pakistan

to 400,000 B.P.) and persisted till the termination of the Pleistocene (14,000–12,000 B.P.), spanning the entire Palaeolithic. Their tools are mostly found on river terraces along the valleys of the Indus, Sohan, Sutlej, Beas, Banganga and Markanda in the western sub-Himalayan flank. The Sohanian cultural material has also been found along the Ghaggar, Chenab, Ravi and Sirsa and also on the slopes above the Punjab Plain, which are largely late assemblages. The Sohanian culture is represented by pebble tools such as choppers (unifacial) and chopping (bifacial) tools, crafted by hitting and striking stones with stones, called 'free flaking'. The faunal remains found in the context of Early and Late Sohan cultures include wild Pleistocene-fauna including horse, hippopotamus, straight tusked elephant, buffalo, wolf, bovids and camel. They bespeak of a perennial drainage, tree thickets and grass steppes which existed in the past. Magnetic polarity stratigraphy has dated Sohanian culture between 700,000-400,000 years from now.

The Acheulian culture covered the beginning of Early Middle Pleistocene to Mid-Upper Pleistocene. The fluvial, colluvial, littoral and lacustrine deposits with which Acheulian remains are associated indicate the climatic fluctuations, sea-level changes and tectonic movements during the Quaternary Period. The Acheulian cultural remains have been found in the terraces or flat surfaces of the Siwalik Frontal Range, semi-arid Western Rajasthan, Mewar Plains, Saurashtra Plains, Central Indian Deciduous Woodlands, Deccan and Chhota Nagpur Plateaus, Hunsgi and Baichbal Valleys in Karnataka, Eastern Ghats, and Southeast Coastal Region.

The Acheulian toolkit consists of choppers, scrapers, flakes, polyhedrons, handaxes, cleavers, denticulates, blades, spheroids and discoids, largely obtained from Narmada Valley. In the Plateau surface of Hunsgi and Baichbal Valleys, there is a predominance of cores and debitage with only a few finished tools. Tools were made on the availability of raw materials. Quartzite was generally preferred. In Northern Bundelkhand it was coarse-grained quartzite, in Western Deccan basalt or dolerite, and in Hunsgi and Baichbal Valleys the choice was siliceous limestone. Three techniques were adopted for making tools. The block-on-block technique to obtain large wide-angled flakes, stone hammer technique for outlining of the tools and soft hammer technique for final finishing and trimming. The tools were used for hunting, butchering, breaking and pulverizing bones for marrow extraction, scraping of tree barks, crushing and processing tubers and plant food, as well as crafting wooden tools and weapons.

The faunal evidence from Acheulian sites is represented by *Equus namadicus, Bos namadicus, Elephas hysudricus, Hexaprotodon palaeindicus, Sus namadicus* and *Stegodon insignis -ganesa* all of which propose a humid climate.

The cranium of a *Homo erectus* or *true human* was found at Hathnora in the gravels of Narmada. It suggests the involvement of man during the Quaternary Period. Thermo-luminiscence, U/Th decay series techniques and K/Ar dates have placed the Acheulian chronology within the time-span of 600 Kyr and 66 Kyr B.P.(K=thousand). Radiometric, and fluorine analysis suggests a time-span of 200,000 to 350,000 years, and fossil tooth samples suggest a time-spread of 500,000 to 600,000 years to the site at Isampur in the Hunsgi and Baichbal Valleys of Karnataka.

Middle Palaeolithic

The Acheulian tradition transformed into the Middle Palaeolithic culture, covering the terminal Middle Pleistocene and greater part of the Upper Pleistocene (Fig1.2). The Middle Palaeolithic remains are sparse in Western Rajasthan and Gujarat Plains, but rich in Siwalik Hills, Chambal, Son and Narmada Valleys, Deccan and Chhota Nagpur Plateaus, Hunsgi and Baichbal Valleys and Eastern Ghats. Tools became smaller in size than those of the Lower Palaeolithic periods. The use of

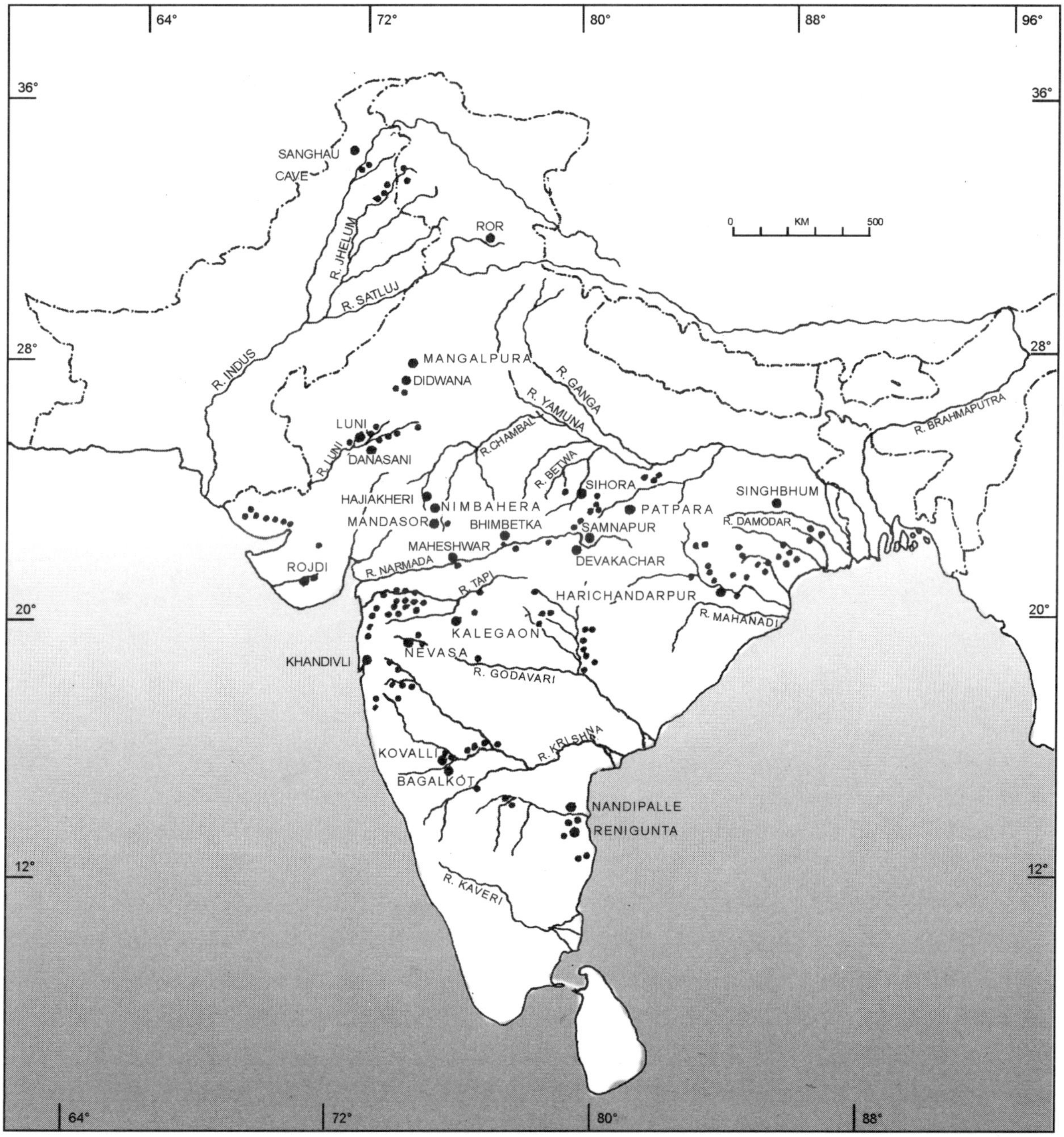

Fig. 1.2 Major Middle Palaeolithic Sites in India and Pakistan

bifaces and heavy core tools got denominated. They were supplanted by tools made on flakes and blades fashioned by the application of retouch as well as levallois and discoid core techniques. Side and end scrapers were common tools. Scrapers were used for processing animal hides and forging wooden tools. While quartzite was still in use, jasper, an opaque variety of quartz, and chert, available as small nodules in limestone formations, were preferred, which imposed a natural constraint on the size of the tools.

The faunal remains comprise *Equus namadicus, Bos namadicus, Elephas hysudricus, Hexaprotodon palaeindicus, Cervus sp.* and *Stegodon insignis -ganesa* from Narmada Valley,

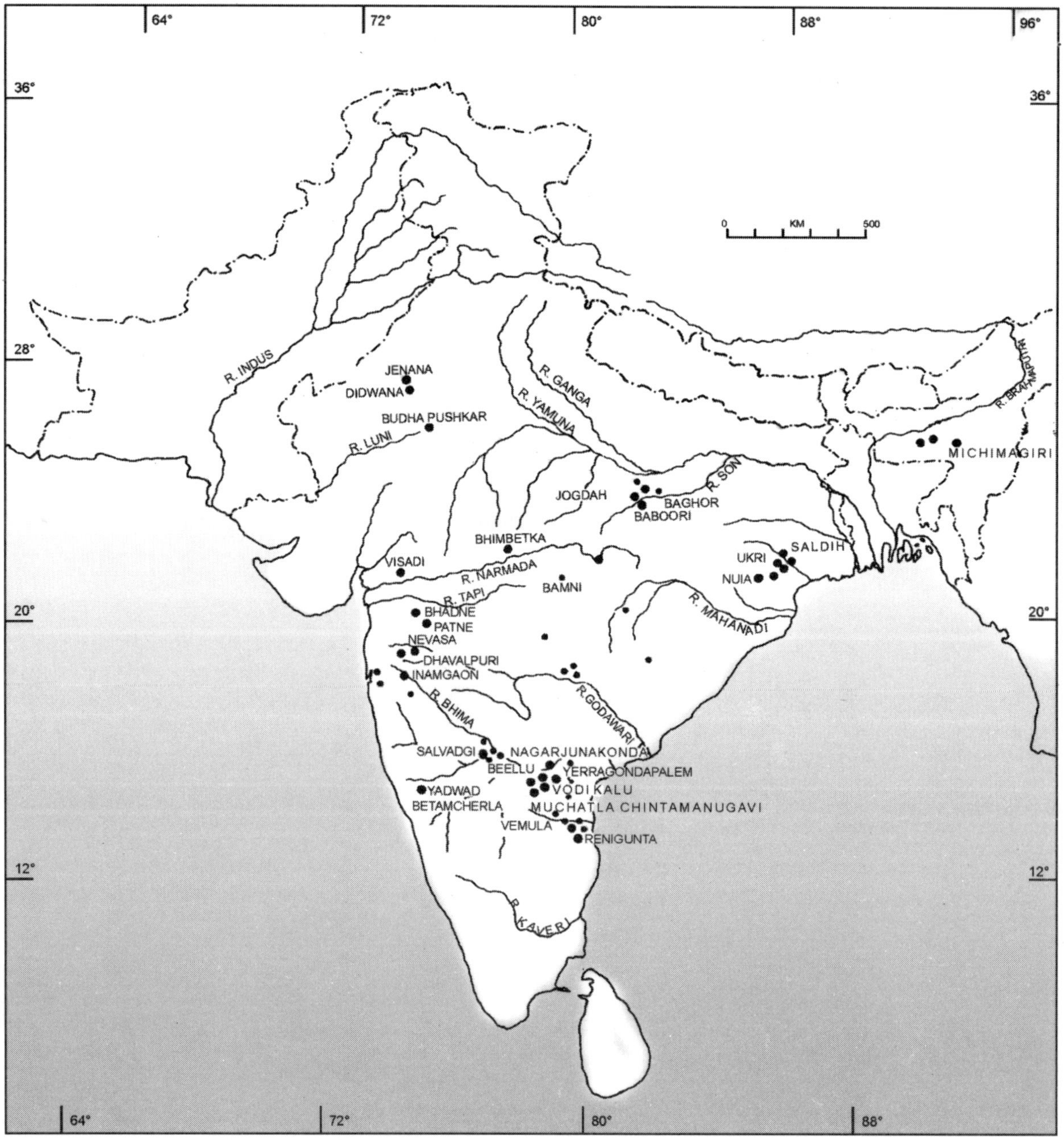

Fig. 1.3 Major Upper Palaeolithic Sites in India

and bone remains of wild cattle and pond turtle from Hunsgi and Baichbal Valleys. It suggests a savanna grassland environment and also a perennial drainage system. Plant fossils have been found at Wajjal in the Hunsgi Valley in Karnataka. Radiocarbon dates on shells and bones from Central India and Deccan, range from 40,000 B.P to 10,000 B.P., while Radiocarbon and Uranium /Thorium decay series dates in western Rajasthan attribute a time spread ranging from 150,000 B.P to 100,000 B.P. Radiometric and Fluorine analysis suggest a time-span of 200, 000 to 350, 000 years to the Middle Palaeolithic site at Isampur in the Hunsgi and Baichbal Valleys of Karnataka.

Upper Palaeolithic

The Terminal Pleistocene cultures are grouped under Upper Palaeolithic (Fig 1.3). It is associated with *Homo sapiens*. Upper Palaeolithic remains are sparse in Western and Central India, but has a dense concentration in Eastern Ghats. Principal tools such as scrapers are made on flakes, flake-blades and cores. Bone tools mark their presence with varities such as scrapers, backed blades, backed knives, and choppers obtained from the Kurnool caves. The bone harpoon from Belan Valley provides cogent evidence of a highly sophisticated tradition of bone-working.

The faunal remains comprise nilgai, chinkara, horse, buffalo, sambar, chital, mouse, hare, monitor lizard, cattle, turtle tortoise, elephant, ox and rhinoceros obtained from Kurnool caves as well as Belan and Son Valleys. Ostrich shells have been found from Yamuna, Chambal, Kalisindh, Banas, Tapi, Bhima and Narmada Valleys which confirm the presence of ostriches in India from the Lower Pliocene to Late Pleistocene times. They formed part of diet, while the empty shells might have been used as vessels. Disc beads have been crafted from ostrich egg-shells as well as engraved. The processing of plant food was done by grinding stones found from sites in Eastern Ghats. Along East Coast, the sites spread along Chennai and Vishakhapatnam Coastal Regions. Radiocarbon and Thermo-luminiscence dates attribute to it a time spread ranging between 40,000B.P. to 10,000 B.P.

Mesolithic

The Mesolithic culture covered the Early and Middle Holocene (Fig. 1.4.). The cultural remains are found in the plains of Gujarat and Mewar Plains, Vindhyan Woodlands, Kurnool Caves, and the Chennai and Vishakhapatnam Coastal Regions. Quartzite, silica, crystal and milky quartz were preferred as raw materials. Blade and bladelet technology was used to manufacture tools. Mesolithic working-floors, quadrangular and oval, have been found at Albaka on Godavari.

Subsistence pattern drastically changed with widespread appearance of grinding stones and bone tools.The temporary settlements on Middle Ganga Valley have provided evidence of grinding stones, ring stones, hammer stones, mullers, pits used for storing food, and plastered floors used for habitation. Nodules of haematite and ochre used for ornamental crafting have also come from these sites. Such cultural evidences mark the beginning of community life during the Holocene. Crude hand- made bowls and vases of red ware and burnished grey ware, from Northern Vindhyas, show the early attempts to introduce pottery during the

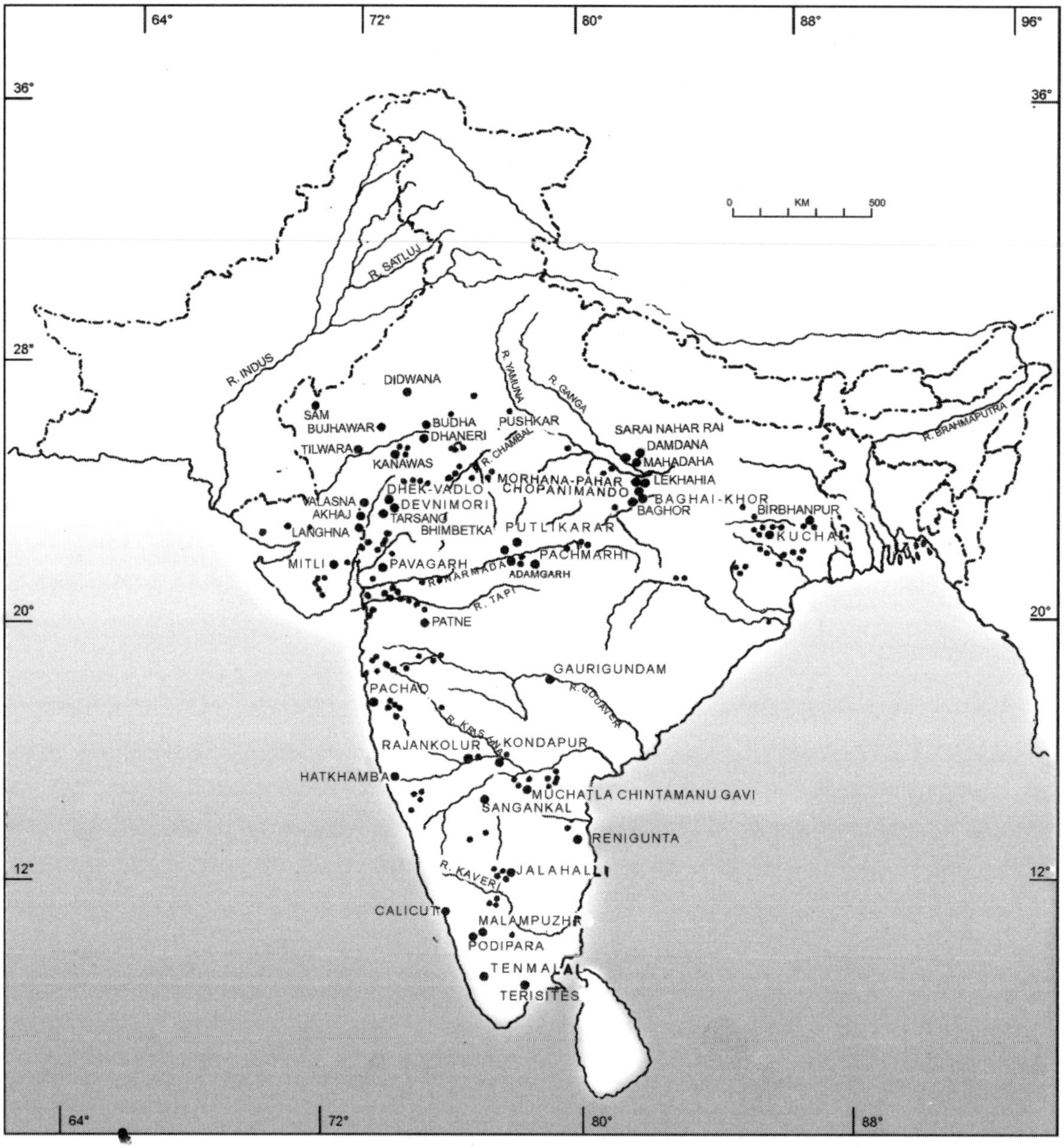

Fig. 1.4 Major Palaeolithic Sites in India

terminal phase of the Mesolithic. The petroglyphs, including cup-marks, in Vindhya and Kaimur Hills depict the Mesolithic subsistence strategies such as hunting and fishing and several unknown features. Along the Eastern Coastal Region, subsistence was relied on marine resources. Mesolithic sites in Vindhya Hills and the Middle Ganga Valley provide evidence on archaeozoological remains of sheep, dog, buffalo, goat, cattle, tortoise, fish, chital, hog deer, black buck, gazelle, elephant, rhinoceros and porcupine. Palaeodietary studies suggest a plant-based diet of the Mesolithic people. The double and multiple burials are found in extended or crouched position. C-14 dates place the Mesolithic culture from the beginning of Holocene, i.e., from 2000 B.C to 8000 B.C.

CATALOGUE

1. **Handaxe**
Lower Palaeolithic, 200,000-350 000 B.P.
Adamgarh, Madhya Pradesh.
Quartzite
Acc. No.01.

2. **Cleaver**
Lower Palaeolithic, 200,000-350 000 B.P.
Quartzite
Acc. No. 03.

3. **Chopping tool**
Lower Palaeolithic, 200,000-350 000 B.P.
Quartzite
Acc. No. 02.

4. **Handaxe**
Middle Palaeolithic,150, 000-100,000 B.P.
Barkhera,Raisen
Quartzite
Acc. No. 04.

5. **Chopper**
Middle Palaeolithic, 150 000-100 000 B.P.
Jasper
Acc. No.05.

6. **Scrapers**
Agate
Middle Palaeolithic,
150, 000-100, 000 B.P.
Acc. No.06.

7. **Flakes**
Upper Palaeolithic, 400,00-100,00 B.P.
Jasper and agate
Acc. No.07.

8. **Blades**
Mesolithic, 8000-2000 B.P.
Jasper and agate
Acc. No.08.

2 Neolithic Period or New Stone Age

THE TRANSITION FROM MESOLITHIC TO Neolithic in India took place in the seventh millennium B.C., in the Bolan Valley of Baluchistan, the evidence of which has come from the site of Mehrgarh, although in other regions it was rather late, around 5000 to 3000 B.C. (Fig 2.). The Neolithic culture is characterised by the gradual transition to sedentary life, more intensive domestication of animals, pastoralism, including seasonal grazing, agriculture, and larger settlements, increased inter and trans-regional interactions, manufacture of hand-made followed by wheel-made pottery, and a diverse variety of tools and ornaments of shell, stone, terracotta, bone and gold. Domestic and professional tools were made of stone and bone, and copper makes a marginal presence.

Remains of Neolithic cultures are found in Kashmir, Bolan and Belan Valleys, Vindhyan Plateau, Mid-Ganga, Narmada, Vindhyas, Northern Bihar, Assam, North-Cachar and Garo Hills, Shillong Plateau, Chota Nagpur and its Peneplains extending to West Bengal and Orissa, Karnataka and Andhra Plateaus, and the Kaveri Valley. Inter- and trans-regional communications gathered momentum as between Burzahom in Kashmir Valley with Swat, and Karnataka and Andhra Plateaus with Deccan and Central India postulated from cultural remains.

The Neolithic sites in India thus display an apparent diversity, both in terms of ecology and culture(Fig. 5) as well as chronology. Hunting, fishing, stock breeding and agriculture, were means of subsistence. Hunting scenes have been engraved on stone slabs as in Burzahom in Kashmir valley on the Karewas. Burzahom has rare features such as pit-dwellings, dog burials and rectangular holed sickles.

Peninsular Indian Neolithic, which spreads along 180 sites, are located away from major water sheds, in proximity to streams. Areas suited for rain- fed gravity flow irrigation were preferred and a few sites are located along river basins which provided scope for water management through canal irrigation. The Telengana and Mysore Plateaus and the Rayalseema Tract has a rich concentration of Neolithic sites. Soil analysis at Kupgal ashmound in Raichur Doab suggests a humid climate with scrub forest and grassland in the past, which facilitated the growth of Neolithic settlements. There were circular and rectangular wattle and daub houses. A few sites provide evidence of artificially plastered floors laid with sandstone blocks, probably used for butchering and dismembering animals.

The stone tools are bifurcated into pecked and ground industry made on coarse grained rocks. They are further categorized as two-edges tools and non-edge tools. Triangular stone axes come in the first category. It has been shaped

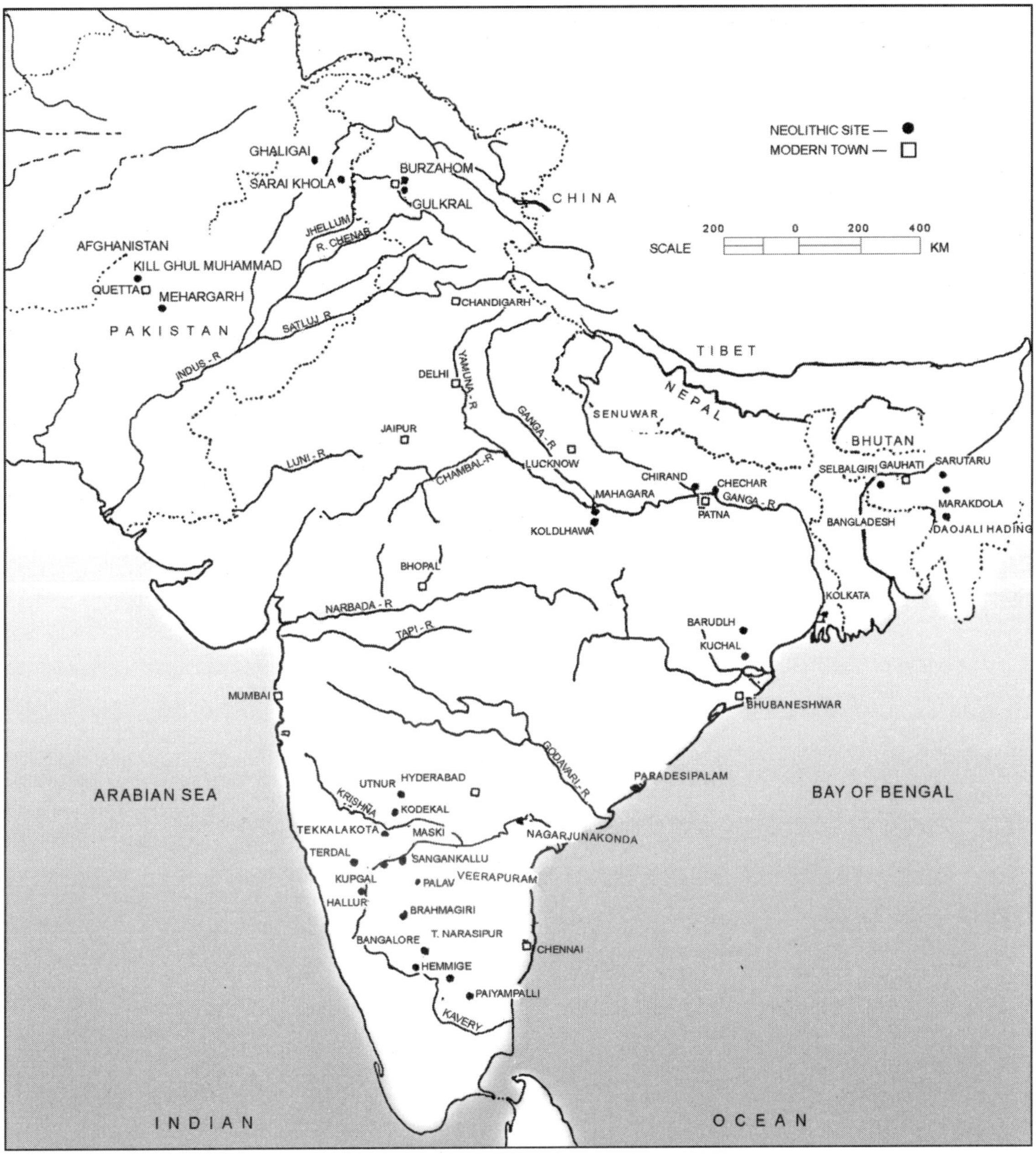

Fig. 2.1 Major Neolithic Sites in India and Pakistan

by flaking and pecking which was followed by partial or full grinding and polishing. Large and small grinding grooves were used for processing ground stone industry. New tool types, such as chert blades, copper and bronze objects with post-Harappan affinities, and Jorwe type pottery show increasing trans-regional interactions by the Peninsular Neolithic cultures with Deccan, Central and Western India. Bone, crafted into scrapers and points through flaking and grinding, were probably used for marrow extraction and hide working. The turn-table and beater and anvil techniques were used to manufacture the Neolithic red and grey ceramics. The hand-made dull burnished grey ware and wheel-made dull red ware are the dominant ceramic types. Beads of steatite, shell, agate, carnelian, gold and pendants of gold and stones were also manufactured. Copper bangles, spirals, pins, terracotta beads and burnt clay clods with bamboo impressions also form the characteristic crafts of Peninsular Neolithic.

The Neolithic people domesticated cattle, sheep, horse, buffalo, goat, dog, pig and ass. Other archaeo-zoological remains include bones of hare, nilgai, gazelle, sambhar, tortoise, fish, crab, and molluscus. They provide evidence of domestication, hunting, fishing and stock-breeding. Ash mounds formed by the accumulation of cow-dung in open and hilly tracts near perennial streams, show the existence of regular pastoral settlements around them. Remains of rice, wheat, barley, kodo millet, finger- millet, bulrush-millet, great millet, horse gram, green gram, red gram, legumes, and date palm relate to the gravity flow irrigation agriculture. Fractional and complete inhumation, ordinary and extended pit-burials, urn and jar burials were practiced by the Neolithic people. Corpses of adults were usually buried in an extended position and those of infants in urns. On the basis of C-14 dating, Neolithic culture in Peninsular India is attributed a time-spread ranging from 2500 B.C. to 1000 B.C. In the Ganga valley its antiquity goes back to 5000 B.C. In the Bolan basin its date is placed in 7000 B.C.

CATALOGUE

1. **Ground stone axe**
Neolithic, 2000-1700 B.C.
Tekkalakkota, Karnataka
Basalt
Acc. No.12.

2. **Potsherd**
Neolithic, 2000-1700 B.C.
Tekkalakkota, Karnataka
Red Ware
Acc. No. 13.

3. **Potsherd**
Neolithic, 2000-1700 B.C.
Tekkalakkota, Karnataka
Grey Ware
Acc. No. 14.

3 The Indus-Saraswati Civilization

THE INDUS-SARASWATI OR HARAPPAN Civilization represents the first urban culture in India whose antiquity goes back in time to 4th millennium B.C. although its roots can be traced back to at least 1000 years more in the Chalcolithic culture of Mehrgarh in the Bolan Valley of Baluchistan. The area of settlements of this civilization extends for more than 1600 kms. from west to east and almost equally, 1600 kms from north to south, covering a total area of about 2. 5 million sq. kms. (Fig. 3). The northern-most site is Manda, in J.&K. on R. Beas, near Jammu; the southern-most site is Bhagatrav in Gujarat on R. Tapi the eastern-most sites are Mandi in Muzaffar nagar, U.P., Bhorgarh in East Delhi and Alamgirpur in Meerut, Uttar Pradesh; and western-most site is Sutkagendor in southern Baluchistan, Pakistan, on the Arabian Sea-coast, near the eastern border of Iran. The civilization developed from chalcolithic phase in the Bolan and Quetta Valleys.

The Neolithic and Chalcolithic cultures of the Bolan and Quetta valleys were denominations of a well integrated cultural system, operating on an inter-regional basis. The growth of Aceramic Neolithic habitats of Mehrgarh and Kili Ghul Mohammad, in the Bolan and Quetta Valleys, respectively, during seventh millennium B.C., laid the foundation on which the later developments of the civilization rest. Barley, wheat, jujube and dates were now regularly cultivated. The animal economy included domesticated sheep and goat, and wild gazelle, wamp deer, chital and onager. The architecture was simple with single and multi-rooms. Primary and secondary burials were practiced. Besides the beads of several materials, like clay, copper, stones, and bone there were turquoise and shell beads the materials for which came from far off places. The sixth millennium B.C. marks the introduction of copper in the region. Similarly, soft buff chaff-tempered pottery and harder plain red ceramics were introduced.

The dawn of the urban phase of the civilization developed in the late fifth millennium B.C. with an extensive settlement. However, the major metropolis of the civilization developed at a site called 'Nausharo', some six to ten kms away from Merhgarh, in the Bolan piedmont region, and at Harappa, Mohenjadaro, Kalibangaṇ, Lothal, Dholavira, etc. in the early to mid-third millennium, had a 'citadel', middle town and lower town. Some of the fortified towns had simple entrances while others had small guard rooms in addition. They were usually laid out with bastions or corner towers, gateways and perhaps moats. When such architectural features come together, the defensive character of the complex is displayed. The fortification represents elite and bureaucracy and also served disaster management such as floods as well as human and animal encroachments. There were public as well as residential buildings. The houses show a combined use of unbaked and baked brick and wooden architecture. The roofing was mud plastered reed matting supported by timber. The houses had baths and privies. Baths were built with burnt, sun-dried and sawn bricks. The bath is evinced by a fine brick sawn pavement, carefully edged, often with surrounding curb, linked by a drainage channel to sloping chutes emptying into main street drains. There were bathing platforms.

The main streets were considerably wide

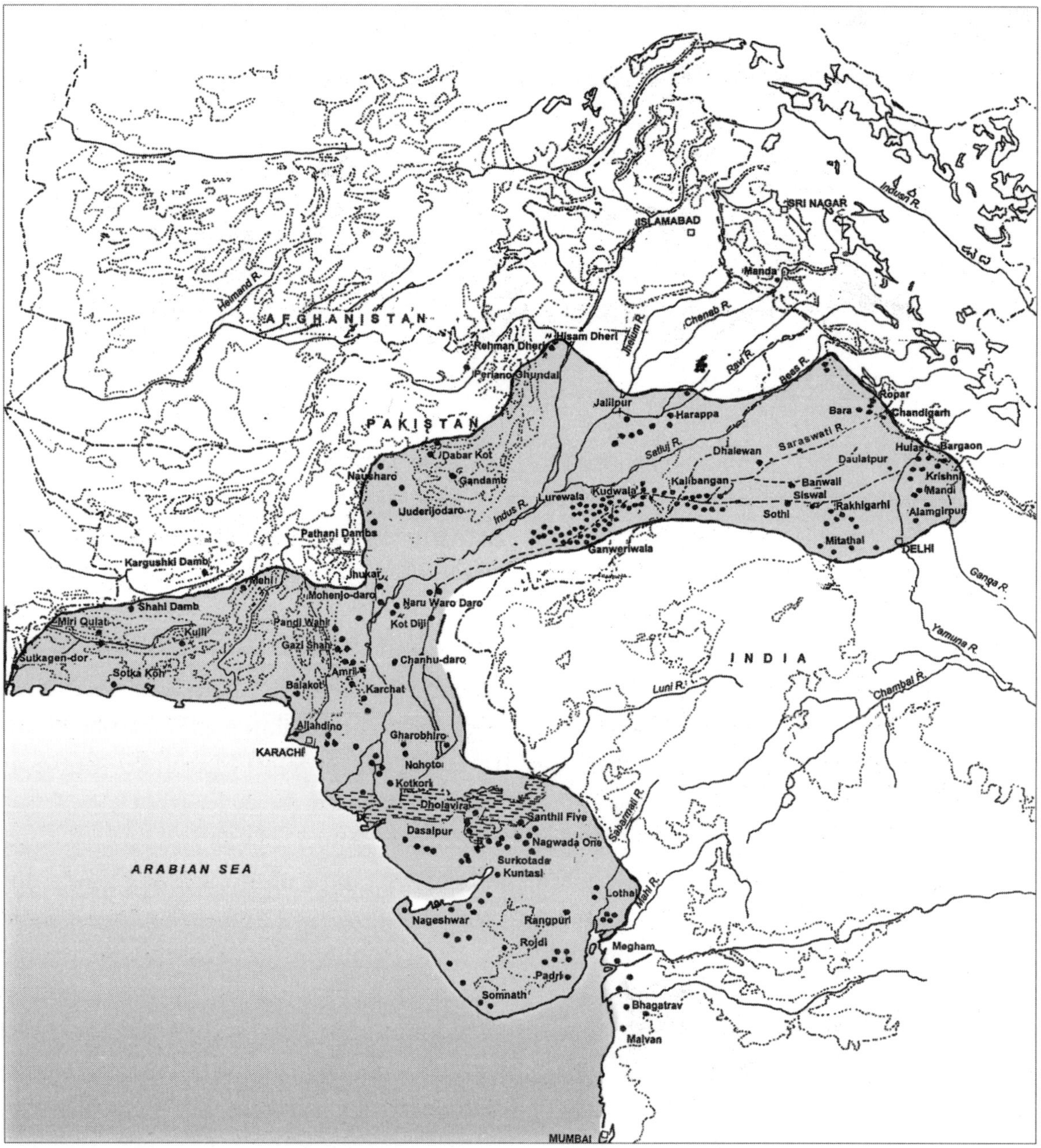

Fig. 3.1 Area Covered by the Indus-Saraswati Civilization

and the lanes were narrower. The streets and drains made of burnt bricks make a salient feature. Drains had manholes and were constructed using burnt and sun dried bricks and joined with mud mortar; occasionally with lime and gypsum mortar. The sewerage was built between the bath and the street for the convenient disposal of the faecal matter. There were cess-pits, privies and also soakage jars. The recent-most excavated site is Rakhigarhi (29° 16" N and 76° 10" E), a very large Indus-Saraswati metropolis located in the Saraswati-Drishadvati divide in Hissar district of Haryana.

A few other sites in India such as Dholovira in Gujarat, the most majestic site, had reservoirs, with partition bunds, inlet channels and dams within a circumvallation. The wells were small in diameter to enable water level rise higher and would indeed overflow in artesian fashion. Usually round, the wells made of burnt bricks were sometimes elliptical, and occasionally with a square coping. Lothal in Gujarat has given to the world the remains of an artificially made dock-yard and a warehouse. Kalibangan in northern Rajasthan has yielded the evidence of an Early Indus-Saraswati cultivated-field just outside the fortification in which twin-crops system of the present day was followed. It has also given the evidence of a group of seven fire-altars placed on high platforms in the citadel area. Banawali in Haryana has yielded on oblong mud-brick platform with several fire-altars. Mandi in UP has yielded several kilos of gold, silver and semi-precious stone jewellery. Kunal in Haryana yielded even the tiaras of silver in the Early Harappan context.

The history of craft specialization goes back to the fifth millennium B.C. at sites like Mehrgarh. Later on it developed much more. It includes a wide variety such as domestic and professional tools, mathematical instruments, pottery, weights and measures, weapons, seals and miscellaneous objects. Secondary exploitation of terrestrial and aquatic animals for subsistence and industries, such as leather, shell, ivory, bone, tanning, horn and glue is evidenced from the large quantity of objects made of these materials.

Along with bronze, copper, gold, silver and lead, a wide range of other raw materials such as steatite, alabaster, coral, agate, jasper, lapis lazuli,carnelian, chalcedony, chert, jade, calcite, garnet, turquoise, bitumen, faience, sandstone, yellow Jaisalmer stone, flint, haematite, quartzite, basalt, marble, limestone, granite, serpentine, slate, feldspar, hornblende, shell and bone were used to manufacture objects. They have been used to manufacture personal ornaments, professional and domestic tools, ritual objects, objects of domestic utility, combat, privy decoration, toys, and agricultural purposes. Lapidiaries had both tapered and constricted cylindrical drills for crafting of semi-precious stones into beads. Shell industry was quite large and specific techniques were applied in chipping and cutting the shell.

Great heights were achieved in the art of bronze and stone sculptures of human beings and animals. The so-called 'Priest' in stone and 'Dancing Girl' in bronze from Mohenjodaro are well known. But nothing like the square seals of steatite with figures of animals like bull and unicorn and human beings shown as decties, such as the famous 'pashupati' from Mohenjodaro, and inscriptions carved in intaglio since the workmanship in them is high level glyptic art.

Ceramics constitute terracotta, software, refractory ceramics and faience. Pyrotechnological objects include baked and fired mud-bricks, terracotta cakes and nodules, kiln and hearth wall fragments as well as vitrified pottery and crucible sherds. They can be extensively sub-classified based on the type of objects manufactured and techniques of production. The pottery is marked by a very characteristic sturdy red ware, often with a red slip and painted over in black pigment with geometric, floral and faunal designs. Terracotta objects display variety and ingenuity such as lids, disc, pestles, bangles, beads, cartframes, cakes, *mustikas* as well as animal and human figurines. Processing, fabrication and manufacture of objects were conducted in around twenty five industrial sites such as Merhgarh, Harappa, Dholavira, Rakhigarhi, Banawali, Kalibangan, Kuntasi and Lothal.

The inter- and trans-regional exchange network of the civilization extended fromWestern and Central India to Afghanistan, Central Asia, Iranian Plateau, Persian Gulf and Mesopotamia. Maritime trade is postulated from the dockyard at Lothal and other ports located on the India's West Coast.

We have fair archaeobotanical and archaeozoological evidence on the Indus-Saraswati subsistence.

The cereal crops cultivated were barley, wheat, rice and millet. They also cultivated lentils and leguminous plants such as the horse gram, green gram, chick pea, field pea, cow pea, grass pea and green pea. Oil seeds such as mustard, castor and sesame, and spices, and tubers such as garlic were also cultivated. Indus-Saraswati sites have provided evidence of fruits such as grapes, dates, water melon, lemon, walnut, almond, *kundru*, coconut, pomegranate, lotus fruit, Indian ber, syconium mulberry and the Indian jujube. Fibre plants such as cotton and oil seeds were cultivated as *kharif* crops. There is enough evidence on herbals such as henna, shikakai, Indian soap-nut, amla and babul. Wood charcoal remains reveal the use of timber by the Indus-Saraswati people for various purposes. They include teak, deodar, rose-wood and jujube. Medicinal plants such as *kareel* and ornamental ones such as *parijata* and jasmine have also been reported.

There was a unique and varied storage system consisting of granaries and chambers, storage jars, storage bins, corn bins, cubicles, storage pits, grain silos, underground silos and grain pounding platforms. Warehouses were also maintained as in Lothal and Kuntasi.

Cattle, sheep, goat, horse, camel, ass, dog, pig, cat, and fowl were domesticated. The remains of a large quantity of aquatic faunal remains of fish-mollusca and oysters suggests that marine food resources constituted about half of the dietary intake particularly in the coastal sites.

The dead were disposed of in oblong pits dug in cemeteries located 200-300 m outside the habitation. The burial practices include primary and secondary deposition of the deceased in graves with some corpses placed in wooden coffins or brick lined pits. Large globular pots without bones have also found buried in pits in the graveyard at Kalibangan, perhaps denoting memorial burials. There are evidences of post-cremation urn burial, as well as flexed, jar and multiple burials. At Dholavira mound burial, somewhat similar to megalithic cairn burials, has also been found.

Recent developments in osteobiographical analyses, taphonomical sciences, and forensic anthropology have rejected the earlier notions of a hypothesized Aryan invasion and massacre of the local people at Harappa and Mohanjodro which ultimately subsided the civilization into quietude.

The Late phase of the Indus-Saraswati Civilization witnessed further migrations into the Ganga plains, Central and Western India, which stimulated the spread of non-urban chalcolithic cultures in those regions.

CATALOGUE

1. **Circular cake**
Mature Harappan, 2500 B. C.
Rakhigarhi, Haryana.
Terracotta.
Acc. No. 34.

2. **Oblong cake**
Mature Harappan, 2500 B. C.
Rakhigarhi, Haryana.
Terracotta.
Acc. No. 35

3. **Triangular cake**
Mature Harappan, 2500 B. C.
Rakhigarhi, Haryana.
Terracotta.
Acc. No. 33.

4. **Circular mustika**
Mature Harappan, 2500 B. C.
Rakhigarhi, Haryana.
Terracotta.
Acc. No. 45.

5. **Oblong mustika**
Mature Harappan, 2500 B. C.
Rakhigarhi, Haryana.
Terracotta.
Acc. No. 46.

6. **Bangles**
Mature Harappan, 2500 B. C.
Rakhigarhi, Haryana.
Terracotta.
Acc. No. 36

7. **Painted bangles**
Mature Harappan, 2500 B. C.
Rakhigarhi, Haryana.
Terracotta.
Acc. No. 37

8. **Goblet**
Mature Harappan, 2500 B. C.
Rakhigarhi, Haryana.
Burnt clay.
Acc. No. 38.

9. **Beaker**
Mature Harappan, 2500 B. C.
Rakhigarhi, Haryana.
Burnt clay.
Acc. No. 39.

10. **Dish**
Mature Harappan, 2500 B. C.
Rakhigarhi, Haryana.
Burnt clay.
Acc. No. 43.

11. **Painted potsherds**
Mature Harappan, 2500 B. C.
Rakhigarhi, Haryana.
Fired clay.
Acc. No. 41 and 42.

12. **Perforated potsherd**
Mature Harappan, 2500 B. C.
Rakhigarhi, Haryana.
Fired clay.
Acc. No. 40.

4 Chalcolithic Period

The transition from Neolithic to Chalcolithic in India took place by the fifth millennium B.C., in the Bolan Valley of Baluchistan, although in other regions it was rather late, around 3500–2500 B.C. and continuing till 1000 B.C. The growth of chalcolithic complexes in Western and Northwestern India and the Indus-Saraswati Phase was followed by a momentous diffusion of different techno-cultural traditions which permeated into western and central India, Ganga-Yamuna doab and further east. They are called the non-urban chalcolithic or the Post-Harappan Chalcolithic or Neolithic-Chalcolithic cultures which fill the gap between the Late Harappan Phase and dawn of the Historical Period (1700 B.C.–1000 B.C.).

The principal Neolithic-Chalcolithic cultures are Mehrgarh, Ahar, Balathal, and Ganeswar-Jodhpura complex of Rajasthan, Chalcolithic Coastal Saurashtra, North Gujarat and Kachch, Savalda culture along the Tapi and Pravara, Kayaṭha in the Chambal, Malwa in Narmada, Jorwe in Godavari and Bhima and the Copper Hoard cultures along the Ganga-Yamuna doab and beyond towards the east and south-east (Fig 7).

Inter- and trans-regional communications gathered further momentum during this period. Along with intervening opportunity, complimentarity and transferability facilitated spread out of chalcolithic cultures. There was a meteoric rise in arts and crafts. The painted ceramics with geometric, animal and plant motifs are classic types of Indian ceramic industry.

Tools and ornaments were made of bronze, copper, gold, ivory, agate, amazonite, faience, glass, steatite, terracotta, quartz, shell, carnelian, chalcedony, lapis lazuli, jasper, jade, chert, garnet, opal, malachite, crystal, calcite, quartzite and sandstone. Where copper was scarce chalcopyrite was used to extract it. Raw materials for manufacturing a wide variety of objects were acquired from western, central and peninsular India, through an extensive communication channel.

The chalcolithic cultures had some homogeneity regarding technology and subsistence, but were distinguished by painted ceramics. Some settlements became more sophisticated, obvious from size, internal planning and architecture. A few sites such as Balathal and Inamgaon are somewhat planned settlements. The other villages do not appear to have been planned at all. There was a well furnished storage system with granaries, storage jars, pit silos and storage bins. Mud ramparts were built as in Awra, for protection against floods.

The subsistence was based on agriculture, hunting-fishing and pastoralism. Barley, rice, dwarf wheat, bread wheat, sorghum,millet, chick pea, gram pea, lentil, green gram, black gram, horse gram, grass pea, sesame and linseed were cultivated for extracting oil. Channel irrigation facilitated agriculture at least at Inamgaon. Cattle, sheep, goat, pig, deer, fowl, pea-fowl, fish and molluscus are the common archaeozoological remains from chalcolithic sites. The chalcolithic cultures are attributed a time-span from 2300 B.C. to 1000 B.C.

Chalcolithic Rajasthan

The type-site of Ahar (24° 43" N and 73° 59" E) also known as *Tambavati* is one among around one hundred known chalcolithic sites of Mewar Plateau in south Rajasthan. There are more than fifty Banas culture sites, including Ahar, in the Banas and Berach Valleys. More than a regional chalcolithic settlement, Ahar had cultural transactions with Bagor, Ganeswar-

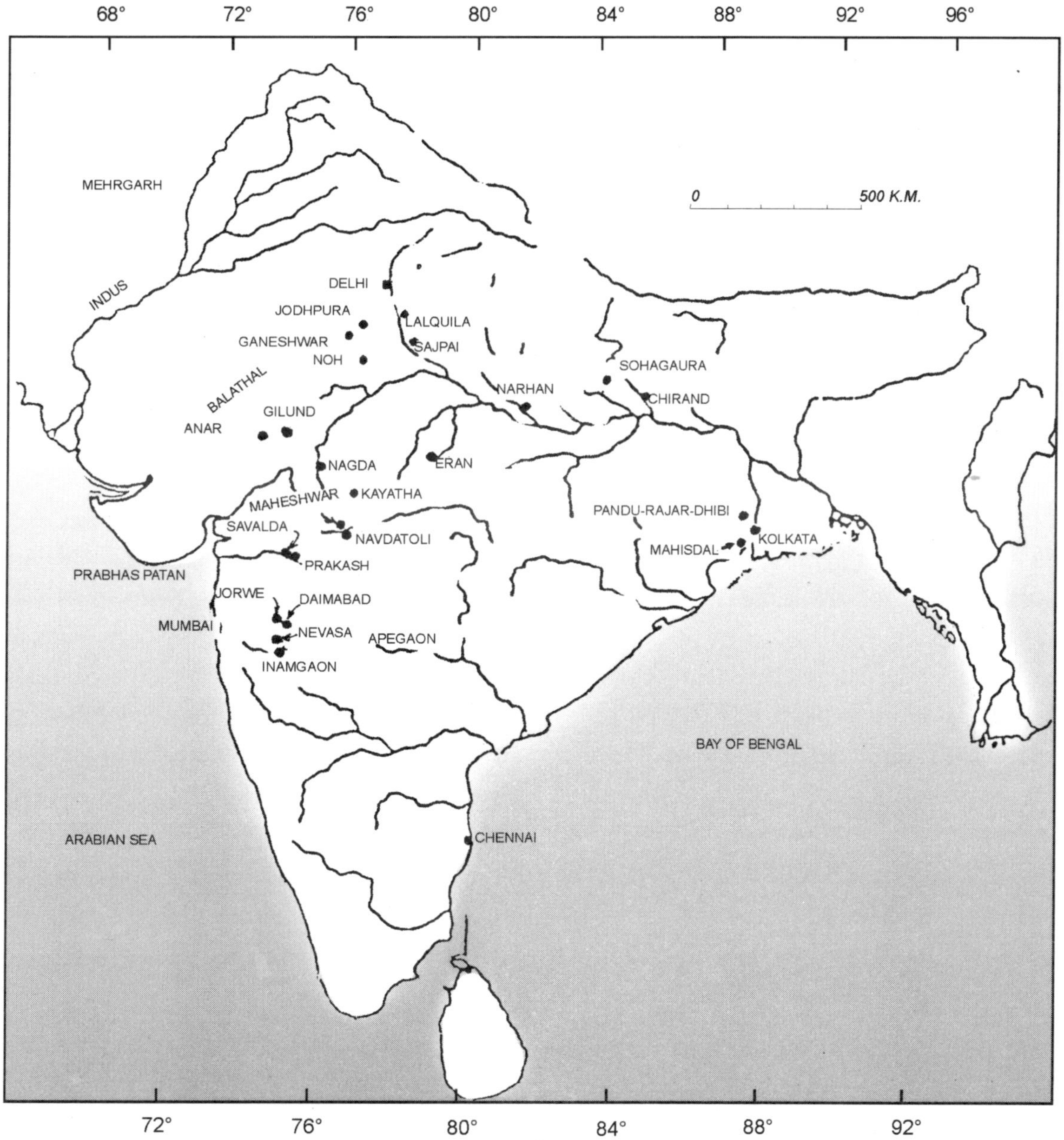

Fig. 4.1 Major Chalcolithic Sites in India

Jodhpura complex, Chalcolithic Gujarat and the Indus -Saraswati Civilization.

Stone and mud and also wattle and daub were used for making houses. The foundations were made of stone rubble, and mud house walls were strengthened with quartz nodules. At Balathal, and Gilund, near Ahar, structures were made of stone, mud, sun dried and burnt bricks.

The plain and white painted black-and-red ware with typical bowls and dishes became the hallmark of Ahar culture. The Ahar Ware consists of seven types. It is distinguished by its wheel-made white painted black-and-red ware, coarse in fabric, the other associated ceramics include the buff and buff slipped, the grey and red wares. The convex-sided bowl with geometrical designs is the type form of Ahar Ware. Storage jars were decorated with cut, appliqué and incised ornamentation.

Jorwe Ware has also been found at Ahar. Similarly, the Tan Ware from Chalcolithic Balathal has affinity with wares of the Late Indus-Saraswati sites in Gujarat. Harappan contacts with Ahar also come from spherical and barrel etched carnelian beads.The Late Indus-Saraswati Lustrous Red Ware found at Ahar has as many as eight categories.

The craft and technology of Ahar is observed from shell bead necklaces and short bicone terracotta beads bearing punctured patterns.There is a rich collection of well baked terracotta bull figurines made of fine clay. *Chulhas* and saddle querns were abundant.

Interestingly, the stone blade industry is absent. Plano-convex stones were used for grinding. Copper objects and beads of agate, shell, jasper, carnelian, chalcedony, steatite, crystal, calcite and lapis lazuli or azurite also constitute the craft of Ahar. Other objects such as sling balls, sandstone and quartzite mullers and a blade industry also display the status of Aharian craft and technology.

It appears that the Indus-Saraswati sites in Gujarat supplied shells, carnelian beads and lapis lazuli for Ahar. Millet, wheat and rice provide evidence of agriculture. Archaeozoological remains include bones of cattle, sheep, goat, pig, deer, fowl, turtle and fish. The site was deserted probably because of floods as evidenced from Awra in Mandsor district. Chalcolithic Ahar goes back to 2300 B.C.

Chalcolithic Malwa

The region of Malwa is situated on the Malwa Plateau between Chambal in the north and Narmada in the south. It was the corridor through which inter- and trans-regional communications to western India and Deccan were mediated. The Malwa Culture, identified by its ceramic, the Malwa Ware, a red ware with paintings of men, women, animals, birds and geometric designs in black, is distributed along Chambal, Narmada, Tapi, Godavari and Betwa basins.The principal sites are Navdatoli, Maheshwar, Eran and Nagda. Navdatoli (27° 70" N and 79° 14" E) located in the Nimar district of Madhya Pradesh, is a principal site of this culture. Here the Narmada has carved out a broad valley, with rich alluvial deposits on either side of its banks. It has remained a major junction linking *Uttarapatha* and *Dakshinapatha*.

The houses of Chalcolithic Malwa were of wattle-and-daub, circular and oblong. Mud bricks have sometimes been used for construction. The huts were provided with *chulas*. Mud plastered fire altars are present as well as terracotta bull figurines. The wheel-made painted pottery is extremely rich in decoration with around 600 designs, confined to the neck, rim or outer part of the vessel. There are linear, geometric, animal, plant and human motifs.The fine sturdy ceramic dressed with a thick brown slip, the red painted Buff Ware and the Combed Ware are principal ceramic types. Globular vessels with high neck and flaring mouth, concave-sided bowls, channel spouted cups, storage jars and pedastalled goblets are charecteristic ceramic forms. Chalcolithic Malwa interacted over a wide area, postulated from the presence of the Late Indus-Saraswati Lustrous Red Ware from Kaothe to Tuljapur.

Copper objects consist of axes, arrow-heads, chisels, daggers, fish-hooks and engravers. The presence of stone tools, such as flakes, cores, blades and scrapers, highlight the technological tradition of Chalcolithic Malwa. Stone tools such as blades and points are numerous and over 23,000 of them have been reported from Navdatoli alone. Copper, bronze, gold and ivory ornaments are present. Beads were crafted from as many as twelve materials such as agate, amazonite, carnelian, chalcedony, faience, glass, jasper, azurite, lapis lazuli, sandstone, steatite, shell and terracotta. Ordinary stone objects include trapstone pestles, rubber stones and hammer stones. Malwa maintained cultural affinities with Chalcolithic Ahar, as well as Chalcolithic and Late Indus-Saraswati sites in Gujarat. Malwa imported coral, lapis lazuli, marine shell, jasper, agate, and amazonite from Gujarat, and copper, quartz, steatite, from Rajasthan, and sandstone from Vindhyas besides several other sites and regions. Chalcolithic Malwa cultivated wheat, barley, rice, lentil, black gram, green gram, grass pea, linseed, ber and amla. Cattle constituted a major share of the economy. Remains of goat, pig, deer, rat, turtle and fish have also been reported. Chalcolithic Malwa has the chronology of 1600-1400 B.C.

Chalcolithic Deccan : Inamgaon

Settled life in Deccan developed with the Savalda Culture (Period 1) in west Khandesh district of Dhule in Maharashtra. Chalcolithic Deccan shared a lot of similarities with Chalcolithic and Late Indus-Saraswati Saurashtra, as well as Chalcolithic Aharians and Malwaites. Similarities between Chalcolithic Deccan and Saurashtrian Indus-Saraswati are observed from the manufacture of ceramics made on a fast wheel, firing techniques, forms and painted motifs. Conch shells were acquired from Saurashtra and gold and semi-precious stones were obtained from Karnataka Plateau. The decline of the Late Indus-Saraswati in the Saurashtra Peninsula led to exploration of new regions, and the fertile black cotton soil of Tapi Valley was found ecologically suitable. Burhanpur Gap and Songadh Pass served as itinaries of communication. The Baghlan Pass linked Tapi and Godavari Valleys. Interactions and migrations gathered momentum,which gradually extended as far as Shorapur doab which is a transitional zone between Karnataka and Deccan Plateaus. Chalcolithic Andhra Plateau also developed affinities with Deccan, which can be postulated from Savalda Ware found in the Krishna Valley.

Tapi Valley has a large concentration of chalcolithic sites, but less along Pravara-

Godavari Valley, and sparse along the dry Bhima Valley. The chalcolithic people practised agriculture, stock-breeding, hunting and fishing. The Savalda Ware with its coarse fabric and gritty core due to poor firing is marked by globular pots with high necks and circular bottom, globular pots with high narrow necks and convex sided bowls with featureless rims, microliths and copper objects. The ceramics display a variety of delicately painted motifs, linear and geometric, of animals and birds as well as weapons in black pigment. Stone querns and mullers were used as domestic appliances. Wheat, barley lentil, common pea, black gram, horse gram and hyacinth bean were cultivated.

Nevasa (74° 54" N and19° 34"E) and Inamgaon (18° 36" N and 74° 32" E) are located along Pravara and Bhima in Ahmednagar and Pune districts of Maharashtra. They were large regional centres of a local chalcolithic culture called Jorwe, named after the type-site, which was quite extensive, numbering over 200 sites. Inamgaon was a well fortified settlement. The large rectangular houses were in rows with low mud walls. The Early Jorwe culture, like the preceding Malwa culture, had copper tools, stone axes of dolerite and blades of chalcedony. Drills were made of copper and chalcedony for perforating stone and ivory beads. The pottery was wheel-made and well fired with a fine fabric. There are large kilns built on stone foundation with a huge clay basin. Increase in agricultural production is marked by the presence of an irrigation channel, 118 m long and 4 m wide. A long canal, 120 m long, received water from the river. There is an embankment built of stone rubble set in mud masonry running parallel to the channel.

The Jorwe Ware is characterized by a light to dark red wash over which painted motifs are executed in black pigment. Some of the diagnostic forms of Jorwe Ware include spouted jars with a carinated body, flaring mouth and an outcurved rim. The high necked *lota* has a squat bulging body and an outcurved rim. There are smaller *lotas* with squat body, short neck and an outcurved rim. The bowl in black-and-red ware has a slightly outcurved rim. The Jorwe Ware is found distributed as far as Karnataka and Andhra Plateaus. Affinities of Chalcolithic Deccan with Karnataka Plateau is also observed from morphology of stone axes. The presence of gold, ivory, serpantine, copper and amazonite also suggests the trans-regional exchange system with Gujarat, Rajasthan and Karnataka.

The people subsisted on dry farming, stock-raising and hunting -fishing. Domestic animals included cattle, sheep, goat, buffalo and pig. Archaeobotanical remains include those of of rice, wheat, barley, finger millet, lentil, chick pea, grass pea, horse gram and wild date. The storage system comprised of pit silos, a granary and round mud platforms to support storage bins. Adults were buried in pits dug under the house-floor in north-south direction.

The Late Jorwe phase (Period III) was confined to Bhima Valley. In this phase houses become circular in shape. The pottery is coarse, and pit silos are replaced by four -legged storage jars supported on four flat stones. Lime balls and lime kilns are seen in large numbers. Weeds and herbaceous plants occur and wheat is conspicuously absent suggesting a decline in agriculture in this phase. The irrigation channel got silted and fell in disuse. Archaeozoological remains of sheep and goat constitute maximum and cattle bones few, showing an increase in pastoral means for subsistence. Among the 266 burials at Inamgaon, 171 belong to Late Jorwe, among which 107 are of infant. Corpses of adults were kept in extended position. They are single, double and three urn burials. Associated with the disposal of the dead is a four legged anthropomorphic urn burial made of unbaked black clay. The Jorwe culture had a time-span of 1400-700 B.C.

CATALOGUE

1. **Pot-sherds**
Chalcolithic Ahar, 2100-1400 B.C.
Ahar,Rajasthan.
Acc. Nos. 17, 18 and 19.

2. **Pot-sherds**
Chalcolithic Malwa, 1700-12000-1400 B.C.
Navdatoli, Madhya Pradesh.
Acc. Nos. 20, 21 and 22

3. **Small lota**
Chalcolithic Jorwe, 1000-700 B.C.
Nevasa, Maharashtra.
Painted Red Ware.
Acc. No. 23.

4. **Spouted jar**
Chalcolithic Jorwe, 1000-700 B.C.
Nevasa, Maharashtra.
Painted Red Ware.
Acc. No. 24.

5. **Bowl**
Chalcolithic Jorwe, 1000-700 B.C.
Inamgaon, Maharashtra.
Black and Red Ware.
Acc. No. 25.

6. **High necked lota**
Chalcolithic Jorwe, 1000-700 B.C.
Inamgaon, Maharashtra.
Painted Red Ware.
Acc. No. 26.

7. **Hop-scotch**
Chalcolithic Jorwe, 1000-700 B.C.
Inamgaon, Maharashtra.
Black Ware.
Acc. No. 29.

5 Early Historical Period

THE EARLY HISTORICAL PERIOD BEGAN IN THE first millennium B.C. when iron, which started in India in the mid 2nd millennium B.C., gained the primary status over copper. The period is marked by the presence of colossal structures, including architectural monuments, townships, inscriptional records, coinage, a spurt in technology and crafts, and an extensive communication network with Afghanistan, Central and Southeast Asia as well as Meditterranean. In Peninsular India, the Iron Age was associated with Megalithic Culture which was followed by the ascent of Satavahana and Ikshvaku dynasties during the 2-3rd century A.D. and 3rd-4th century A.D., repectively. In the Indo-Gangetic Plains the Late Indus-Saraswati and Ochre Coloured Pottery people were succeeded by a society associated with ceramics such as black-and-red, the Painted Grey Ware, Black Slipped Ware, and Northern Black Polished Ware during the first millennium B.C.

Early settlements in Ganga Valley grew by the side of tributaries, during Painted Grey Ware Period, which commenced from the late 2nd millennium B.C. Majority of the sites were located near drainage systems of eastern part of the Saraswati, Ravi, Sutlej, Upper Ganga, Gomti and extended upto Besnagar in central India. Among the late Painted Grey Ware-early NBPW sites, fortified settlements, as in Kaushambi, are very few. The pottery was made of well levigated clay. The storage jars, bowls and vases of Painted Grey Ware were well fired, fine slipped and occasionally washed. Geometric designs, and natural motifs were painted in black on the grey surface. It includes types such as straight sided bowls, cups, and dishes with incurved sides and saggar bases, as well as small vases. Polished black ware, black-and-red-ware, brownish-red ware and plain red ware are associated with Painted Grey Ware. These ceramics, at least in certain Late Indus-Saraswati doab sites, display links between the Bronze Age Cultures and Iron Age Cultures.

Cultural remains of the Painted Grey Ware period include terracotta discs, stone-querns, net- sinkers, shell, glass beads and bangles, ivory ear-studs, textiles, bone arrow-heads, awls, pendants and sockets. Tools and weapons of copper include antimony rods and nail-parers, and that of iron are spears and arrow-heads. There were weights made of chert and jasper. A *Syena chiti* shaped brick structure, resembling a flying Garuda, has been found at Purola in Uttaranchal. Barley, rice and pulses were cultivated. Cattle, horse, buffalo, goat, sheep, dog, fowl, pig, bivalve, turtle and fish, also formed part of subsistence.

In the Middle and Lower Ganga Plains urbanization gathered momentum with the introduction of Northern Black Polished Ware, the deluxe ceramic of the Buddha's Period, by 600 B.C.–500 B.C. Sole dependence on agiculture for subsistence decreased and large number of settlements came up away from drainage systems. Civil architecture achieved a meteoric rise. Townships established on alluvium had extensive ramparts and moats as at Kaushambi near Allahabad on the Yamuna. However, townships on rocky terrains had stone walls with square bastions of rocks. Single or double ringed fortifications became a common feature, and the core was of mud dug with burnt-brick revetments constructed later as at Rajgriha in Bihar.

Townships were either oblong or square in shape and a wide moat encircled the settlements. Moat and ramparts are essential parts of fortification. The ramparts had gateways, watch towers and guard rooms. Ramparts defended settlements not only from invasional threats but also from natural disasters such as floods. Burnt bricks and *kankar* lime were used for constructional purposes. Timber was extensively used for palisades, basements, ceilings, platforms for ramparts as well as *chaitya* arch in rock-cut caves.

Roads were built of burnt bricks. There was a regular grid pattern of constructing main streets as at Taxila, near Islamabad, Pakistan. The drainage system was not extensive like that of the Indus-Saraswati civilization but there were burnt brick drains, terracotta ring- wells and stone and wooden drains with corbelled arches at the mouth. Houses were built on street-sides paved with bricks and roofed with terracottas tiles. A good number of rooms surrounded the courtyard. Houses had an entrance room, bathrooms and wells. In some cases, there were terracotta soak-wells attached to houses. Terracotta slabs with a central hole and raised foot emplacements, as well as cess-pits and pottery drain-pipes have been found in the Ganga Valley sites such as Ahichchhatra and Rajaghat.

Mauryan Period

Among the monumental architectural remains, are the Mauryan columns, which are monolithic shafts with a capital attached to it. They are made of polished sandstone and represent one of the finest elements of Mauryan art. Polished stone pillars with bulls seated back to back and other types of capitals were used in the palace-complexes of the Mauryas such as these found at Pataliputra, near Patna in Bihar. Among public structures, the hall at Kumrahar in Pataliputra has monolithic pillars of sandstone. The Stupa, the apsidal *chaitya* hall, the circular *chaitya* hall, and the *viharas,* come under religious monumental structures of the Mauryan and post-Mauryan period. The theological seminaries at Vikramasila belong to this period.

There was also much advance in technology, trade and craft. The Northern Black Polished Ware was made on fast wheel with polished surface and lustrous metallic finish. Iron gained a monetory status and tool types include chisels, axes, knives and moulds and large quantity of iron slags has been unearthed from Ujjain, Sambhar and Rairh. Mathura has provided evidence of copper smith's furnaces, and Vidisha and Rajghat of bone-working workshops. Bead factories functioned at Ujjain in Madhya Pradesh, and jeweller's mould in Champa in Bihar. Agate, amethyst, sandstone, carnelian, steatite, chalcedony, garnet, jasper, lapiz lazuli, onyx, quartz, rock crystal, slate, shale, alabaster, shell, bone, ivory, gold, glass, copper, coral and terracotta were the raw materials used to manufacture beads of a very large variety, shaped even in human forms, animals and birds besides geometrical shapes, as at Kaushambi, Mathura, Rajghat and Hastinapur. Quarrying was an important occupation, especially at the sandstone belt at Chunar. Jasper was used to make weights and measures, which were usually in discoidal form. Animals, birds, snake goddesses, and females are represented in Mauryan, Sunga and Kushana terracotta art. The ringstones and discstones in steatite, slate and alabaster display animal, plant and human life withn a framework of geometric patterns during the Mauryan and Sungan times. The round, relief, rock-cut sculptures, architectural fragments of Mauryan and Late Mauryan periods bear the typical Mauryan polish. Stone sculptures

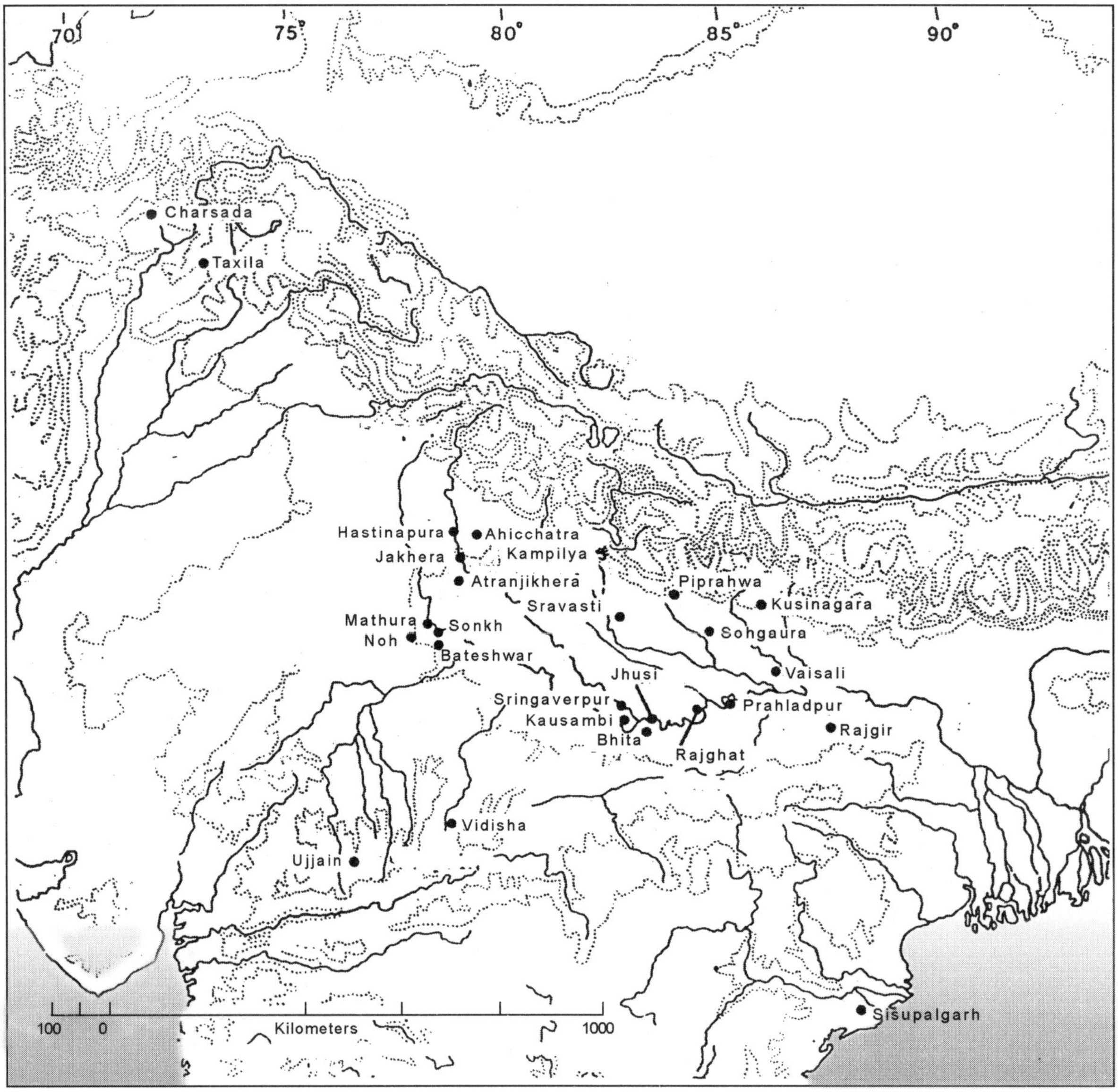

Fig. 5.1 Major Sites of Historical Period in Northern India and Pakistan

include life sized nude male torsos from Lohanipur in Patna of the Mauryan times. The stone brackets, free-standing Yakshas and Yakshis, and the decorative art motifs are some of the other salient features of the Mauryan and Late Mauryan art.

Iron has also been been found associated with black slipped, black-and-red, burnished grey and associated red wares of the pre-mauryan and Mauryan times. Punch marked coins of copper and silver and uninscribed copper cast coins were introduced during this period. Asokan edicts were engraved on rocks and pillars, and other Mauryan inscriptions in caves and on stone slabs, copper plates and relic caskets. Inscribed potsherds, as well as ivory, bone, stone and terracotta seals also give evidence of writing. Brahmi, Kharoshti and Prakrit were the scripts in general use although Greek and Aramaic were also used by Ashoka and others in the north-west.

Irrigation tanks were constructed as at Girnar in Gujarat. Barley, rice, wheat, *kodon* millet, black gram, green gram, peas, khesari, cotton, and sesame were cultivated. The period is marked by the presence of simple but large granaries. Storage jars were placed on circular brick structures. The terminal phase of Northern Black Polished Ware culture provides evidence on the remains of large scale destructions by fire and flood.

Sunga Period

The post-NBP period, from 2nd century B.C. is marked by regular fortified townships with satellite settlements. The Post-Mauryan art comes from gateways, railings, balustrades, coping stones, stone-castings, facades and walls of stupas, *chaityas* and *viharas*. Mauryan stupas were enlarged during the Sunga Period as at Sanchi, with stone railings and gateways. They were adorned with relief carvings, some of them carrying inscriptions. The Brahmi script had a dominant position. Inscriptions in Prakrit language showing Sanskrit influence is seen on the Heliodorus pillar inscription at Vidisha, dated to 120 B.C. The ceramic during the Sunga Period is a red ware decorated with stamped and incised designs. Grey and red wares are other principal types. Common types include bowls and dishes. Varied types of iron tools were manufactured for carving and hewing stones and rocks.

A distinct feature of Sunga art is the spread of terracottas plaques made from single moulds showing female figurines high bejewelled and covering heads with scarfs as well as turbans. Ivory working developed and icons cast in bronze were manufactured. The copper coins were produced from moulds or were struck from dies.

There were two major cultural and commercial focal points. Bharhut, near Satna in Madhya Pradesh, with a large stupa, with huge stone railing and gateways, located on the eastern route connected Sravasti and Kausambi with southern Kosala, and the eastern metropolis of Pataliputra. The Stupa at Vidisha was an important breakpoint in the Ganga Valley on the route linking Mathura and Ujjayini and it further extended to Gandhara and Madradesa in Northwest and Pratishthana in Deccan. The plastic quality of the sculptures in the rock cut-caves at Bhaja shows the range and extent of Sunga-Satavahana craftsmanship. Punch marked copper coins have been found from various places, including Vidisha, the western capital of the Sungas.

Kushana Period

The Kushana Period is marked by great building activity and art as well as opening of new trade diasporas and routes. The inscriptions from Mathura, Sanchi, Kanheri and Jogimara refer to bankers, merchants, carpenters, ivory workers, surveyors, sculptors, gardeners, weavers, jewellers, goldsmiths, iron workers, royal scribes and *devadasis*. They present the range of social stratification as well as economic enterprises. The cultural relics of the Kushana Period include pottery, terracotta objects such as toy carts, votive tanks, bricks, tiles, wheels, terracotta figurines with typical Kushana headdress, plaques and sculptures depicting costumes and ornaments, as well as beads of ordinary stone and semi-precious stones, glass, ivory, terracotta, bone and iron objects.

The pottery is generally of monochrome red ware. The common types found in the Ganga Valley are bowls with tapering sides, lids with central knobs, vases, basins, sprinklers and storage jars, beakers and goblets in Red Polished Ware. The depictions on the pottery include geometric patterns, schematic floral designs and branches of trees. Roman amphora is found in Northwestern, Western and Eastern coastal India such as Hatab and Kamrej in Gujarat, Elephanta and Nevasa in Maharashtra and Pondicherry. There are variations in the pottery at Takshasila (Taxila). Cotton, linen and jute seem to have been used in textile industry as observed from spindle whorls and inscriptions found at excavated sites. Timber was extensively used in construction. Mining and metallurgy thrived as postulated from various objects such as nails, door-knobs, hooks, chains, arrowheads, axes, chisels, knives, and ploughshares. Copper was used to manufacture coins,ornaments, vessels and lamps. Gold was largely used for coins and ornaments. Beads, bangles, finger rings, vessels and mirrors were made of glass. Ivory is confined to plaques. There are evidences of antimony rods, perfume vessels and incense burners at Mathura, Sonkh, Sravasti and other places.

Pataliputra was the terminus of trade routes from Ganga Valley to Afghanistan and Central Asia. Mathura was a junction of two major trade-routes, to West and Northwest India. The Kushana contacts with the Meditterranean world is postulated from large amphorae, bronze statues and silver objects recovered from Sirkap in Taxila and Brahmapuri in Maharashtra. Mathura acquired a meteoric rise as a craft and industrial centre. A considerable number of Vaishnava, Shaiva, Shakta, Buddhist and Jaina sculptures and also of denominative cults such as Naga, Skanda and Surya of the Mathura school of art have been recovered from Mathura and various other sites in the Ganga-Yamuna *doab*. The stone quarries at Agra, Sikri, Rupbas and Karauli supplied red mottled sandstone for carving sculptures. Along with their copper coinage, the Kushanas issued a golden dinar on the pattern of the Roman aureus. Distinct deities were depicted on the coinage issued by Kushana and his successors such as the Shiva, Buddha, Greek and Egyptian deities and the Iranian pantheon like Ordoksho with corncopia. From the second century B.C. Brahmi inscriptions are found used on coins. Now even Kharoshti and Greek inscriptions are found on them. Names of kings and gods and their images adorned the coinage of the period.

The gold coins of the later Kushanas show

a standing monarch wearing a long coat, holding the trident at an altar on the obverse and goddess Ordoksho seated on a throne on the reverse. During the Kushana Period Sanskrit inscriptions made much progress. Trees, serpents and hills were elaborately depicted in Kushana sculptures.

Archaeobotanical remains of the Kushana Period include rice, barley, wheat,green gram, black gram, horse gram, lentils, grass pea, black pepper, *tulsi,* jujube, date, almond, grapes, custard apple fruit and walnut. Wood charcoal of pipal, deodar, camphor, sandalwood and *kaith* have also been identified.

In peninsular India, Arikamedu has yielded a ware-house and tanks. This site, which represents an Indo-Roman trade-centre, has yielded lapidiaries as well as red Arretine Ware, Rouletted Ware, and the two handled amphorae as well as Roman lamp and glass ware.The chronology of the site goes to the first century B.C.

Larger fortifications and streets marked the township of Nagarjunakonda in the Krishna Valley in the 3rd–4th century A.D. The sculptures at Nagarjunakonda, Ghantasala, Gummadi-durru, Goli and Amaravati show the range of mutual cultural interaction. There are *stupa* and *chaitya* remains at Nagarjunakonda and at Amaravati. The Jataka themes depicted in Goli, and the story of Nanda and Janapadakalyani and others are depicted at Nagarjunakonda. The visit of Indra as well as Ajatasatru to the Buddha are depicted at Amaravati, scenes of temptation at Ghantasala, flying figures over stupa at Gummadi-durru and the panel depicting Vissantara's story at Goli are unique. Sannati in Karnataka has also yielded a large number of sculptured panels belonging to the Satavahana period (2nd century B.C.–2nd century A.D.) as Amaravati had also yielded.

Gupta Period

Large fortifications, brick wells, streets, drains, libation slabs linked with drains through earthenware pipes are some features of Gupta townships. Nalanda, Pataliputra, Vaisali, Kausambi, Sravasti, Sarnath, Bhita and Rajghat offer abundant scope for study on Gupta architecture. The stone and iron pillars at Mathura and Mehrauli respectively represent the best specimen of the period. Copper and stone images and shell inlays also display the craftsmanship of the Gupta Period. There were ornamental as well as inscribed bricks. Burnt clay images and plaques were skillfully manufactured. Large size terracotta plaques were used for decorating walls of temples such as those at Ahichhatra, Bhitargaon, etc. Red ware is the principal type and ornamental pottery was popular. The shapes are round, ellipsoid, flat-bottomed, open at the top and receding at the base and rims are plain. Pottery spouts included heads of animal such as lion, horse, elephant, boar and *makara.* Large number of motifs and designs such as lotuses, rosettes, and floral patterns are found incised on face or in relief among red ware pottery, terracottas and bricks. Terracotta art and casting figures in stucco achieved great heights during the Gupta Period. Gupta terracottas include gods and goddesses, male and female figurines, animal figurines, and miscellaneous objects.

Epigraphic evidence of the Gupta Period shows popularity of the Vaishnava cults.

Paintings are well represented in the Bedsa, and Ajanta and Bagh-cave-walls and they are world-famous. Besides the Buddhist themes, these multi-coloured murals depict secular themes like banquets and the animal and vegetal worlds. These are known for their shade-and-light effect, *mudras* or gestures and flowing linear quality. They are in tempere technique. Architecture of the Gupta Period is well represented in stupas, and rock-cut caves with Hindu temples as at Vidisha. Temples were excavated in rocks, and as independent structures they were built in dressed stone as at Bhumara in Madhya Pradesh, and in bricks as at Bhitargaon near Kanpur in Uttar Pradesh. Some temples were flat roofed and sanctum square with a shallow pillared porch in front, as at Sanchi, Temple No. 17; or with a covered ambulatory around the sanctum and preceded by a pillared porch. The other group included either rectangular or circular with an apsidal back as for example the Durga temple of Aihole, or with shallow rectangular projection at the four cardinal faces. The most famous of the Gupta stone temples with spire or pointed *shikhara* is of Deogarh near Jhansi in which sculptures of Nara-Narayana is world famous. Gold coins were common showing the monarch, *Garuddhwaja*, deities such as Sri and Skanda as well as the sacrificial horse. There were a few coins of copper and lead. The designs on Gupta seals include *Sri*, vases, lions, trees and altars. Sculptures on the various manifestations of Vishnu show the popularity of Vaishnavism during the Gupta Period. The Gupta kings called themselves as *Parama-Bhagavatas.*

After the Indus-Saraswati Period, we find a revitalization of core elements such as extensive town-planning, spurt in technology, arts and crafts, and internal and trans-regional trade which were lying in quietude for more than a thousand years.

Some Excavations

Kamrej Excavation

The ancient site of Kamrej (21 16' 55 N; 72 58' 0] E), Dist. Surat, Gujarat, is situated on the left bank of the river Tapi. The site falls within the precincts of the modern village of Kamrej which is also the headquarters of the Taluka of the same name. Kamrej lies about 15 km upstream of Surat. From the Surat Railway Station, the village of Kamrej is approximately 20 km. The Graeco-Roman records of the early centuries AD, such as the *Periplus*, indicate the existence of ancient Kamrej, called 'Kammoni', as a port-town. The site was excavated by the Indian Archaeological Society under the directorship of S.P. Gupta and Sunil Gupta with assistance from Tejas Garge, Ms. Sonali Gupta, Anuja Geetali and Rohini Pandey.

The site could be excavated this year only upto a depth of 82 cm which revealed three levels or phases of occupation. Antiquities from layer 1 of level I on what is called 'cliff mound' include monochrome drawn glass beads, hopscotch made from pottery and arecanut shaped terracotta beads and spindles belonging to the early centuries of the Christian era. Some terracotta stamps were recovered from layer 2 along with fragmented terracotta figurines, shell bangle fragments and worked columella shells, a few fragments of crucibles and iron slags. Bangle fragments of glass, fragments of a copper vessel, a polished piece of shell and shell fragments, copper beads were the other finds.

A number of other antiquities associated with several burnt-brick structures, including a wall, all belonging to the same period, of the cliff section, were also recovered. Level III yielded a burnt brick wall. Most part of the wall is destroyed. It is difficult to explain the function of the wall. The mortar used was thick coarse lime. The second phase of the cliff section showed remains of a large fired brick structure held up by rammed brick and mud foundations. There are seven courses of bricks joined with thick coarse lime mortar.

The artefacts associated with them include finished beads of glass and semiprecious stones, iron nails as well as handfuls of cotton thread. A good number of other antiquities include fragmented terracotta figurine of an animal and also of human beings and fragments of black, yellow and white glass bangles.

The excavations also yielded a rich variety of artifacts which are indicators of water vessels plying on the Tapi in Early Historic times. For example, a number of thick iron nails from the excavations were bent almost ninety degrees. These thick iron nails, hammered and bent upwards, are still used to secure the planking of riverboats on the Tapi. A piece of burnt rope with the knot still in place was recovered near the Kiln in trench Al/l. Knotted ropes near major water bodies signify, among other things, a maritime function. Various types of knots are necessary for binding masts, yardarms, oars, etc. of riverine and deep-sea watercraft.

A particular bead-type included faceted glass beads imitating precious stones. These 'imitation' beads were actively traded across the Indian Ocean and are to be found in far flung sites such as Ban Don Ta Phet (Thailand), Arikamedu (south India) and Tissamaharama (Sri Lanka). Beads of stone, terracotta and glass were also recovered from the same level. Also worked fragments of agate and carnelian recovered from excavated contexts point to bead crafting at the site. Stone beads include melon shaped orange coloured carnelian beads, spheroid reddish white carnelian, spheroid orange red carnelian, spheroid white-red carnelian, and Collar bead of crystal. These types of beads were first categorized by Mortimer Wheeler in his excavations at Arikamedu. Glass beads recovered include an emerald green glass bead, short and cylindrical square with chamfered edges. This was most likely made in imitation of emerald or beryl. Such faceted beads, imitating precious stones, were exported from India to Southeast Asia and the Mediterranean world. There is a reference to 'counterfeit' beads in the *Natural History* of Pliny. Others include a cylinder hexagonal made from drawn glass and faceted ink blue in colour, faceted glass beads cylinder hexagonal, and turquoise blue in colour. Finally, a dark brown drawn glass bead of the Indo-Pacific type and an orange paste glass drawn bead, also of the Indo-Pacific type, have made the collection of beads from Kamrej very important. Agate nodules and unfinished agate beads, on the other hand, indicate stone bead-making activity at the site

The prolific finds of columella shells in various stages of being finished into bangles leave no doubt about a rich shell crafting industry at Kamrej. Pieces of a green and blue glass were also excavated. The terracotta finds comprised of roof tiles, spindles and terracotta figurines. The roof tiles, mainly recovered from Trench Al, are diagnostic artefacts of the early centuries AD. These tiles are ubiquitous in Early

Historic sites in western and northern India.

Sanjan Excavations

There is a strong tradition, as codified in *Kisseh Sanjan,* a text of 1600 A.D., that the forefathers of the Indian Parsis came to Sanjan, some 60 km from Mumbai, on the sea-coast and settled down there with the goodwill of the local ruler, one Jadi Rana. It happened sometimes in the 8th century. The World Zarathushti Cultural Foundation, Mumbai, through its office-bearers, Mrs. Mani Kamerkar and Dr. Homi Dhalla, requested the Indian Archaeological Society to excavate the site for them. Dr. S.P. Gupta, the Chairman, agreed to direct the excavations with Dr. Kurush Dalal as the Field Director and assistance in the field-work from Dr. Abhijit Denekar, Ms. Rhea Mitra, Ruksana Nanji and Rohini Pandey.

The excavations revealed housing complexes and ringwells along with a large amount of potteries, plain and gazed wares, glass beads and vessels, iron implements, copper and silver coins, datable to the period bracketed between 8th century and 13th centuries. Some antiquities belong to the first five early centuries of thc Christian era also.

Kampilya Excavation

Kampilya (27° 36N 79° 17"E), the capital of erstwhile Dakshina Panchala of the Mahabharata Period, is located in Farukhabad district of Uttar Pradesh. The antiquity of this site goes back to the Mahabharata Period. The site was jointly excavated by the Indian Archaeological Society and the Venitian Academy of Indian Studies. Geoarchaeological observations of the region was carried out with the help of Remote Sensing. The Drupad-ka-Kila site of Kampilya spreads out over 900,00 sq m with a fortification wall made of bricks and brickbats. A vast land of flooded area is seen from the top of the ancient mound. At both the ends of the mound, huge dressed stone boulders project out of the deep occupational deposit. The sides of the fortification wall is in a rectangular shape with the longer axis oriented east-west. In the sharp cutting edge of the section mixture of washed flood deposits are seen. Such erosional scars are seen at a few Painted Grey Ware sites such as Hastinapur, Atranjikhera and Jakhera in Upper Ganga basin.

The Painted Grey Ware and Northern Black Polished Ware sherds are seen on the surface of the mound. The cultural material from Kampilya belongs to the Kushana-Gupta Period. Iron objects include chisel, knife and nails. Decorated *kankar* slabs and a sandstone relief with the central figure of Saraswati flanked by attendants were recovered from the site. The main pottery types include sprinklers, vases, spouted pots, bowls, handis and storage jars. The terracotta objects include a cart frame, beads, earlobes, bangles and animal figurines. Kampilya is located on the grand route to Takshasila. A Panchala coin was unearthed from the site. The Panchalas issued a uniform series of copper coins bearing the name of about twenty one rulers. On one side these coins bear three small symbols in a row and the name of the issuer below. The other side has a figure or symbol representing the deity associated with the name of the ruler.

CATALOGUE

1. **Panchala coin**
Kushana-Gupta 200-500 A.D.
Kampilya, Uttar Pradesh
Copper
Acc. No. 62

2. **Nail**
Kushana-Gupta 200-500 A.D.
Kampilya, Uttar Pradesh
Iron
Acc. No.63

3. **Chisel**
Kushana-Gupta 200-500 A.D.
Kampilya, Uttar Pradesh
Iron
Acc. No. 52

4. **Cart frame**
Kushana-Gupta 200-500 A.D.
Kampilya, Uttar Pradesh
Terracotta
Acc. No. 50

5. **Bead**
Kushana-Gupta 200-500 A.D.
Kampilya, Uttar Pradesh
Agate
Acc. No.48

6. **Beads**
Kushana-Gupta 200-500 A.D.
Kampilya, Uttar Pradesh
Terracotta
Acc. No. 47

7. **Earlobe**
Kushana-Gupta 200-500 A.D.
Kampilya, Uttar Pradesh
Terracotta
Acc. No. 51

8. **Bangle**
Kushana-Gupta 200-500 A.D.
Kampilya, Uttar Pradesh
Terracotta
Acc. No. 64

9. **Animal figurine**
Kushana-Gupta 200-500 A.D.
Kampilya, Uttar Pradesh
Terracotta
Acc. No. 49

10. **Lamp**
Kushana-Gupta 200-500 A.D.
Kampilya, Uttar Pradesh
Terracotta
Acc. No. 60

11. **Conch**
Kushana-Gupta 200-500 A.D.
Kampilya, Uttar Pradesh
Shell
Acc. No. 65

12. **Kauri**
Kushana-Gupta 200-500 A.D.
Kampilya, Uttar Pradesh
Shell
Acc. No 66

13. **Bangle**
Kushana-Gupta 200-500 A.D.
Kampilya, Uttar Pradesh
Glass
Acc. No 64

14. **Spouted Vase**
Kushana-Gupta 200-500 A.D.
Kampilya, Uttar Pradesh
Red Ware
Acc. No 53

15. **Handi**
Kushana-Gupta 200-500 A.D.
Kampilya, Uttar Pradesh
Grey Ware
Acc. No 56

16. **Bowl**
Kushana-Gupta 200-500 A.D.
Kampilya, Uttar Pradesh
Coarse Red Ware
Acc. No. 54

6 Medieval Art and Persian Documents

From the 8th through the 13th century A.D. the Arabs traded with India. The Parsis, who were prosecuted by the Muslims in Persia and their fire-temples converted into mosques, fled to India in the 8th century and lived for about twelve years in the island of Diu and then moved to Sanjan located in the mainland on the Western Coast. The museum has a small but representative collection of this early medieval site (9th–13th century).

Excavations at Sanjan: 2002–03: Glazed and Plain Wares

Sanjan, known as the first regular settlement of the Parsis in India, is located on the Varoli basin near the tidal limit of the creek in Valsad district of southern Gujarat. The site was jointly excavated in January 2002 and January 2003 by the World Zarathusti Cultural Foundation headed by Homi Dhalla and Mrs. Mani Kamerkar, and the Indian Archaeological Society with Dr. S.P. Gupta as the overall Director and Dr. Kurush Dalal as the Field Director, and Dr. Abhijit Dandekar, Ms. Rukshana Nanji, Ms. Rohini Pandey and Ms. Rhea Mitra as field supervisors. Sarvashri M.S. Mani and Lakshmi Narain were the chiefs of the Graphics and Photo Divisions of the Indian Archaeological Society, respectively. The site now nestles a village of fishermen called 'Machchivada'.The excavations brought to light rich habitational deposits, classified into the Early and Late Periods. The Upper level deposits are characterized by hearths and burnt brick structures. Both periods have revealed ring-wells made of large bottomless terracotta jars placed one above the other. They possibly served as toilets. The artifacts recovered include utilitarian grey ware pottery, green and blue glazed ware, turquoise glazed ware, white glazed ware, buff/ kaolin ware, Chinese wares, fine glass ware fragments, silver coins, iron, lumps of carnelian and garnet and shell bangle fragments. The glazed sherds include a few bearing appliqué designs. The description of representative samples of sherds are as follows: body sherd with thick turquoise glaze on surface, sandy buff fabric and black coating on the interior, shoulder fragment of jar having coarse buff exterior, similar core and black sooty coating in the interior; body sherd with blue-green glaze, nearly eroded, and having compact pinkish core; body sherd with red polished slip and well levigated reddish fabric.

The upper levels of Period II have yielded a large number of opaque and transparent glass ware and glass beads, many of them are opaque and in variegated colours. A bright Red Ware spout of a sprinkler of the 1st–2nd century A.D. is a significant find from Period II debris. One of the silver coins is datable to 7- 8th century A.D. and it resembles a Sassanian issue of undetermined date but possibly 7th century.

A fragmented Gadhiya copper coin of the 11/ 12 century A.D. has also been suspected. There is a coin with Brahmi inscription of 2nd century A.D. also. In the absence of absolute dates, the tentative dating of the site on the basis of historical and artefactual data is between 2nd century A.D. and 13th century A.D. On further comparitive studies the dates may go beyond this time-bracket particularly because Sanjan still has the remains of a large stone-and-brick built fortification on the joint sea and river waters front built by the Portuguese for negotiating long-distance trade.

The Glazed wares came from Iran and Iraq along with the Arab trade while greenish porcelain belong to the Chinese trade.

In the excavations of 2003 a house complex and a few human skeletal remains have also been found on the creek burnt-brick walls of a jetty have also been found.

Late Mughal Period Documents

Hand-written documents form an important source material for the Mughal administrative and economic history. There are five valuable and administrative orders from the period of Akbar.They are *Jaridata-i-Farman-i-Salatan-i-Delhi*, Imperial farmans granted by Akbar and his successors to Vithal Nath Goswami of Mathura and Vrindavana and his decendants. The Mughals and the Jogis of Jakhbar containing farmans of Akbar and his successors relating to free grants of lands to the Nath Jogis of Jakhbar in Punjab, The Parsees at the court of Akbar and Dastur Meharji Rana which includes copies of Akbar's and Jahangir's farmans of *Madad-i-Maash* grant to the Parsee priests of Navsari. A descriptive list of farmans, manshurs and nishans addressed by the imperial Mughals to the princes of Rajasthan. The farmans were also issued by Aurangazeb and Bahadur Shah I. There are some *nishans* also, handwritten administrative orders regarding land-grants.

CATALOGUE

1. **Glazed Wares**
900 A.D.
Sanjan,Gujarat.
Acc. No. Lot No. 02.1

2. **Document of Aurangazeb**
1658-1680 A.D.
Persian, Paper
Landgrant
Acc. No. 71.
Manuscript

3. **Painted Manuscript**
1900 A.D.
Persian, Paper
Acc. No.72.

SOME PERSIAN EXECUTIVE DOCUMENTS

I: *Parwana*, (Official document) to Mutasaddis of present and future (account officer) Pargana Narsi, Sarkar Manakpur, Suba Allahabad, regarding the grant of 55 bighas of land, tax-free, around the village Kesri under above said Pargana. On the request of Mir Saheb Sayyed Mohammad Baqar Ali Khan to Syed Shabbir Ali from the beginning to 1206 Fasli. Further directing the said officers that they will not impose any type of tax and will not enter into any sort of dispute with them. All the income of the land may be left to him and paper of the grant will not be demanded for renewal each year. So that he may bestow blessings on the royal dynasty; dated 26 Zilajja 1212 year.
Note:- The forehead of the document bears a seal which is not decipherable being unclear. Also a remark for particular Imams.

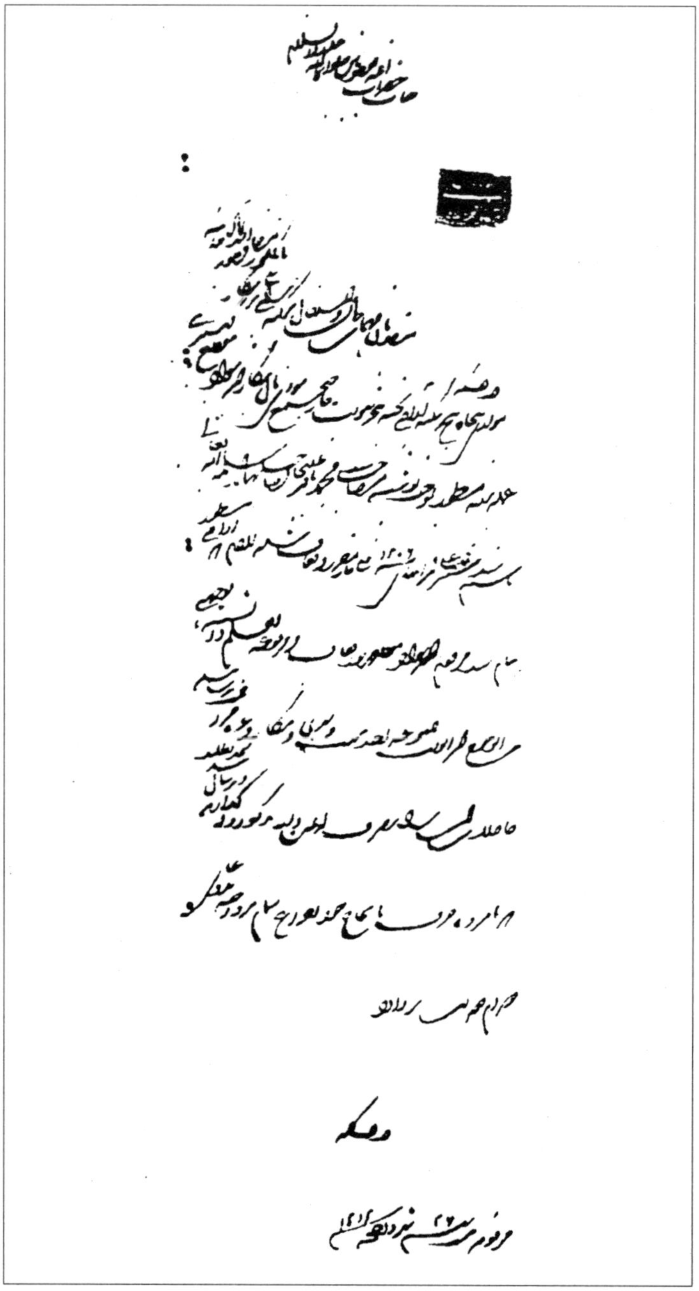

II: *Copied accordinq to the original Parwana* with the seal of Qazi Syed Nasiruddin Ibn Syed Rahamat Ullaha Khadim-i-Shar-e-Mohammad Rasul-Allah. Parwana with the seal of Mohammed Darab Ali Khan Bahadur dated 11th Ziliajja 1215 A.H. addressed to Rai Desh Mukh Rai regarding grant of 16 Bigha land with the standard measurement, tax-free, in the village of Miranpur to Syed Shabbir Ali since a long time and this land is under his possession. Now as usual in 1208 Fasli is granted to him. You are instructed that you will not confront and raise any objections and leave the land in his possession for his daily food. So that he always be busy for the blessings for the government. You are stressed to act according to the instructions.

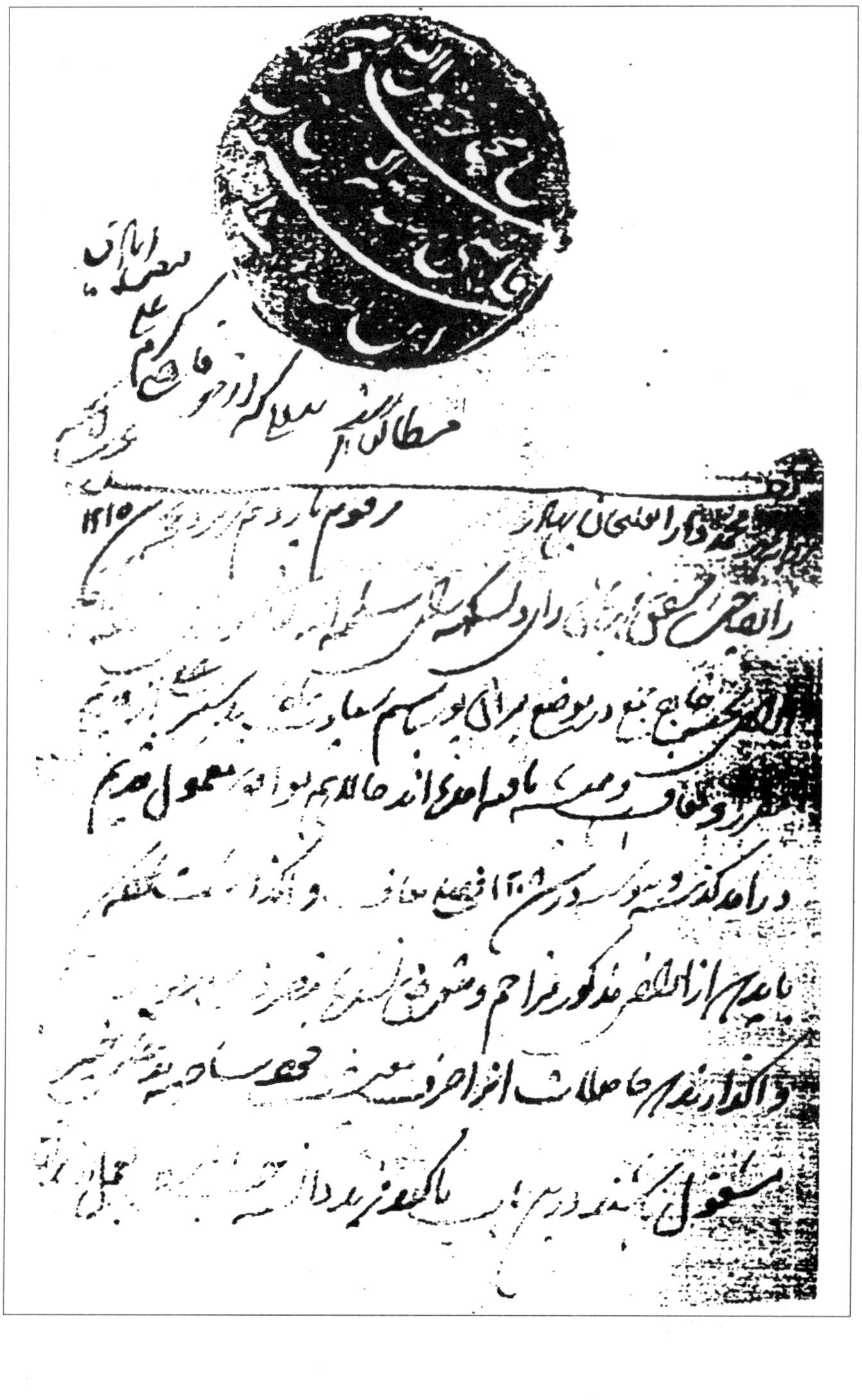

III: The detail of two pieces of land granted to Syed Shabbir Ali, with the seal of Mirza Aziz- Ullah-Beig.
Dated 1211 A.H. Kumbe-3gaz. Ouser 10 bighas

Kheti	3 bighas.	
Qusar	1 bigha	10 biswa
Bulkha	1 bigha	2 bighas
Wazih	10bigha	
Malhoo	1 bigha	- biswa
Sian	2 bigha	
Bhasi	1 bigha.	
Bakarna	1 bigha,	5 biswa
Shian	1 bigha	12 biswa
Birya do Balat	2	- biswa

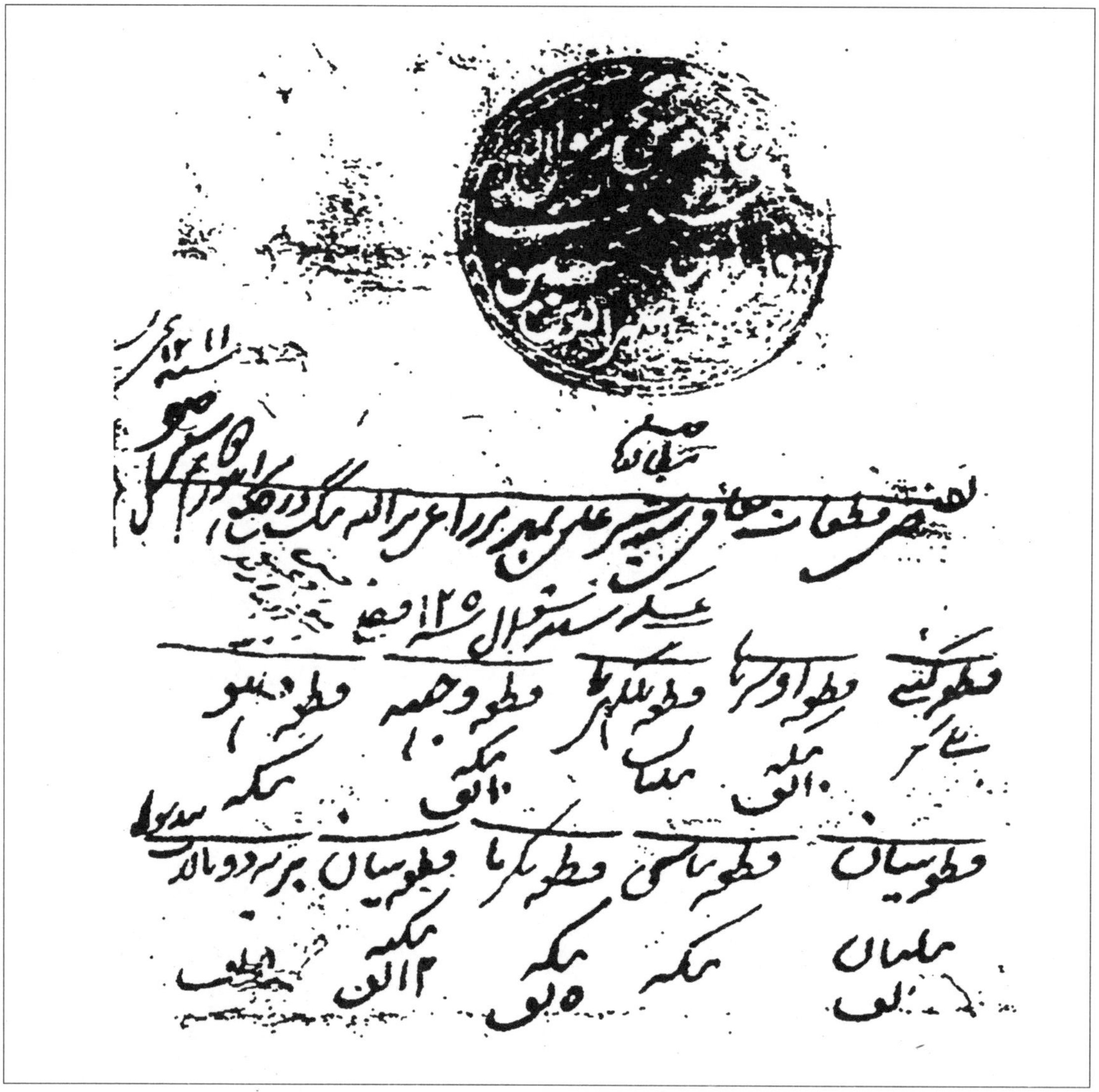

IV: *Copy according to the original Parwana* with the seal of "Princess God bless her" addressed to Khawaja Shakhrullah officer of Ceylon, informing Khawaja Shakhrullah, Tahsildar of Ceylon, etc. that 16 bigha land according to the standard measurement, tax-free, besides Govt grants, from village Miranpur under Jais is granted to Syed Shabbir Ali since a long period. So that in the year 1225 Fasli after investigation it was found that the said land is granted to him since a long period. Therefore, the land should be left to him for his daily food, to get the blessing of the saint. This is stressed to act according to the order. Dated 17 Ziqada/1213 A.H. The document is decorated with the seal of Raisul Mashaikh Mufti Ul Mulk Hazrat Gulam Ahmad.

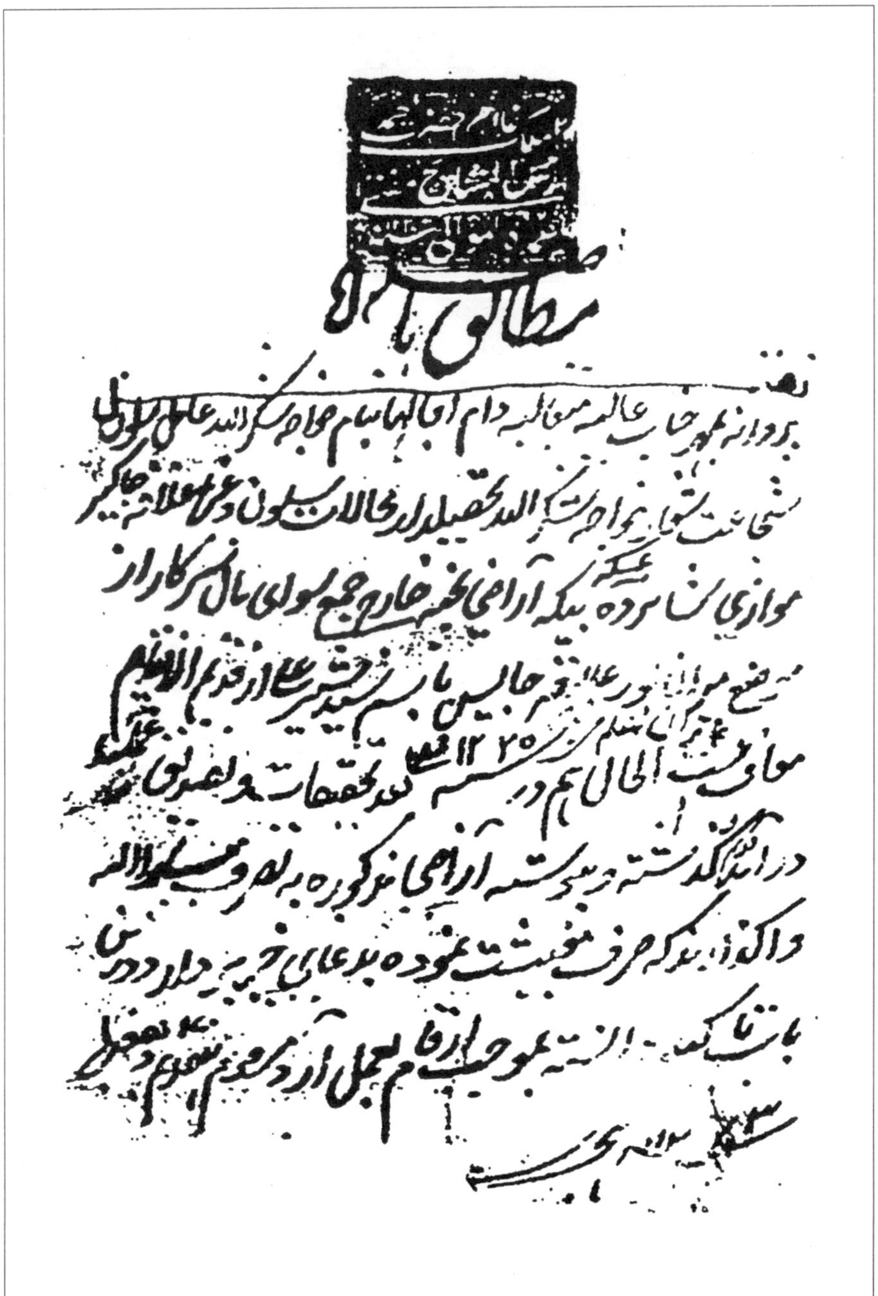

V: *Copy of Parwana* with the seal of Darab Ali Khan Bahadur written on 11 Zilijja 1215 A.H. (1802 AD) addressed to Rai Sahab Rai Desh Mukh, informing him that 16 Bigha land, tax-free, situated in the village Miranpur is granted to Syed Shabbir Ali since a long time and is always under his control. Now again as previously granted to him you are instructed not to raise any objections or confrontation; it may be left to him, the produce of the land may be left for his daily food, so that he always may busy for the blessings in favour of royal dynasty, you are stressed to act accordingly.

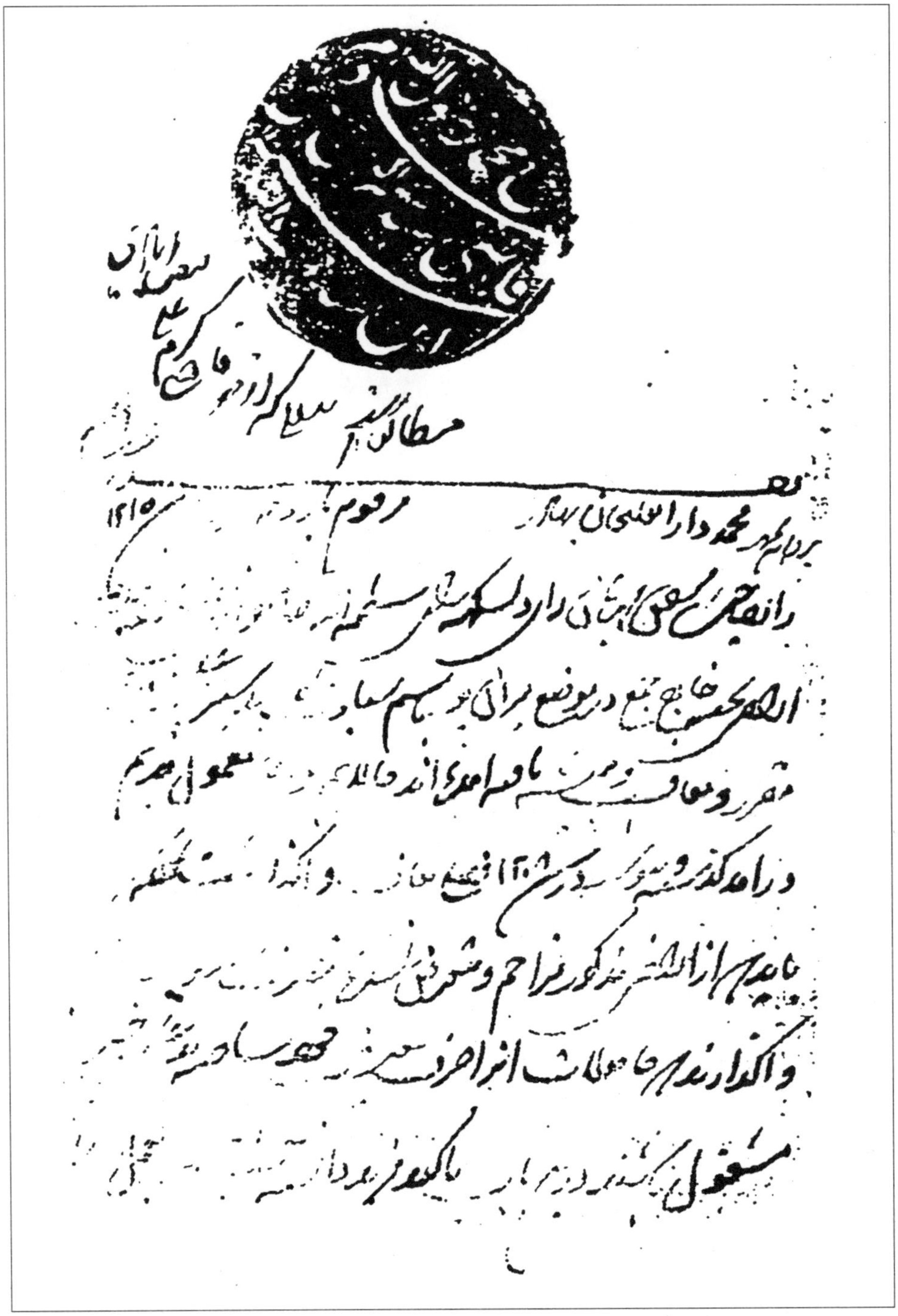

VI: *Parwana* with the seal of Rai Jai Singh dated 17th Rabi Awwal, 1224 A. H. addressed to Sheikh Faiz-Ullah-and-Bhola Nath-Jeo. Regarding individual details of village Qasimpur. The amount should be written off. You are instructed that written off amount will not be demanded and you are instructed to do as told.

The forehead of the document is decorated with the seal of Ali Mustafa Khadiṃ-E-Shara-Mohammadi Syed Gulzur Musavi.

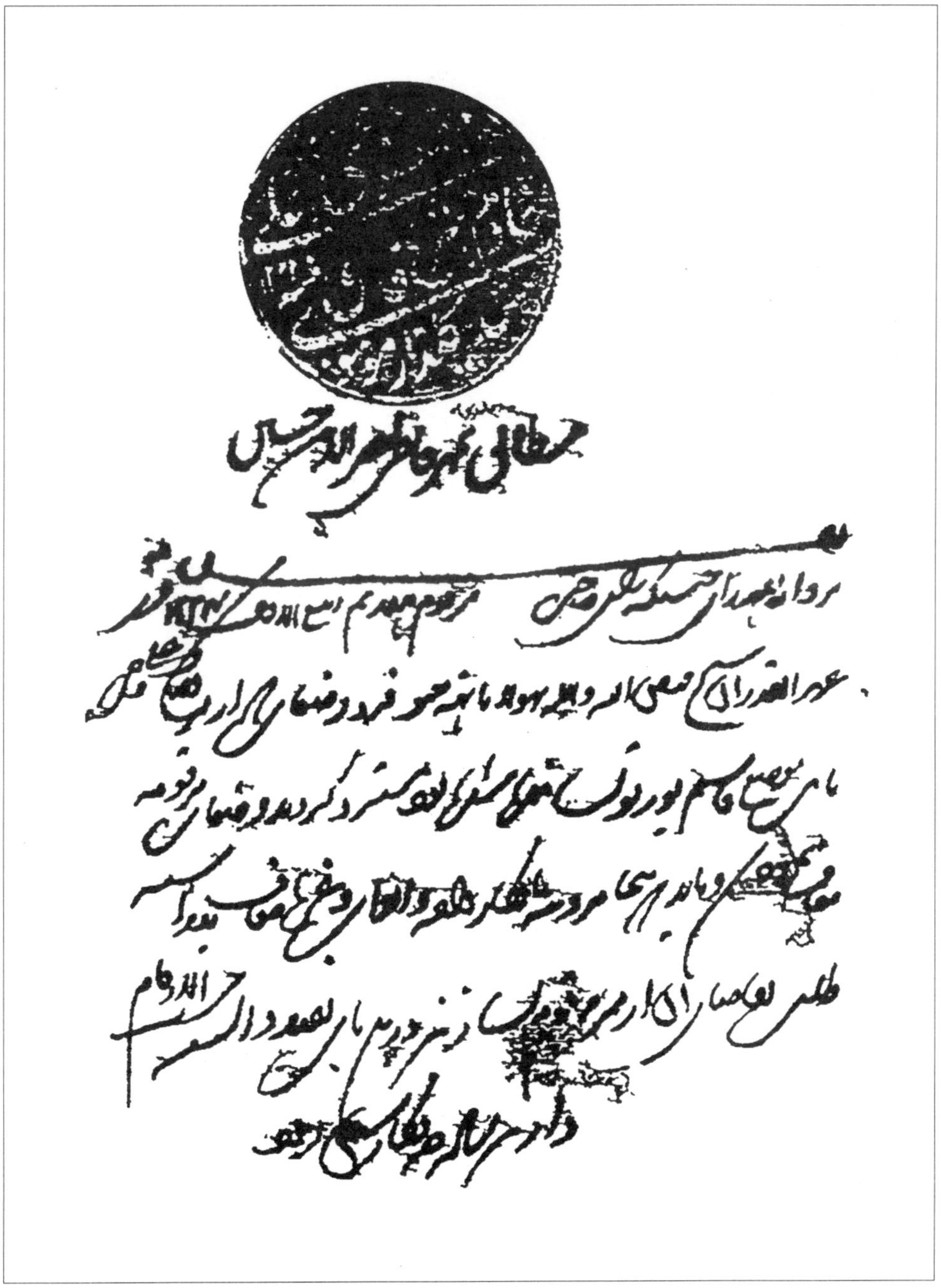

VII: *Copied Parwana* with seal of Mohammad Darab Ali Khan Bahadur dated 11th Zihijja 1215 A.H./ addressed to Rai Deshmukh Rai regarding 16 Bighas land, measured according to the standard measurement, tax free, in the village Miranpur is granted to Syed, Shabbir Ali since a long time. He always possessed this land. Now, according to the previously made Parwana in 1208 Fasli, again it is granted to him. You will not raise any objection or make confrontation with him, the land should be left to him for his daily food, so that he may be able to bless the royal dynasty forever, this is a stressed letter and you are to act according to the instruction.

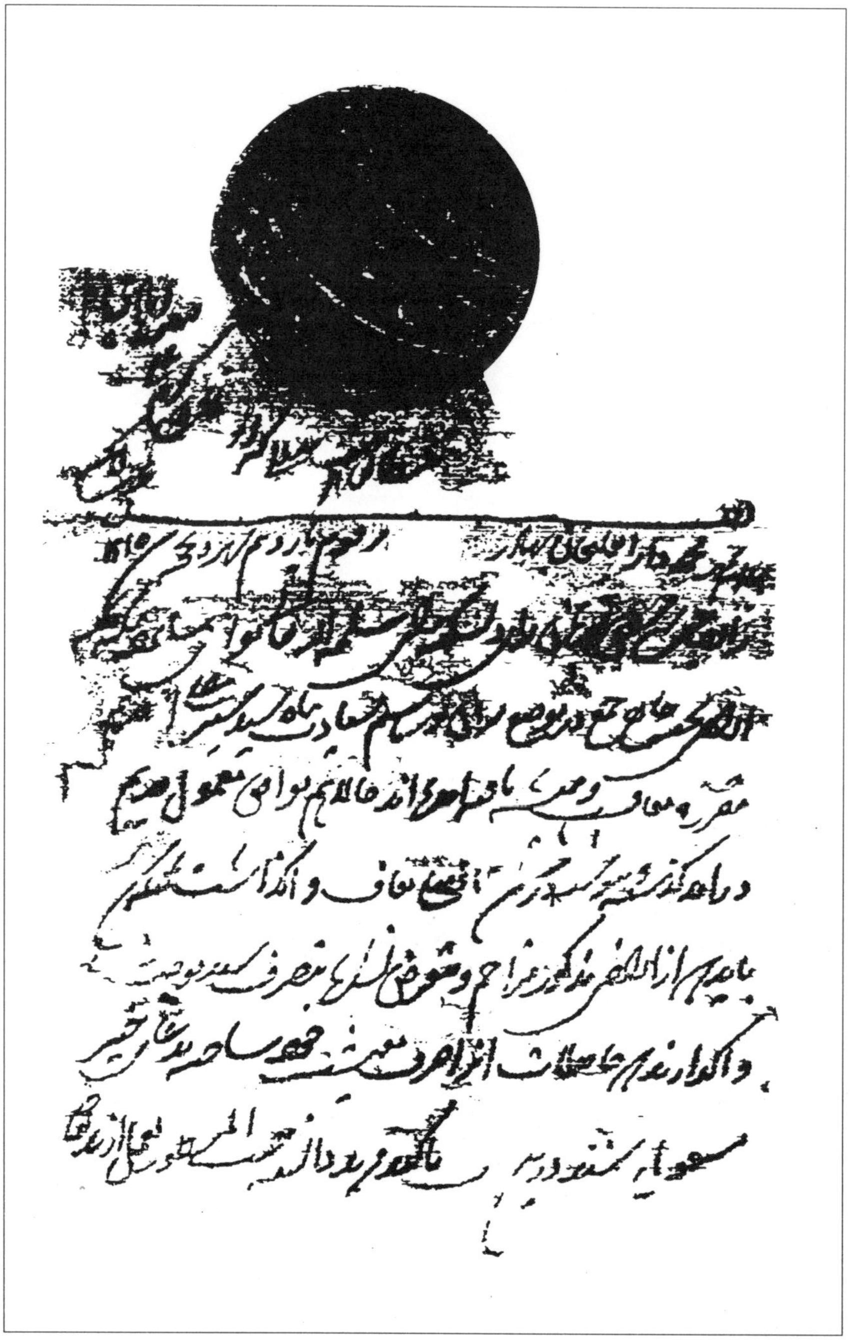

VIII: *Copy of Parwana* with seal of Qutbul Mulk addressed to.................... resident of Qasba Jais, Sarkar Manakpuri Suba Allahabal, instructing him to take 5000 tanka from Mohammad Isa Faujdar (Suspended) who had received from the people of Jais forcibly and distribute the said amount to the persons from whom the amount was collected.

— **Nasim Akhtar**

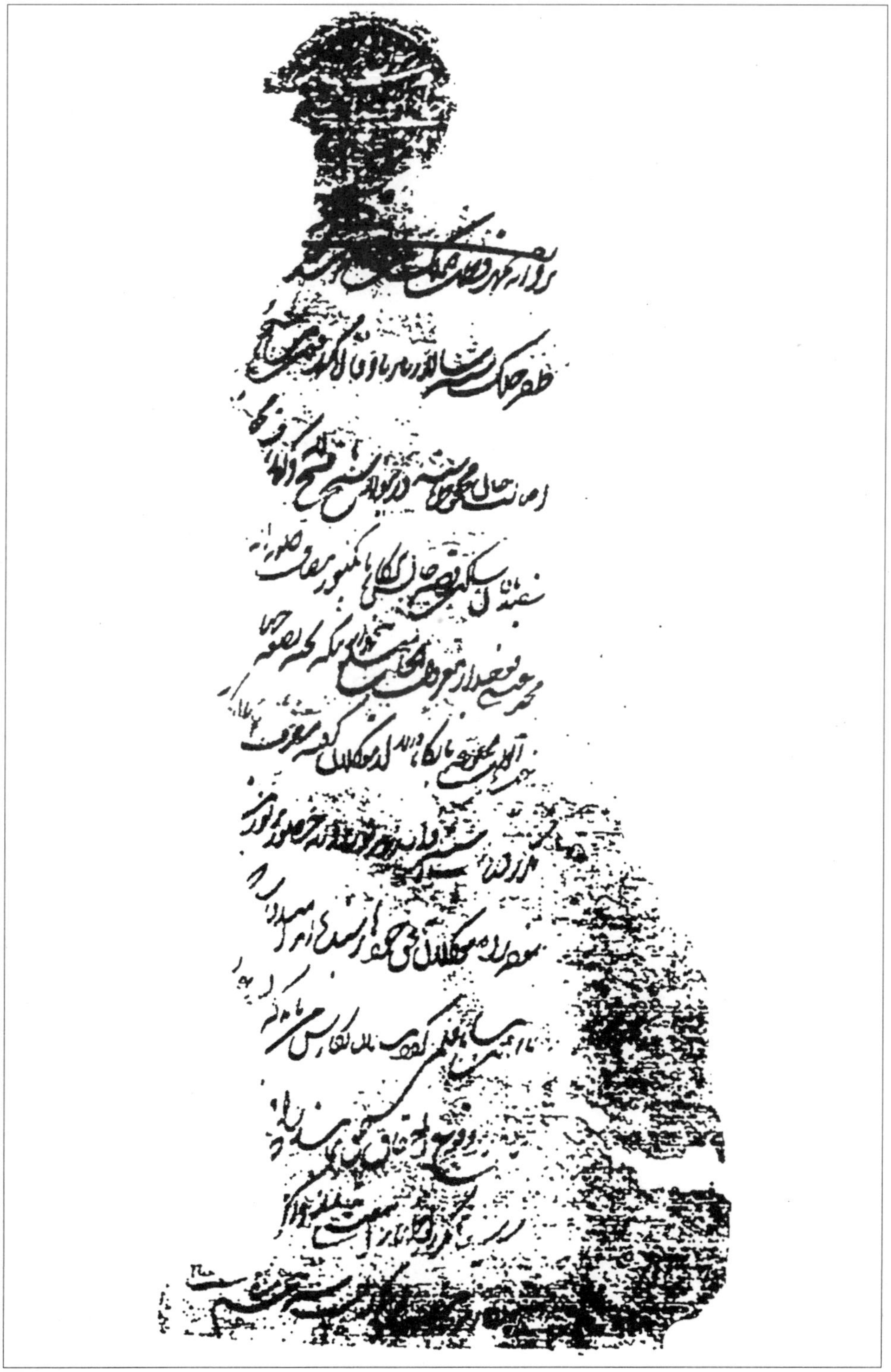

7 Late Medieval Art

DURING THE FIRST HALF OF THE SIXTEENTH century, Indo-Persian styles influenced paintings patronized in Muslim courtly circles, especially by the Early Mughals. The Rajasthani School of paintings, also confined to Rajasthan, developed several distinct schools. Notable among them are those of Mewar, Bundi, Kotah, Marwar, Kishangarh, Jaipur and Bikaner. Among them, Bikaner and Bundi are much influenced by the Mughal School. Contemporary with the Mughal School, the Deccani style developed a school containing Persian and Turkish styles as well as the tradition of the Vijayanagara empire.

The paintings from Jaipur, Mewar, Kishangarh and Bundi shed considerable light on the popularity of the Krishna-Vasudeva cult. The *sringara* of Radha and Krishna is a unique portrayal of the *Krishna-giti* composed by Somanatha in the 16th century. The fervours of *bhakti, virya* and *sringara,* illustrating Radha and Krishna, Nala and Damayanti and the triumphs of Durga are found at many places. Themes with a terrestrial touch, such as the longing of the separated wife *Proshitabhartrika*, ego of the wronged wife, *Khandita*, the expectant wife *Vasakasajjika*, the damsel *Abhisarika* and the shy bride *Mugdha* were also popular. The temporal aspects of nature lends credence to the themes.

The Pahari paintings, which developed in the Himalayan foothills, are distinguished by two broad phases. The Early Pahari paintings, known as Basohli style paintings, are marked by bold colours, like yellow, blue and brown, vigorous drawing and intense expressions. The later phase, known as Kangra style, developed by the third quarter of the eighteenth century, has given us a large number of beautiful paintings on Radha and Krishna themes.

Local patronage was extended in centres such as Cuddappah, Kurnool, Arcot, Mysore and Thanjavur. The Gujarati school of text illustrations influenced Malwa, although Persian influence held sway over Malwa. The Vijayanagara influence was strong in Ahmadnagar, Golconda and Bijapur schools of painting. In the eighteenth century, Hyderabad, the capital of the Asaf Jahi dynasty, became a centre of Deccan paintings.

Ravi Varma, in the early 20th century, was more inclined towards Indian traditions in themes but was greatly influenced by the Western oil paintings. No other Indian could learn this technique better than Ravi Verma. By the mid 20th century, Bengali artists led by Abanindranath Tagore attempted to develop a new style based on the murals of Ajanta and Bagh as well as other miniature schools but in water colour, rarely in other mediums. Later, Jamini Roy developed a personal style based on folk art of Bengal. His lineage was inherited by Nandalal Bose, A.K. Haldar and S.N. Gupta. Although paintings of Amrita Sher Gil developed an aesthetic individual style in 1930s, with Indian ethos it was much inspired by European traditions where she had the first training, particularly in France.

Contemporary paintings are no more true Indian; they are trans-regional in theme and Western in touch. Only a few have some originality, like M.F. Hussain and Rama Kinkar.

The Dutch warship on high sea represents the Dutch and Flemish painting of the Baroque era. During the 17th century, the Dutch developed their undecorated class of warships. The two gun-decks of Dutch warships are shown ventilated by spacious deck gratings covered with tarpaulins. When Peter the Great of Russia visited Holland to learn ship-building, he invited ship-builders to his newly found capital at St. Petersburg. Russian artists then learnt this Dutch School of high sea ship building and style in oil painting on large canvas.

Among the six systems of Indian philosophy, the Sankhya-*darsana* by Kapila interprets the cosmos as a cyclic manifestation caused by the Absolute Brahman (*Purusha*) and its Primordial Nature (*Prakrti*). The concept has been portrayed by S.P. Gupta in one of his paintings done in 1959 at Nagpur in the Nagpur School of Art.

8 Painted Manuscript

PERSIAN PAINTING AND CALLIGRAPHY developed during the Abbasid Period (700–800 A.D.) that first appeared in the form of a book. By the end of the seventh century, Koran manuscripts were executed on parchment at Basra and Kufa. Persian calligraphers contributed to the development of various forms of *Naskh;* the decorative *thuluth* was derived from it. The Baghdad, Timurid, Tabriz and Isfahan were the major schools of painting in Persia. By the nineteenth century much impetus was given to lacquer painting. Miniature paintings in Persian manuscripts are marked by a spectacular technique of precise drawings and subtle colours. The growing demand for Persian miniatures has led to the mushrooming of workshops for the production of fakes where even complete manuscripts are concocted in the archaic style.

The present manuscript contains fourteen paintings. They display landscapes, royal durbar, palanquins, recreation, learning, quietus, parturition, as well as animals and birds such as elephants, horses and doves.

CATALOGUE

1. **Painted Manuscript**
1700 A.D.
Persian, Paper.
Loan from "Bangali Babu" from Bihar
Acc. No.8.01.

9 European Art

Archaeology was a well established discipline in Tzarist Russia, especially with the Russian colonization of Steppe lands, stretching from Ukraine to Siberia. Interest developed in the Kurgan tombs and Classical Greek settlements along the north shore of the Black Sea. Russian aristocrats were more interested in Kurgan and Greek art rather than Slavic prehistory. Treasure hunting was common among aristocracy. Peter I, same as Peter the Great of Russia, issued orders that bureaucrats should collect and forward to St. Petersburg old and rare objects. His interests included archaeological as well as geological materials and by 1721, the Imperial Art Collection had a prestigious collection of antiquities. When Peter the Great visited Holland to learn about the famous Dutch ship-building techniques, he was much impressed by the Dutch warships which were were powerful at that paint of time and invited ship-builders to St. Petersburg. He found the two gun-decks of warships in the Dutch painting which are shown ventilated by spacious deck gratings covered with tarpaulins. It reflects the Dutch and Flemish art of the Baroque era, which was the concluding phase of Renaissance in Europe. The Dutch artistic traditions developed in Holland, where local schools of art flourished at Amsterdam, Haarlem, Utrecht, Leyden and Delft. Customers preferred themes such as landscapes, and awareness of natural forces dominated the best creations such as that of the 'Netherlands threatened by the Sea' or the 'Thunder clouds passing over a deserted mountain valley', which were portrayed by Jan Van Goyen and Jacob Van Ruisdael.

Catherine the Great, who succeeded Peter III, was a patron of art and opened academies for literature and art. By 1859 the rapid development in archaeology led to the establishment of the Imperial Archaeological Commission at St. Petersburg. In 1864, Count Aleksey Uvarov organized the Imperial Russian Archaeological Society in Moscow, which was followed by the establishment of regional archaeological societies in the provincial cities of Russia by 1900.

All these developments in the Russian nobility led to the creation of some of the best paintings in Russia itself although the source of their inspiration laid in Holland. There is a rare oil painting of this school of Russia with the museum which is the donation of Dr. S.P. Gupta.

CATALOGUE

1. **Dutch Warship on High Sea before Cloud Burst**
1900 A.D.
St. Petersburg, Russia
Oil on Canvas
105x 65 cms, Green, white, grey, and black
Gift of Dr. S.P. Gupta
Acc . No 9.01.

10 Contemporary Art

THE INFLUENCE OF THE EUROPEAN PAINTINGS on Indian painting is evident from the development of a distinct Indo-Anglian style in the late eighteenth and nineteenth centuries. To a great extent it was through the efforts of E.B. Havell, who was Principal of the Government School of Art at Calcutta, that Colonial art got denominated in favour of the classical Indian art. The early to mid 20th century is known as the period of Renaissance in India. There was an urge to rediscover the roots of Indian aesthetic traditions, both ancient and medieval. Institutions also responded to the national awakening and Gandhi's call of national pride in nation's heritage. Society for the Improvement of Oriental Painting and Sculpture (1842), The Indian Association for the Promotion of Fine Arts and Natural Gallery (1892), Bangiya Kala Samsad (1905) and The Indian Society of Oriental Art (1907) were some amongst them. By the last century, Abanindranath Tagore, Principal of the Calcutta School of Art, attempted to develop a new style based on the murals of Ajanta and Bagh as well as Rajasthani and Pahari schools of miniature paintings. He urged that the technique of the Western art cut the Indian painter from the past. The Japanese revivalist Kakuzo Okakura, who visited Calcutta in 1902, influenced his perspectives. Some of Abanindranath's paintings include the 'Banished Yaksha,' and 'Siddhas of the Upper Air', Meghaduta, 'Passing away of Shah Jahan'. His brother Gaganendranath's 'Peace Declared in the Punjab', depicting the Jallianwalahbagh massacre, was exhibited at the annual conference of the Indian Society of Oriental Art. Nandalal Bose and Kshitindranath Mazumdar guided students at the newly found studio of the Society. The commonly available reproductions were brought out by the Calcutta Art Studio.

The Indian Society of Oriental Art produced some of the eminent painters like Debiprosad Roy- Chowdhury, Mukul De, Lalit Mohan Sen, Pramod Kumar Chatterjee, Chintamoni Kar and Prankrishna Pal. Annie Besant and James Cousins were two ardent propogators of the Bengal School of Art. At the initiative of Sister Nivedita, the Society deputed Nandalal and Asit Kumar to work with her at Ajanta, the copies of which were printed by the London India Society. Schools of art were established in Mumbai, Chennai and Kolkata during the Colonial rule. These Schools introduced techniques of realistic painting in oil colour. The Bombay School of Art as well as the J.J. School of Art and Architecture at Mumbai were major centres which patronized the movement of modern painting. Abdur Rahman Chaghatai of Punjab and some members of the Ukil family were renowned artists from Northwest India.

The introduction of Western style of oil

paintings was adopted most forcefully and skillfully in India by Ravi Varma, the most famous oil colour painter from the erstwhile princely state of Travancore in Kerala. He mastered the western technique of oil painting to depict not only royal personages but also epic and puranic themes the prints of which became very popular with the Indian masses. Jamini Roy developed a personal style based on folk art of Bengal. His lineage was inherited by Nandalal Bose, A.K.Haldar and S.N. Gupta. The paintings of Amrita Sher Gil developed an individual aesthetic style, but was much inspired by European traditions as developed in France since she had her schooling in Paris. However, her themes were based upon Indian villages and Indian folk with the hidden pathos and child-like joy.

Following various schools of painting in the West, such as Impressionistm, Abstractionism and Intimist school, the young painters of the twentieth century developed a radical new style termed 'Fauvism'. It was full of violent colours and bold distortions and depended on anthropological and archaeological collections. Its leading member was Herry Matisse. By 1910 Cubism was established as an alternative to Fauvism. It derived its models from nature and geometric patterns and solids. Cubism was led by Pablo Picasso and Georges Braque. It had its variants such as Negroid, analytical and synthetic. Following the inception of Cubism, there were minor schools such as Rayonism, Suprematism and Constructivism. Among the nineteenth century paintings, Fantasy was a major current. During 1924, Surrealism became a more boldly imaginative branch in painting. There were other schools as well, such as Futurism, Orphism, Synchronism and Vorticism. After the Second World War, Action Painting gave a leverage to American Art but got denominated after mid fifties. With its imagery based on American mass media, Pop Art started in London during the same period. Photo Realism is an offshoot of Pop Art , since photographs have been utilized by some nineteenth century painters. The urge to endow works of art with a new identity by blurring the difference between image and reality has produced new techniques in painting such as environment. Another current that has gathered momentum in contemporary painting is Op Art, so termed because of its concern with optics. Western paintings have experimented methodologies such as Engaustic, Tempera, Fresco, Oil Painting as well as Water Colour and its variants such as Gouache and Poster Colour.

With the passing away of the Nationalist Movement and the Gandhian era, Indian painting lost the ideological mooring. Most of the contemporary paintings are no more true Indian, they also follow other modes of experimentation in modern Western art such as the Neoplasticism, Purism, Dadaism and Surrealism. Contemporary paintings are accommodated in Central and State Lalit Kala Academies, National Gallery of Modern Art, New Delhi and various other institutions of fine arts as well as Universities.

The paintings display a wide range of themes, from aspirations, womanhood, aesthetics, cosmic evolution, Neo-Tantrism and habitat .

CATALOGUE

1. **Creation according to Sankhyadarsana**
1959 A.D., S.P. Gupta
Nagpur, Maharashtra
Pastle colour on paper
37X 29 cms, Green, yellow, white, grey and pink
Acc. No. 80.

2. **Confronting dilemmas : Feminine determination**
2000 A.D.
Delhi
Etching on Oil Canvas
73 x 52 cms, Black, pink and grey
Gift by Dr. S.P. Gupta
Acc. No. 10.01.

3. **Man, Women and moon**
2000 A.D.
Delhi
Pastle on Canvas
44 x 27 cms, yellow, black, grey, blue and brown
Gift by Dr. S.P. Gupta
Acc. No.10.02.

4. **The Cycle of cosmic manifestation : Sankhyadarsana**
1959 A.D. S.P. Gupta's painting
Nagpur, Maharashtra
Pastle colour on paper
37X 29 cms, Green, yellow, white, grey and pink
Gift by Dr. S.P. Gupta
Acc .No 10.03.

5. **Dancing peacock**
2000 A.D.
Jaipur
Pastle on Cloth
88 x 45 cms, Pink, grey, blue, yellow and bronzy - green
Gift by Dr. S.P. Gupta
Acc. No.10.04.

6. **Reclining boy- A fugitive farewell to juvenile quandaries**
2000 A.D.
Delhi
Oil on Canvas
95 x 68cms, Green, blue, grey, brown and white
Gift of the artist Ms. Poonam Sehgal
Acc. No 10.05.

7. **Fenced hut**
2000 A.D.
53 X 85 cms, Blue, green, yellow, grey and white
Gift by Dr. S.P. Gupta
Acc. No. 10.05.

11 Decorative Art

Persia and India have long remained manufacturing and marketing centers of exquisite oriental carpets. Influence of Persian rug/ carpets is observed in India largely from the sixteenth century and they share many common characteristics. The great court carpets of the sixteenth century in Persia are classified in accordance with their presumed themes, such as Hunting carpets, Garden carpets, Compartment carpets, Medallion and Animal carpets of Northwest Persia, and Vase carpets of Joshaghan. The Hunting carpet is historically important and is preserved in the Poldi Pezzoli Museum in Milan with the inscription of Giyath-ud-Din in the year 1522-23. Silk animal rugs were woven at Kashan in the second half of the sixteenth century. The carpets were further enriched by gold and silver threads.

During the time of Shah Abbas I (1571-1629), carpets were woven from silk, interspersed with silver and gold. The Coronation carpet is among the most prestigious one of this variety. The majority of the important carpets of the sixteenth century belongs to a variety of schools as observed from the colours, patterns, materials and techniques. The East Persian Heart carpets, which reached Europe through India, is generally termed as the typical 'Persian Carpet' and was quite extensively marketed.

Carpet weaving spread in India with the advent of the Mughals. Akbar set up looms to manufacture an exquisite quality of carpets. During the late sixteenth century, delicate silk carpets were woven at the site of sarcophagus of Shah Abbas II, particularly in the shrine at Qim in Persia. By the seventeenth century there was a general decline in the designing and weaving of carpets. Tabriz in the northwest, Joshaghan in central Persia, Kerman and Ravar in the southeast, and Meshed in northeast were the principal weaving centers of Persia during the nineteenth century. Dye methods were used to manufacture such humbler rugs belonging to the so-called 'Low Schools' of Persia which were ruined by European colonial markets by the later half of the nineteenth century.

The present carpet, a contemporary one, displays hunting of deers and tigers using arrows, spears and swords.

CATALOGUE

1. **Iranian Carpet**
Contemporary
Tehran
60 x 100 cms, Silk
Gift by Dr. S.P. Gupta
Acc. No. 11.01.

Handlist of Select Antiquities in the Indraprastha Museum of Art and Archaeology

1. PALAEOLITHIC

1. **Handaxe**
Lower Palaeolithic, 200,000–350,000 B.P.
Adamgarh, Madhya Pradesh
Quartzite
Gift by Deccan College, Pune
Acc. No. 1. 01

2. **Cleaver**
Lower Palaeolithic, 200,000–350,000 B.P.
Quartzite
Gift by Deccan College, Pune
Acc. No.1. 02

3. **Chopping Tool**
Lower Paleolithic, 200,000–350,000 B.P.
Quartzite
Gift by Deccan College, Pune
Acc. No.1. 03

4. **Handaxe**
Middle Palaeolithic, 150,000–100,000 B.P.
Barkhera, Raisen
Quartzite
Gift by Deccan College, Pune
Acc. No.1.04

5. **Chopper**
Middle Palaeolithic, 150,000–100,000 B.P.
Jasper
Gift by Deccan College, Pune
Acc. No.1.05

6. **Scraper**
Middle Palaeolithic,
150,000–100,000 B.P.
Agate
Gift by Deccan College, Pune
Acc. No.1.06

7. **Scraper**
Middle Palaeolithic,
150,000–100,000 B.P.
Agate
Gift by Deccan College, Pune
Acc. No.1.07

8. **Scraper**
Middle Palaeolithic,
150,000–100,000 B.P.
Agate
Gift by Deccan College, Pune
Acc. No.1.08

9. **Flake**
Upper Palaeolithic, 400,00–100,00 B.P.
Jasper
Gift by Deccan College, Pune
Acc. No.1.09

10. **Flake-blade**
Mesolithic, 8000–2000 B.P.
Jasper
Gift by Deccan College, Pune
Acc. No.1.10

11. **Flake-blade**
Mesolithic, 8000–2000 B.P.
Jasper
Gift by Deccan College, Pune
Acc. No.1.11

12. **Flake-blade**
Mesolithic, 8000–2000 B.P.
Jasper
Gift by Deccan College, Pune
Acc. No.1.12

13. **Flake-blade**
Mesolithic, 8000–2000 B.P.
Jasper
Gift by Deccan College, Pune
Acc. No.1.13

14. **Flake-blade**
Mesolithic, 8000–2000 B.P.
Jasper
Gift by Deccan College, Pune
Acc. No.1.14

15. **Flake-blade**
Mesolithic, 8000–2000 B.P.
Jasper

Gift by Deccan College, Pune
Acc. No.1.15

16. **Flake-blade**
Mesolithic, 8000–2000 B.P.
Jasper
Gift by Deccan College, Pune
Acc. No.1.16

17. **Flake-blade**
Mesolithic, 8000–2000 B.P.
Jasper
Gift by Deccan College, Pune
Acc. No.1.17

18. **Flake-blade**
Mesolithic, 8000–2000 B.P.
Jasper and Agate
Gift by Deccan College, Pune
Acc. No.1.18

19. **Flake-blade**
Mesolithic, 8000–2000 B.P.
Jasper
Gift by Deccan College, Pune
Acc. No.1.19

20. **Flake-blade**
Mesolithic, 8000–2000 B.P.
Jasper
Gift by Deccan College, Pune
Acc. No.1.20

21. **Flake-blade**
Mesolithic, 8000–2000 B.P.
Jasper
Gift by Deccan College, Pune
Acc. No.1.21

22. **Flake-blade**
Mesolithic, 8000–2000 B.P.
Jasper
Gift by Deccan College, Pune
Acc. No.1.22

23. **Flake-blade**
Mesolithic, 8000–2000 B.P.
Jasper
Gift by Deccan College, Pune
Acc. No.1.23

24. **Flake-blade**
Mesolithic, 8000–2000 B.P.
Jasper
Gift by Deccan College, Pune
Acc. No.1.24

25. **Flake-blade**
Mesolithic, 8000–2000 B.P.
Jasper
Gift by Deccan College, Pune
Acc. No.1.25

26. **Flake-blade**
Mesolithic, 8000–2000 B.P.
Jasper
Gift by Deccan College, Pune
Acc. No.1.26

27. **Flake-blade**
Mesolithic, 8000–2000 B.P.
Jasper
Gift by Deccan College
Acc. No.1.27

28. **Flake-blade**
Mesolithic, 8000–2000 B.P.
Jasper
Gift by Deccan College
Acc. No.1.28

29. **Flake-blade**
Mesolithic, 8000–2000 B.P.
Jasper
Gift by Deccan College, Pune
Acc. No.1.29

30. **Flake-blade**
Mesolithic, 8000–2000
Jasper
Gift by Deccan College, Pune
Acc. No.1.30

31. **Flake-blade**
Mesolithic, 8000–2000 B.P.
Jasper
Gift by Deccan College, Pune
Acc. No.1.31

32. **Flake-blade**
Mesolithic, 8000–2000 B.P.
Jasper
Gift by Deccan College, Pune
Acc. No.1.32

33. **Flake-blade**
Mesolithic, 8000–2000 B.P.
Jasper
Gift by Deccan College, Pune
Acc. No.1.33

34. **Flake-blade**
Mesolithic, 8000–2000 B.P.
Jasper
Gift by Deccan College, Pune
Acc. No.1.34

35. **Flake-blade**
Mesolithic, 8000–2000 B.P.
Agate

Gift by Deccan College, Pune
Acc. No.1.35

36. **Flake-blade**
Mesolithic, 8000–2000 B.P.
Agate
Gift by Deccan College, Pune
Acc. No.1.36

37. **Flake-blade**
Mesolithic, 8000–2000 B.P.
Agate
Gift by Deccan College, Pune
Acc. No.1.37

38. **Flake-blade**
Mesolithic, 8000–2000 B.P.
Agate
Gift by Deccan College, Pune
Acc. No.1.38

39. **Flake-blade**
Mesolithic, 8000–2000 B.P.
Agate
Gift by Deccan College, Pune
Acc. No.1.39

40. **Flake-blade**
Mesolithic, 8000–2000 B.P.
Agate
Gift by Deccan College, Pune
Acc. No.1.40

2. NEOLITHIC

41. **Ground stone-axe**
Neolithic, 2000–1700 B.C.
Tekkalakota, Karnataka
Basalt
Gift by Deccan College, Pune
Acc. No.2.01

42. **Potsherd**
Neolithic, 2000–1700 B.C.
Tekkalakota, Karnataka
Red Ware
Gift by Deccan College, Pune
Acc. No.2.02

43. **Potsherd**
Neolithic, 2000–1700 B.C.
Tekkalakota, Karnataka
Grey Ware
Gift by Deccan College, Pune
Acc. No.2.03

3. INDUS-SARASWATI CIVILIZATION

44. **Circular cake**
Mature Harappan, 2500 B.C.
Rakhigarhi,Haryana
Terracotta
Acc. No.3.01

45. **Cake**
Mature Harappan, 2500 B.C.
Rakhigarhi, Haryana
Terracotta
Acc. No.3.02

46. **Circular cake**
Mature Harappan, 2500 B.C.
Rakhigarhi, Haryana
Terracotta
Acc. No.3.03

47. **Oblong cake**
Mature Harappan, 2500 B.C.
Rakhigrahi, Haryana
Terracotta
Acc. No.3.04

48. **Triangular cake**
Mature Harappan, 2500 B.C.
Rakhigarhi, Haryana
Terracotta
Acc. No.3.05

49. **Circular cake**
Mature Harappan, 2500 B.C.
Rakhigarhi, Haryana
Terracotta
Acc. No.3.06

50. **Oblong cake**
Mature Harappan, 2500 B.C.
Rakhigarhi, Haryana
Terracotta
Acc. No.3.07

51. **Bangle fragment**
Mature Harappan, 2500 B.C.
Rakhigarhi, Haryana
Terracotta
Acc. No.3.08

52. **Bangle fragment**
Mature Harappan, 2500 B.C.
Rakhigarhi, Haryana
Terracotta
Acc. No.309

53. **Bangle fragment**
Mature Harappan, 2500 B.C.
Rakhigarhi, Haryana
Terracotta
Acc. No.3.10

54. **Bangle fragment**
Mature Harappan, 2500 B.C.

Rakhigarhi, Haryana
Terracotta
Acc. No.3.11

55. **Bangle fragment**
Mature Harappan, 2500 B.C.
Rakhigarhi, Haryana
Terracotta
Acc. No.3.12

56. **Bangle fragment**
Mature Harappan, 2500 B.C.
Rakhigarhi, Haryana
Terracotta
Acc. No.3.13

57. **Bangle fragment**
Mature Harappan, 2500 B.C.
Rakhigarhi, Haryana
Terracotta
Acc. No.3.14

58. **Bangle fragment**
Mature Harappan, 2500 B.C.
Rakhigarhi, Haryana
Terracotta
Acc. No.3.15

59. **Bangle fragment**
Mature Harappan, 2500 B.C.
Rakhigarhi, Haryana
Terracotta
Acc. No.3.16

60. **Bangle fragment**
Mature Harappan, 2500 B.C.
Rakhigarhi, Haryana
Terracotta
Acc. No.3.17

61. **Bangle fragment**
Mature Harappan, 2500 B.C.
Rakhigarhi, Haryana
Terracotta
Acc. No.3.18

62. **Bangle fragment**
Mature Harappan, 2500 B.C.
Rakhigarhi, Haryana
Terracotta
Acc. No.3.19

63. **Bangle fragment**
Mature Harappan, 2500 B.C.
Rakhigarhi, Haryana
Terracotta
Acc. No.3.20

64. **Bangle fragment**
Mature Harappan, 2500 B.C.

Rakhigarhi, Haryana
Terracotta
Acc. No3.21

65. **Bangle fragment**
Mature Harappan, 2500 B.C.
Rakhigarhi, Haryana
Terracotta
Acc. No.3.22

66. **Bangle fragment**
Mature Harappan, 2500 B.C.
Rakhigarhi, Haryana
Terracotta
Acc. No.3.23

67. **Painted bangles**
Mature Harappan, 2500 B.C.
Rakhigarhi, Haryana
Terracotta
Acc. No. 3.24

68. **Painted bangle**
Mature Harappan, 2500 B.C.
Rakhigarhi, Haryana
Terracotta
Acc. No. 3.25

69. **Painted bangle**
Mature Harappan, 2500 B.C.
Rakhigarhi, Haryana
Terracotta
Acc. No.3.26

70. **Painted bangle**
Mature Harappan, 2500 B.C.
Rakhigarhi, Haryana
Terracotta
Acc. No.3.27

71. **Painted bangle**
Mature Harappan, 2500 B.C.
Rakhigarhi, Haryana
Terracotta
Acc. No.3.28

72. **Goblet**
Mature Harappan, 2500 B.C.
Rakhigarhi, Haryana
Terracotta
Acc. No.3.29

73. **Beaker**
Mature Harappan, 2500 B.C.
Rakhigarhi, Haryana
Pottery
Acc. No.3.30

74. **Dish**
Mature Harappan, 2500 B.C.

Rakhigarhi, Haryana
Pottery
Acc. No.3.31

75. **Painted potsherd**
Mature Harappan, 2500 B.C.
Rakhigarhi, Haryana
Pottery
Acc. No.3.32

76. **Perforated potsherd**
Mature Harappan, 2500 B.C.
Rakhigarhi, Haryana
Pottery
Acc. No.3.33

77. **Fragment of a Dish**
Mature Harappan, 2500 B.C.
Rakhigarhi, Haryana
Pottery
Acc. No.3.34

78. **Ribbed potsherd**
Mature Harappan, 2500 B.C.
Rakhigarhi, Haryana
Pottery
Acc. No.3.35

79. **Fragment of a goblet**
Mature Harappan, 2500 B.C.
Rakhigarhi, Haryana
Pottery
Acc. No.3.36

80. **Fragmented beaker**
Mature Harappan, 2500 B.C.
Rakhigarhi, Haryana
Pottery
Acc. No.3.37

81. **Painted potsherd**
Mature Harappan, 2500 B.C.
Rakhigarhi, Haryana
Pottery
Acc. No.3.38

82. **Painted potsherd**
Mature Harappan, 2500 B.C.
Rakhigarhi, Haryana
Pottery
Acc. No.3.39

4. CHALCOLITHIC

83. **Potsherd**
Chalcolithic Ahar, 2500–1400 B.C.
Ahar, Rajasthan
Grey Ware
Gift by Deccan College, Pune
Acc. No.4.01

84. **Potsherd**
Chalcolithic Ahar, 2500–1400 B.C.
Ahar, Rajasthan
Black-and-Red Ware
Gift by Deccan College, Pune
Acc. No.4.02

85. **Potsherd**
Chalcolithic Ahar, 2500–1400 B.C.
Ahar, Rajasthan
Black-and-Red Ware
Gift by Deccan College, Pune
Acc. No. 4.05

86. **Potsherd**
Chalcolithic Ahar, 2500–1400 B.C.
Ahar, Rajasthan
Black-and-Red Ware
Gift by Deccan College, Pune
Acc. No.4.04

87. **Potsherd**
Chalcolithic Ahar, 2500–1400 B.C.
Ahar, Rajasthan
Black-and-Red Ware
Gift by Deccan College, Pune
Acc. No.4.05

88. **Potsherd**
Chalcolithic Ahar, 2100–1400 B.C.
Ahar, Rajasthan
Black-and-Red Ware
Gift by Deccan College, Pune
Acc. No.4.06

89. **Painted potsherd**
Chalcolithic Malwa, 1700–1400 B.C.
Navdatoli, Madhya Pradesh
Black on Red Ware
Gift by Deccan College, Pune
Acc. No. 4.07

90. **Painted potsherd**
Chalcolithic Malwa, 1700–1400 B.C.
Navdatoli, Madhya Pradesh
Black on Red Ware
Gift by Deccan College, Pune
Acc. No.4.08

91. **Painted potsherd**
Chalcolithic Malwa, 1700–1400 B.C.
Navdatoli, Madhya Pradesh
Black on Red Ware
Gift by Deccan College, Pune
Acc. No.4.09

92. **Painted potsherd**
Chalcolithic Malwa, 1700–1400 B.C.
Navdatoli, Madhya Pradesh

Black on Red Ware
Gift by Deccan College, Pune
Acc. No.4.10

93. **Painted potsherd**
Chalcolithic Malwa, 1700–1400 B.C.
Navdatoli, Madhya Pradesh
Cream Slipped Ware
Gift by Deccan College, Pune
Acc. No.4.11

94. **Painted potsherd**
Chalcolithic Malwa, 1700–1400 B.C.
Navdatoli, Madhya Pradesh
Cream Slipped Ware
Gift by Deccan College, Pune
Acc. No.4.12

95. **Painted potsherd**
Chalcolithic Malwa, 1700–1400 B.C.
Navdatoli, Madhya Pardesh
Black on Red Ware
Gift by Deccan College, Pune
Acc. No.4.13

96. **Small *lota***
Chalcolithic Jorwe, 1000–700 B.C.
Nevasa, Maharashtra
Painted Red Ware
Gift by Deccan College, Pune
Acc. No. 4.14

97. **Spouted jar**
Chalcolithic Jorwe, 1000–700 B.C.
Nevasa, Maharashtra
Painted Red Ware
Gift by Deccan College, Pune
Acc. No.4.15

98. **Bowl**
Chalcolithic Jorwe, 1000–700 B.C.
Inamgaon, Maharashtra
Black-and-Red Ware
Gift by Deccan College, Pune
Acc. No.4.16

99. **High-necked lota**
Chalcolithic Jorwe, 1000–700 B.C.
Inamgaon, Maharashtra
Painted Red Ware
Gift by Deccan College, Pune
Acc. No.4.17

100. **Hop scotch**
Chalcolithic Jorwe, 1000–700 B.C.
Inamgaon, Maharashtra
Black Ware
Gift by Deccan College, Pune
Acc. No.4.18

5. EARLY HISTORICAL PERIOD

101. **Panchala coin**
Kushana-Gupta 200–500 A.D.
Kampilya, Uttar Pradesh
Copper
Gift by Indian Archaeological Society, New Delhi
Acc. No.5.01

102. **Unidentified object**
Kushana-Gupta 200–500 A.D.
Kampilya, Uttar Pradesh
Copper
Gift by Indian Archaeological Society, New Delhi
Acc. No.5.02

103. **Unidentified object**
Kushana-Gupta 200–500 A.D.
Kampilya, Uttar Pradesh
Copper
Gift by Indian Archaeological Society, New Delhi
Acc. No.5.03

104. **Copper fragment**
Kushana-Gupta 200–500 A.D.
Kampilya, Uttar Pradesh
Copper
Gift by Indian Archaeological Society, New Delhi
Acc. No.5.04

105. **Chisel**
Kushana-Gupta 200–500 A.D.
Kampilya, Uttar Pradesh
Iron
Gift by Indian Archaeological Society, New Delhi
Acc. No.5.05

106. **Nail**
Kushana-Gupta 200–500 A.D.
Kampilya, Uttar Pradesh
Iron
Gift by Indian Archaeological Society, New Delhi
Acc. No.5.06

107. **Nail**
Kushana-Gupta 200–500 A.D.
Kampilya, Uttar Pradesh
Iron
Gift by Indian Archaeological Society, New Delhi
Acc. No.5.07

108. **Nail**
Kushana-Gupta 200–500 A.D.
Kampilya, Uttar Pradesh
Iron
Gift by Indian Archaeological Society, New Delhi
Acc. No.5.08

109. **Nail**
Kushana-Gupta 200–500 A.D.
Kampilya, Uttar Pradesh
Iron
Gift by Indian Archaeological Society, New Delhi
Acc. No.5.09

110. **Nail**
Kushana-Gupta 200–500 A.D.
Kampilya, Uttar Pradesh
Iron
Gift by Indian Archaeological Society, New Delhi
Acc. No.5.10

111. **Nail**
Kushana-Gupta 200–500 A.D.
Kampilya, Uttar Pradesh
Iron
Gift by Indian Archaeological Society, New Delhi
Acc. No.5.11

112. **Nail**
Kushana-Gupta 200–500 A.D.
Kampilya, Uttar Pradesh
Iron
Gift by Indian Archaeological Society, New Delhi
Acc. No. 5.12

113. **Nail**
Kushana-Gupta 200–500 A.D.
Kampilya, Uttar Pradesh
Iron
Gift by Indian Archaeological Society, New Delhi
Acc. No.5.13

114. **Nail**
Kushana-Gupta 200–500 A.D.
Kampilya, Uttar Pradesh
Iron
Gift by Indian Archaeological Society, New Delhi
Acc. No.5.14

115. **Nail**
Kushana-Gupta 200–500 A.D.
Kampilya, Uttar Pradesh
Iron
Gift by Indian Archaeological Society, New Delhi
Acc. No.5.15

116. **Unidentified object**
Kushana-Gupta 200–500 A.D.
Kampilya, Uttar Pradesh
Iron
Gift by Indian Archaeological Society, New Delhi
Acc. No.5.16

117. **Unidentified object**
Kushana-Gupta 200–500 A.D.
Kampilya, Uttar Pradesh
Iron
Gift by Indian Archaeological Society, New Delhi
Acc. No.5.17

118. **Unidentified object**
Kushana-Gupta 200–500 A.D.
Kampilya, Uttar Pradesh
Iron
Gift by Indian Archaeological Society, New Delhi
Acc. No.5.18

119. **Unidentified object**
Kushana-Gupta 200–500 A.D.
Kampilya, Uttar Pradesh
Iron
Gift by Indian Archaeological Society, New Delhi
Acc. No.5.19

120. **Iron fragments** (4 Nos.)
Kushana-Gupta 200–500 A.D.
Kampilya, Uttar Pradesh
Iron
Gift by Indian Archaeological Society, New Delhi
Acc. No.5.20

121. **Slag**
Kushana-Gupta 200–500 A.D.
Kampilya, Uttar Pradesh
Iron
Gift by Indian Archaeological Society, New Delhi
Acc. No.5.21

122. **Slag**
Kushana-Gupta 200–500 A.D.
Kampilya, Uttar Pradesh
Iron
Gift by Indian Archaeological Society, New Delhi
Acc. No.5.22

123. **Bar**
Kushana-Gupta 200–500 A.D.
Kampilya, Uttar Pradesh
Iron
Gift by Indian Archaeological Society, New Delhi
Acc. No.5.23

124. **Cart frame**
Kushana-Gupta 200-500 A.D.
Kampilya, Uttar Pradesh
Terracotta
Gift by Indian Archaeological Society, New Delhi
Acc. No.5.24

125. **Bead**
Kushana-Gupta 200–500 A.D.
Kampilya, Uttar Pradesh
Agate
Gift by Indian Archaeological Society, New Delhi
Acc. No.5.25

126. **Bead**
Kushana-Gupta 200–500 A.D.
Kampilya, Uttar Pradesh
Terracotta
Gift by Indian Archaeological Society, New Delhi
Acc. No.5.26

127. **Bead**
Kushana-Gupta 200–500 A.D.
Kampilya, Uttar Pradesh
Terracotta
Gift by Indian Archaeological Society, New Delhi
Acc. No.5.27

128. **Bead**
Kushana-Gupta 200–500 A.D.
Kampilya, Uttar Pradesh
Terracotta
Gift by Indian Archaeological Society, New Delhi
Acc. No.5.28

129. **Bead**
Kushana-Gupta 200–500 A.D.
Kampilya, Uttar Pradesh
Terracotta
Gift by Indian Archaeological Society, New Delhi
Acc. No.5.29

130. **Bead**
Kushana-Gupta 200–500 A.D.
Kampilya, Uttar Pradesh
Terracotta
Gift by Indian Archaeological Society, New Delhi
Acc. No.5.30

131. ***Ghata*-shaped Bead**
Kushana-Gupta 200–500 A.D.
Kampilya, Uttar Pradesh
Terracotta
Gift by Indian Archaeological Society, New Delhi
Acc. No.5.31

132. **Ear-lobe**
Kushana-Gupta 200–500 A.D.
Kampilya, Uttar Pradesh
Terracotta
Gift by Indian Archaeological Society,
Acc. No.5.32

133. **Bangle**
Kushana-Gupta 200–500 A.D.
Kampilya, Uttar Pradesh
Terracotta
Gift by Indian Archaeological Society, New Delhi
Acc. No.5.33

134. **Hip portion of an animal**
Kushana-Gupta 200–500 A.D.
Kampilya, Uttar Pradesh
Terracotta
Gift by Indian Archaeological Society, New Delhi
Acc. No.5.34

135. **Lamp (small)**
Kushana-Gupta 200–500 A.D.
Kampilya, Uttar Pradesh
Terracotta
Gift by Indian Archaeological Society, New Delhi
Acc. No.5.35

136. **Lamp**
Kushana-Gupta 200–500 A.D.
Kampilya, Uttar Pradesh
Terracotta
Gift by Indian Archaeological Society, New Delhi
Acc. No.5.36

137. **Circular lamp**
Kushana-Gupta 200–500 A.D.
Kampilya, Uttar Pradesh
Terracotta
Gift by Indian Archaeological Society, New Delhi
Acc. No.5.37

138. **Lid knob**
Kushana-Gupta 200–500 A.D.
Kampilya, Uttar Pradesh
Terracotta
Gift by Indian Archaeological Society, New Delhi
Acc. No.5.38

139. **Circular base**
Kushana-Gupta 200–500 A.D.
Kampilya, Uttar Pradesh
Terracotta
Gift by Indian Archaeological Society, New Delhi
Acc. No.5.39

140. **Ball**
Kushana-Gupta 200–500 A.D.
Kampilya, Uttar Pradesh
Terracotta
Gift by Indian Archaeological Society, New Delhi
Acc. No.5.40

141. **Fragmented bangle**
Kushana-Gupta 200–500 A.D.
Kampilya, Uttar Pradesh
Glass
Gift by Indian Archaeological Society, New Delhi
Acc. No.5.41

142. **Bangle fragment**
Kushana-Gupta 200–500 A.D.
Kampilya, Uttar Pradesh
Glass
Gift by Indian Archaeological Society, New Delhi
Acc. No.5.42

143. **Bangle fragment**
Kushana-Gupta 200–500 A.D.
Kampilya, Uttar Pradesh
Glass
Gift by Indian Archaeological Society, New Delhi
Acc. No.5.43

144. **Bangle fragment**
Kushana-Gupta 200–500 A.D.
Kampilya, Uttar Pradesh
Glass
Gift by Indian Archaeological Society, New Delhi
Acc. No.5.44

145. **Bangle fragment**
Kushana-Gupta 200–500 A.D.
Kampilya, Uttar Pradesh
Glass
Gift by Indian Archaeological Society, New Delhi
Acc. No.5.45

146. **Bangle fragment**
Kushana-Gupta 200–500 A.D.
Kampilya, Uttar Pradesh
Glass
Gift by Indian Archaeological Society, New Delhi
Acc. No.5.46

147. **Bangle fragment**
Kushana-Gupta 200–500 A.D.
Kampilya, Uttar Pradesh
Glass
Gift by Indian Archaeological Society, New Delhi
Acc. No.5.47

148. **Bangle fragment**
Kushana-Gupta 200–500 A.D.
Kampilya, Uttar Pradesh
Glass
Gift by Indian Archaeological Society, New Delhi
Acc. No.5.48

149. **Bangle frabment**
Kushana-Gupta 200–500 A.D.
Kampilya, Uttar Pradesh
Glass
Gift by Indian Archaeological Society, New Delhi
Acc. No.5.49

150. **Animal head**
Kushana-Gupta 200–500 A.D.
Kampilya, Uttar Pradesh
Terracotta
Gift by Indian Archaeological Society, New Delhi
Acc. No.5.50

151. **Conch**
Kushana-Gupta 200–500 A.D.
Kampilya, Uttar Pradesh
Shell
Gift by Indian Archaeological Society, New Delhi
Acc. No.5.51

152. **Cowrie**
Kushana-Gupta 200–500 A.D.
Kampilya, Uttar Pradesh
Shell
Gift by Indian Archaeological Society, New Delhi
Acc. No.5.52

153. **Cowrie**
Kushana-Gupta 200–500 A.D.
Kampilya, Uttar Pradesh
Shell
Gift by Indian Archaeological Society, New Delhi
Acc. No.5.53

154. **Cowrie**
Kushana-Gupta 200–500 A.D.
Kampilya, Uttar Pradesh
Shell
Gift by Indian Archaeological Society, New Delhi
Acc. No.5.54

155. **Cowrie**
Kushana-Gupta 200–500 A.D.
Kampilya, Uttar Pradesh
Shell
Gift by Indian Archaeological Society, New Delhi
Acc. No.5.55

156. **Cowrie**
Kushana-Gupta 200–500 A.D.
Kampilya, Uttar Pradesh
Shell
Gift by Indian Archaeological Society, New Delhi
Acc. No.5.56

157. **Shell fragment**
Kushana-Gupta 200–500 A.D.
Kampilya, Uttar Pradesh
Shell
Gift by Indian Archaeological Society, New Delhi
Acc. No.5.57

158. **Bangles**
Kushana-Gupta 200–500 A.D.
Kampilya, Uttar Pradesh
Glass
Gift by Indian Archaeological Society, New Delhi
Acc. No.5.58

159. **Spouted Vase**
Kushana-Gupta 200–500 A.D.
Kampilya, Uttar Pradesh
Red ware
Gift by Indian Archaeological Society, New Delhi
Acc. No.5.59

160. **Handi**
Kushana-Gupta 200–500 A.D.
Kampilya, Uttar Pradesh
Grey Ware
Gift by Indian Archaeological Society, New Delhi
Acc. No.5.60

161. **Bowl**
Kushana-Gupta 200–500 A.D.
Kampilya, Uttar Pradesh
Coarse Red Ware
Gift by Indian Archaeological Society, New Delhi
Acc. No.5.61

162. **Vase with out-turned rim**
Kushana-Gupta 200–500 A.D.
Kampilya, Uttar Pradesh
Red Ware
Gift by Indian Archaeological Society, New Delhi
Acc. No.5.62

163. **Vase with elongated rim and small neck**
Kushana-Gupta 200–500 A.D.
Kampilya, Uttar Pradesh
Red Ware
Gift by Indian Archaeological Society, New Delhi
Acc. No.5.63

164. **Storage vase with out-turned rim**
Kushana-Gupta 200–500 A.D.
Kampilya, Uttar Pradesh
Red Slipped Ware
Gift by Indian Archaeological Society, New Delhi
Acc. No.5.64

165. **Vase with out-turned rim**
Kushana-Gupta 200–500 A.D.
Kampilya, Uttar Pradesh
Red Slipped Ware
Gift by Indian Archaeological Society, New Delhi
Acc. No.5.65

166. **Rim with groves**
Kushana-Gupta 200–500 A.D.
Kampilya, Uttar Pradesh
Red Slipped Ware
Gift by Indian Archaeological Society, New Delhi
Acc. No.5.66

167. **Rim**
Kushana-Gupta 200–500 A.D.
Kampilya, Uttar Pradesh
Red Slipped Ware
Gift by Indian Archaeological Society, Delhi
Acc. No.5.67

168. **Vase with bevelled rim**
Kushana-Gupta 200–500 A.D.
Kampilya, Uttar Pradesh
Red Slipped Ware
Gift by Indian Archaeological Society, New Delhi
Acc. No.5.68

169. **Rim of a *handi***
Kushana-Gupta 200–500 A.D.
Kampilya, Uttar Pradesh
Red Slipped Ware
Gift by Indian Archaeological Society, New Delhi
Acc. No.5.69

170. **Vase**
Kushana-Gupta 200–500 A.D.
Kampilya, Uttar Pradesh
Red Ware
Gift by Indian Archaeological Society, New Delhi
Acc. No.5.70

171. **Everted rim of spouted vase**
Kushana-Gupta 200–500 A.D.
Kampilya, Uttar Pradesh
Coarse Red Ware
Gift by Indian Archaeological Society, New Delhi
Acc. No.5.71

172. **Vase with out-turned rim**
Kushana-Gupta 200–500 A.D.
Kampilya, Uttar Pradesh
Coarse Red Ware
Gift by Indian Archaeological Society, New Delhi
Acc. No.5.72

173. ***Handi***
Kushana-Gupta 200–500 A.D.
Kampilya, Uttar Pradesh
Coarse Red Ware
Gift by Indian Archaeological Society, New Delhi
Acc. No.5.73

174. **Rim of a pot**
Kushana-Gupta 200–500 A.D.
Kampilya, Uttar Pradesh
Red Slipped Ware
Gift by Indian Archaeological Society, New Delhi
Acc. No.5.74

175. **Vase**
Kushana-Gupta 200–500 A.D.
Kampilya, Uttar Pradesh
Coarse Red Ware
Gift by Indian Archaeological Society, New Delhi
Acc. No.5.75

176. **Vase**
Kushana-Gupta 200–500 A.D.
Kampilya, Uttar Pradesh
Red Slipped Ware
Gift by Indian Archaeological Society, New Delhi
Acc. No.5.76

177. **Spout of a Vase**
Kushana-Gupta 200–500 A.D.
Kampilya, Uttar Pradesh
Coarse Red Ware
Gift by Indian Archaeological Society, New Delhi
Acc. No.5.77

178. **Vase**
Kushana-Gupta 200–500 A.D.
Kampilya, Uttar Pradesh
Coarse Red Ware
Gift by Indian Archaeological Society, New Delhi
Acc. No.5.78

179. **Handi with nail impressions**
Kushana-Gupta 200–500 A.D.
Kampilya, Uttar Pradesh
Grey Ware
Gift by Indian Archaeological Society, New Delhi
Acc. No.5.79

180. ***Handi***
Kushana-Gupta 200–500 A.D.
Kampilya, Uttar Pradesh
Plain Grey Ware
Gift by Indian Archaeological Society, New Delhi
Acc. No.5.80

181. ***Handi***
Kushana-Gupta 200–500 A.D.
Kampilya, Uttar Pradesh
Grey Ware
Gift by Indian Archaeological Society, New Delhi
Acc. No.5.81

182. **Bowl**
Kushana-Gupta 200–500 A.D.
Kampilya, Uttar Pradesh
Polished Red Ware
Gift by Indian Archaeological Society, New Delhi
Acc. No.5.82

183. **Vase with straight sided rim**
Kushana-Gupta 200–500 A.D.
Kampilya, Uttar Pradesh
Coarse Red Ware
Gift by Indian Archaeological Society, New Delhi
Acc. No.5.83

184. ***Handi***
Kushana-Gupta 200–500
Kampilya, Uttar Pradesh
Grey Ware
Gift by Indian Archaeological Society, New Delhi
Acc. No.5.84

185. **Out-turned rim of a *handi***
Kushana-Gupta 200–500 A.D.
Kampilya, Uttar Pradesh
Grey Ware
Gift by Indian Archaeological Society, New Delhi
Acc. No.5.85

186. **Out-turned rim of a vase**
Kushana-Gupta 200–500 A.D.
Kampilya, Uttar Pradesh
Red Ware
Gift by Indian Archaeological Society, New Delhi
Acc. No.5.86

187. **Grooved rim of a vase**
Kushana-Gupta 200–500 A.D.
Kampilya, Uttar Pradesh
Painted Micaceous Red Ware
Gift by Indian Archaeological Society, New Delhi
Acc. No.5.87

188. **Carinated *handi***
Kushana-Gupta 200–500 A.D.
Kampilya, Uttar Pradesh
Plain Red Ware
Gift by Indian Archaeological Society, New Delhi
Acc. No.5.88

189. **Carinated *handi***
Kushana-Gupta 200–500
Kampilya, Uttar Pradesh
Slipped Grey Ware
Gift by Indian Archaeological Society, New Delhi
Acc. No.5.89

190. **Vase with incurved rim**
Kushana-Gupta 200–500 A.D.
Kampilya,Uttar Pradesh
Red Polished Ware
Gift by Indian Archaeological Society, New Delhi
Acc. No.5.90

191. **Vase**
Kushana-Gupta 200–500 A.D.
Kampilya, Uttar Pradesh
Coarse Red Ware
Gift by Indian Archaeological Society, New Delhi
Acc. No.5.91

192. **Rim of *handi***
Kushana-Gupta 200–500 A.D.
Kampilya, Uttar Pradesh
Plain Grey Ware
Gift by Indian Archaeological Society, New Delhi
Acc. No.5.92

193. **Vase with featureless out-turned rim**
Kushana-Gupta 200–500 A.D.
Kampilya, Uttar Pradesh
Coarse Red Ware
Gift by Indian Archaeological Society, New Delhi
Acc. No.5.93

194. **Vase with featureless out-turned rim**
Kushana-Gupta 200–500 A.D.
Kampilya, Uttar Pradesh
Coarse Red Ware
Gift by Indian Archaeological Society, New Delhi
Acc. No.5.94

195. **Straight-sided dish**
Kushana-Gupta 200–500 A.D.
Kampilya, Uttar Pradesh
Red Polished Ware
Gift by Indian Archaeological Society, New Delhi
Acc. No.5.95

196. **Straight-sided bowl with incurved rim**
Kushana-Gupta 200–500 A.D.
Kampilya, Uttar Pradesh
Coarse Red Ware
Gift by Indian Archaeological Society, New Delhi.
Acc. No.5.96

197. **Vase with out-turned rim**
Kushana- Gupta 200–500 A.D.
Kampilya, Uttar Pradesh
Coarse Red Ware
Gift by Indian Archaeological Society, New Delhi
Acc. No.5.97

198. **Bowl with featureless rim**
Kushana-Gupta 200–500 A.D.
Kampilya, Uttar Pradesh
Coarse Red Ware
Gift by Indian Archaeological Society, New Delhi
Acc. No.5.98

199. **Vase with out-turned rim**
Kushana-Gupta 200–500 A.D.
Kampilya, Uttar Pradesh
Coarse Red Ware
Gift by Indian Archaeological Society, New Delhi
Acc. No.5.99

200. **Dish with straight-sides**
Kushana-Gupta 200–500 A.D.
Kampilya, Uttar Pradesh
Red Ware
Gift by Indian Archaeological Society, New Delhi
Acc. No.5.100

201. **Dish with featureless rim**
Kushana-Gupta levels
Kampilya, Uttar Pradesh
Northern Black Polished Ware
Gift by Indian Archaeological Society, New Delhi
Acc. No.5.101

202. **Bowl**
Kushana-Gupta 200–500 A.D.
Kampilya, Uttar Pradesh
Coarse Red Ware
Gift by Indian Archaeological Society, New Delhi
Acc. No.5.102

203. **Dish**
Kushana-Gupta 200–500 A.D.
Kampilya, Uttar Pradesh
Red Ware
Gift by Indian Archaeological Society, New Delhi
Acc. No.5.103

204. **Bowl with featureless rim**
Kushana-Gupta 200–500 A.D.
Kampilya, Uttar Pradesh
Coarse Red Ware
Gift by Indian Archaeological Society, New Delhi
Acc. No.5.104

205. **Miniature lamp**
Kushana-Gupta 200–500 A.D.
Kampilya, Uttar Pradesh
Coarse Red Ware
Gift by Indian Archaeological Society, New Delhi
Acc. No.5.105

206. **Bowl with featureless rim**
Kushana-Gupta 200–500 A.D.
Kampilya, Uttar Pradesh
Coarse Red Ware
Gift by Indian Archaeological Society, New Delhi
Acc. No.5.106

207. **Bowl with incurved rim**
Kushana-Gupta 200–500 A.D.
Kampilya, Uttar Pradesh
Coarse Red Ware
Gift by Indian Archaeological Society, New Delhi
Acc. No.5.107

208. **Pedestalled bowl**
Kushana-Gupta 200–500 A.D.
Kampilya, Uttar Pradesh
Coarse Red Ware
Gift by Indian Archaeological Society, New Delhi
Acc. No.5.108

209. **Lid with central knob**
Kushana-Gupta 200–500 A.D.
Kampilya, Uttar Pradesh
Coarse Red Ware
Gift by Indian Archaeological Society, New Delhi
Acc. No.5.109

210. **Sherd with impressed designs**
Kushana-Gupta 200–500 A.D.
Kampilya, Uttar Pradesh
Micaceous Red Ware
Gift by Indian Archaeological Society, New Delhi
Acc. No.5.110

211. **Out-turned rim of vase**
Kushana-Gupta 200–500 A.D.
Kampilya, Uttar Pradesh
Plain Grey Ware
Gift by Indian Archaeological Society, New Delhi
Acc. No.5.111

212. **Rim of vase**
Kushana-Gupta 200–500 A.D.
Kampilya, Uttar Pradesh
Slipped Red Ware
Gift by Indian Archaeological Society, New Delhi
Acc. No.5.112

213. **Handi with out-turned rim**
Kushana-Gupta 200–500 A.D.
Kampilya, Uttar Pradesh
Coarse Red Ware
Gift by Indian Archaeological Society, New Delhi
Acc. No.5.113

214. **Obliquely cut rim of *handi***
Kushana-Gupta 200–500 A.D.
Kampilya, Uttar Pradesh
Red Ware
Gift by Indian Archaeological Society, New Delhi
Acc. No.5.114

215. **Lipped rim of a vase**
Kushana-Gupta 200–500 A.D.
Kampilya, Uttar Pradesh
Red Ware
Gift by Indian Archaeological Society, New Delhi
Acc. No.5.115

216. **Out-turned rim**
Kushana-Gupta 200–500 A.D.
Kampilya, Uttar Pradesh
Grey Ware
Gift by Indian Archaeological Society, New Delhi
Acc. No.5.116

217. **Obliquely cut rim of *handi***
Kushana-Gupta 200–500 A.D.
Kampilya, Uttar Pradesh
Coarse Red Ware
Gift by Indian Archaeologicl Society,
New Delhi
Acc. No.5.117

218. **Out-turned rim of handi**
Kushana-Gupta 200–500 A.D.
Kampilya, Uttar Pradesh
Grey Ware
Gift by Indian Archaeological Society, New Delhi
Acc. No.5.118

219. **Vase with long neck**
Kushana-Gupta 200–500 A.D.
Kampilya, Uttar Pradesh
Red Ware
Gift by Indian Archaeological Society, New Delhi
Acc. No.5.119

220. **Vase with under-cut rim**
Kushana-Gupta 200–500 A.D.
Kampilya, Uttar Pradesh
Slipped Red Ware
Gift by Indian Archaeological Society, New Delhi
Acc. No.5.120

221. **Rim of *handi***
Kushana-Gupta 200–500 A.D.
Kampilya, Uttar Pradesh
Grey Ware
Gift by Indian Archaeological Society, New Delhi
Acc. No.5.121

222. **Obliquely cut rim of vase**
Kushana-Gupta 200–500 A.D.
Kampilya, Uttar Pradesh
Grey Ware
Gift by Indian Archaeological Society, New Delhi
Acc. No.5.122

223. **Out-turned rim of *handi***
Kushana-Gupta 200–500 A.D.
Kampilya, Uttar Pradesh
Grey Ware
Gift by Indian Archaeological Society, New Delhi
Acc. No.5.123

224. **Rim of *handi***
Kushana-Gupta 200–500 A.D.
Kampilya, Uttar Pradesh
Grey Ware
Gift by Indian Archaeological Society, New Delhi
Acc. No.5.124

225. **Rim of Vase**
Kushana-Gupta 200–500 A.D.
Kampilya, Uttar Pradesh
Coarse Red Ware
Gift by Indian Archaeological Society, New Delhi
Acc. No.5.125

226. **Dish with nail marks on th side**
Kushana-Gupta 200–500 A.D.
Kampilya, Uttar Pradesh
Red Ware
Gift by Indian Archaeological Society, New Delhi
Acc. No.5.126

227. **Straight Sided jar**
Kushana-Gupta 200–500 A.D.
Kampilya, Uttar Pradesh
Slipped Red Ware

Gift by Indian Archaeological Society, New Delhi
Acc. No.5.127

228. **Bowl with out-turned rim**
Kushana-Gupta 200–500 A.D.
kampilya, Uttar Pradesh
Red Ware
Gift by Indian Archaeological Society, New Delhi
Acc. No.5.128

229. **Dish**
Kushana-Gupta 200–500 A.D.
Kampilya, Uttar Pradesh
Slipped Red Ware
Gift by Indian Archaeological Society, New Dehli
Acc. No.5.129

230. **Vase with obliquely-cut rim**
Kushana-Gupta 200–500 A.D.
Kampilya, Uttar Pradesh
Plain Red Ware
Gift by Indian Archaeological Society, New Delhi
Acc. No.5.130

231. **Upper portion of bowl**
Kushana-Gupta 200–500 A.D.
Kampilya, Uttar Pradesh
Coarse Red Ware
Gift by Indian Archaeological Society, New Delhi
Acc. No.5.131

232. **Bowl with featureless rim and concave body**
Kushana-Gupta 200–500 A.D.
Kampilya, Uttar Pradesh
Coarse Red Ware
Gift by Indian Archaeological Society, New Delhi
Acc. No.5.132

233. **Dish with featureless rim**
Kushana-Gupta 200–500 A.D.
Kampilya, Uttar Pradesh
Plain Grey Ware
Gift by Indian Archaeological Society, New Delhi
Acc. No.5.133

234. **Bowl with oblique body**
Kushana-Gupta 200–500 A.D.
Kampilya, Uttar Pradesh
Coarse Red Ware
Gift by Indian Archaeological Society, New Delhi
Acc. No.5.134

235. **Bowl with out-turned rim**
Kushana-Bupta 200–500 A.D.
Kampilya, Uttar Pradesh
Plain Grey Ware
Gift by Indian Archaeological Society, New Delhi
Acc. No.5.135

236. **Straight-sided bowl with carination**
Kushana-Gupta 200–500 A.D.
Kampilya, Uttar Pradesh
Coarse Red Ware
Gift by Indian Archaeological Society, New Delhi
Acc. No.5.136

237. **Vase with out-turned rim**
Kushana-Gupta 200–500 A.D.
Kampilya, Uttar Pradesh
Slipped Red Ware
Gift by Indian Archaeological Society, New Delhi
Acc. No.5.137

238. **Straight-sided bowl with slightly out-turned rim**
Kushana-Gupta 200–500 A.D.
Kampilya, Uttar Pradesh
Coarse Grey Ware
Gift by Indian Archaeological Society, New Delhi
Acc. No.5.138

239. **Everted rim of vase**
Kushana-Gupta 200–500 A.D.
Kampilya, Uttar Pradesh
Coarse Red Ware
Gift by Indian Archaeological Society, New Delhi
Acc. No.5.139

240. **Vase with out-turned rim**
Kushana-Gupta 200–500 A.D.
Kampilya, Uttar Pradesh
Coarse Red Ware
Gift by Indian Archaeological Society, New Delhi
Acc. No.5.140

241. **Rim of straight-sided jar**
Kushana-Gupta 200–500 A.D.
Kampilya, Uttar Pradesh
Coarse Red Ware
Gift by Indian Archaeological Society, New Delhi
Acc. No.5.141

242. **Rim of a vase**
Kushana-Gupta 200–500 A.D.
Kampilya, Uttar Pradesh
Coarse Red Ware
Gift by Indian Archaeological Society, New Delhi
Acc. No.5.142

243. **Dish with a rib**
Kushana-Gupta 200–500 A.D.
Kampilya, Uttar Pradesh
Coarse Red Ware
Gift by Indian Archaeological Society, New Delhi
Acc. No.5.143

244. **Out-turned rim of a *handi***
Kushana-Gupta 200–500 A.D.
Kampilya, Uttar Pradesh

Plain Grey Ware
Gift by Indian Archaeological Society, New Delhi
Acc. No.5.144

245. **Pedestalled bowl with featureless rim**
Kushana-Gupta 200–500 A.D.
Kampilya, Uttar Pradesh
Plain Red Ware
Gift by Indian archaeological Society, New Delhi
Acc. No.5.145

246. **Out-turned rim of vase**
Kushana-Gupta 200–500 A.D.
Kampilya, Uttar Pradesh
Micaceous Red Ware
Gift by Indian Archaeological Society, New Delhi
Acc. No.5.146

247. **Rim of *handi* with external rib**
Kushana-Gupta 200–500 A.D.
Kampilya, Uttar Pradesh
Slipped Grey Ware
Gift by Indian Archaeological Society, New Delhi
Acc. No.5.147

248. **Rim of vase with a curvilinear neck**
Kushana-Gupta 200–500 A.D.
Kampilya, Uttar Pradesh
Coarse Red Ware
Gift by Indian Archaeological Society, New Delhi
Acc. No.5.148

249. **Beaded rim of *handi* with nail imprerssions**
Kushana-Gupta 200–500 A.D.
Kampilya, Uttar Pradesh
Coarse Red Ware
Gift by Indian Archaeological Society, New Delhi
Acc. No.5.149

250. **Rim of vase**
Kushana-Gupta 200–500 A.D.
Kampilya, Uttar Pradesh
Micaceous Red Ware
Gift by Indian Archaeological Society, New Delhi
Acc. No.5.150

251. **Out-turned rim of *handi* with short neck**
Kushana-Gupta 200–500 A.D.
Kampilya, Uttar Pradesh
Grey Ware
Gift by Indian Archaeological Society, New Delhi
Acc. No.5.151

252. **Rim of vase**
Kushana-Gupta 200–500 A.D.
Kampilya, Uttar Pradesh
Coarse Red Ware
Gift by Indian Archaeological Society, New Delhi
Acc. No.5.152

253. **Rim of jar**
Kushana-Gupta 200–500 A.D.
Kampilya, Uttar Pradesh
Red Ware
Gift by Indian Archaeological Society, New Delhi
Acc. No.5.153

254. **Rim of dish**
Kushana-Gupta 200–500 A.D.
Kampilya, Uttar Pradesh
Dull Red Ware
Gift by Indian Archaeological Society, New Delhi
Acc. No.5.154

255. **Rim of miniature-vase**
Kushana-Gupta 200–500 A.D.
Kampilya, Uttar Pradesh
Dull Red Ware
Gift by Indian Archaeological Society, New Delhi
Acc. No.5.155

256. **Rim of straight sided jar**
Kushana-Gupta 200–500 A.D.
Kampilya, Uttar Pradesh
Polished Red Ware
Gift by Indian Archaeological Society, New Delhi
Acc. No.5.156

257. **Rim of vase**
Kushana-Gupta 200–500 A.D.
Kampilya, Uttar Pradesh
Slipped Red Ware
Gift by Indian Archaeological Society, New Delhi
Acc. No.5.157

258. **Out-turned rim of *handi***
Kushana-Gupta 200–500 A.D.
Kampilya, Uttar Pradesh
Slipped Red Ware
Gift by Indian Archaeological Society, New Delhi
Acc. No.5.158

259. **Bowl with featureless rim**
Kushana-Gupta 200–500 A.D.
Kampilya, Uttar Pradesh
Dull Red Ware
Gift by Indian Archaeological Society, New Delhi
Acc. No.5.159

260. **Rim of dish**
Kushana-Gupta 200–500 A.D.
Kampilya, Uttar Pradesh
Coarse Red Ware
Gift by Indian Archaeological Society, New Delhi
Acc. No.5.160

261. **Sherd of vase**
Kushana-Gupta 200–500 A.D.
Kampilya, Uttar Pradesh

Coarse Red Ware
Gift by Indian Archaeological Society, New Delhi
Acc. No.5.161

262. **Rim of jar**
Kushana-Gupta 200–500 A.D.
Kampilya, Uttar Pradesh
Red Ware
Gift by Indian Archaeological Society, New Delhi
Acc. No.5.162

263. **Vase with out-turned rim**
Kushana-Gupta 200–500 A.D.
Kampilya, Uttar Pradesh
Red Ware
Gift by Indian Archaeological Society, New Delhi
Acc. No.5.163

264. **Tray with thick walls**
Kushana-Gupta 200–500 A.D.
Kampilya, Uttar Pradesh
Red Ware
Gift by Indian Archaeological Society, New Delhi
Acc. No.5.164

265. **Rim of vase**
Kushana-Gupta 200–500 A.D.
Kampilya, Uttar Pradesh
Coarse Red Ware
Gift by Indian Archaeological Society, New Delhi
Acc. No.5.165

266. **Rim of vase**
Kushana-Gupta 200–500 A.D.
Kampilya, Uttar Pradesh
Coarse Red Ware
Gift by Indian Archaeological Society, New Delhi
Acc. No.5.166

267. **Rim of bowl**
Kushana-Gupta 200–500 A.D.
Kampilya, Uttar Pradesh
Coarse Red Ware
Gift by Indian Archaeological Society, New Delhi
Acc. No.5.167

268. **Rim and shoulder of vase**
Kushana-Gupta 200–500 A.D.
Kampilya, Uttar Pradesh
Slipped Red Ware
Gift by Indian Archaeological Society, New Delhi
Acc. No.5.168

269. **Bowl with featureless rim and oblique sides**
Kushana-Gupta 200–500 A.D.
Kampilya, Uttar Pradesh
Coarse Red Wrae
Gift by Indian Archaeological Society, New Delhi
Acc. No.5.169

270. **Rim of miniature vase**
Kushana-Gupta 200–500 A.D.
Kampilya, Uttar Pradesh
Coarse Red Ware
Gift by Indian Archaeological Society, New Delhi
Acc. No.5.170

271. **Rim of storage jar**
Kushana-Gupta 200–500 A.D.
Kampilya, Uttar Pradesh
Red Slipped Ware
Gift by Indian Archaeological Society, New Delhi
Acc. No.5.171

272. **Rim of vase**
Kushana-Gupta 200–500 A.D.
Kampilya, Uttar Pradesh
Coarse Red Ware
Gift by Indian Archaeological Society, New Delhi
Acc. No.5.172

273. **Portion of corrugated stem**
Kushana-Gupta 200–500
Kampilya, Uttar Pradesh
Coarse Red Ware
Gift by Indian Archaeological Society, New Delhi
Acc. No.5.173

274. **Rim of *handi***
Kushana-Gupta 200–500 A.D.
Kampilya, Uttar Pradesh
Coarse Red Ware
Gift by Indian Archaeological Society, New Delhi
Acc. No.5.174

275. **Rim of vase**
Kushana-Gupta 200–500 A.D.
Kampilya, Uttar Pradesh
Coarse Red Ware
Gift by Indian Archaeological Society, New Delhi
Acc. No.5.175

276. **Rim of a dish with external carination**
Kushana-Gupta 200–500 A.D.
Kampilya, Uttar Pradesh
Slipped Red Ware
Gift by Indian Archaeological Society, New Delhi
Acc. No.5.176

277. **Rim and oblique wall of dish**
Kushana-Gupta 200–500 A.D.
Kampilya, Uttar Pradesh
Coarse Red Ware
Gift by Indian Archaeological Society, New Delhi
Acc. No.5.177

278. **Rim of miniature vase**
Kushana-Gupta 200–500 A.D.
Kampilya, Uttar Pradesh

Coarse Red Ware
Gift by Indian Archaeological Society, New Delhi
Acc. No.5.178

279. ***Handi***
Kushana-Gupta 200–500 A.D.
Kampilya, Uttar Pradesh
Grey Ware
Gift by Indian Archaeological Society, New Delhi
Acc. No.5.179

280. **Out-turned rim of *handi***
Kushana-Gupta 200–500 A.D.
Kampilya, Uttar Pradesh
Coarse Red Ware
Gift by Indian Archaeological Society, New Delhi
Acc. No.5.180

281. **Out-turned rim of vase**
Kushana-Gupta 200–500 A.D.
Kampilya, Uttar Pradesh
Coarse Red Ware
Gift by Indian Archaeological Society, New Delhi
Acc. No.5.181

282. **Out-turned beaked rim of *handi***
Kushana-Gupta 200–500 A.D.
Kampilya, Uttar Pradesh
Slipped Red Ware
Gift by Indian Archaeological Society, New Delhi
Acc. No.5.182

283. **Out-turned rim of deep bowl**
Kushana-Gupta 200–500 A.D.
kampilya, Uttar Pradesh
Coarse Red Ware
Gift by Indian Archaeological Society, New Delhi
Acc. No.5.183

284. **Rim of *handi***
Kushana-Gupta 200–500 A.D.
Kampilya, Uttar Pradesh
Coarse Red Ware
Gift by Indian Archaeological Society, New Delhi
Acc. No.5.184

285. **Fragment of pedestalled bowl**
Kushana-Gupta 200–500 A.D.
Kampilya, Uttar Pradesh
Coarse Red Ware
Gift by Indian Archaeological Society, New Delhi
Acc. No.5.185

286. **Beaked rim of *handi***
Kushana-Gupta 200–500 A.D.
Kampilya, Uttar Pradesh
Plain Grey Ware
Gift by Indian Archaeological Society, New Delhi
Acc. No.5.186

287. **Flat basin with straight sided rim**
Kushana-Gupta 200–500 A.D.
Kampilya, Uttar Pradesh
Coarse Red Ware
Gift by Indian Archaeological Society, New Delhi
Acc. No.5.187

288. **Lid with central knob**
Kushana-Gupta 200–500 A.D.
Kampilya, Uttar Pradesh
Red Slipped Ware
Gift by Indian Archaeological Society, New Delhi
Acc. No.5.188

289. **Beaked rim of *handi***
Kushana-Gupta 200–500 A.D.
Kampilya, Uttar Pradesh
Coarse Red Ware
Gift by Indian Archaeological Society, New Delhi
Acc. No.5.189

290. **Beaked rim of *handi***
Kushana-Gupta 200–500 A.D.
Kampilya, Uttar Pradesh
PlainGrey Ware
Gift by Indian Archaeological Society, New Delhi
Acc. No.5.190

291. **Out-turned rim of vase**
Kushana-Gupta 200–500 A.D.
Kampilya, Uttar Pradesh
Plain Red Ware
Gift by Indian Archaeological Society, New Delhi
Acc. No.5.191

292. **Out-turned rim of *handi***
Kushana-Gupta 200–500 A.D.
Kampilya, Uttar Pradesh
Black Slipped Grey Ware
Gift by Indian Archaeological Society, New Delhi
Acc. No.5.192

293. **Beaked Rim of *handi***
Kushana-Gupta 200–500 A.D.
Kampilya, Uttar Pradesh
Grey Ware
Gift by Indian Archaeological Society, New Delhi
Acc. No.5.193

294. **Bowl with featureless rim**
Kushana-Gupta 200–500 A.D.
Kampilya, Uttar Pradesh
Coarse Red Ware
Gift by Indian Archaeological Society, New Delhi
Acc. No.5.194

295. **Out-turned rim of *handi***
Kushana-Gupta 200–500 A.D.
Kampilya, Uttar Pradesh

Coarse Grey Ware
Gift by Indian Archaeological Society, New Delhi
Acc. No.5.195

296. **Rim of a vase**
Kushana-Gupta 200–500 A.D.
Kampilya, Uttar Pradesh
Coarse Red Ware
Gift by Indian Archaeological Society, New Delhi
Acc. No.5.196

297. **Out-turned rim of a vase**
Kushana-Gupta 200–500 A.D.
Kampilya, Uttar Pradesh
Coarse Red Ware
Gift by Indian Archaeological Society, New Delhi
Acc. No.5.197

298. **Out-turned rim of miniature vase.**
Kushana-Gupta 200–500 A.D.
Kampilya, Uttar Pradesh
Coarse Grey Ware
Gift by Indian Archaeological Society, New Delhi
Acc. No.5.198

299. **Vase with splayed-out rim and convex neck**
Kushana-Gupta 200–500 A.D.
Kampilya, Uttar Pradesh
Coarse Red Ware
Gift by Indian Archaeological Society, New Delhi
Acc. No.5.199

300. **Bowl with featureless rim**
Kushana-Gupta 200–500 A.D.
Kampilya, Uttar Pradesh
Coarse Red Ware
Gift by Indian Archaeological Society, New Delhi
Acc. No.5.200

301. **Bowl with featureless rim and oblique sides**
Kushana-Gupta 200–500 A.D.
Kampilya, Uttar Pradesh
Coarse Red Ware
Gift by Indian Archaeological Society, New Delhi
Acc. No.5.201

302. **Deep bowl with out-turned rim**
Kushana-Gupta 200–500 A.D.
Kampilya, Uttar Pradesh
Coarse Red Ware
Gift by Indian Archaeological Society, New Delhi
Acc. No.5.202

303. **Pedestalled bowl with oblique body and featureless rim**
Kushana-Gupta 200–500 A.D.
Kampilya, Uttar Pradesh
Coarse Red Ware
Gift by Indian Archaeological Society, New Delhi
Acc. No.5.203

304. ***Handi* with out-turned rim**
Kushana-Gupta 200–500 A.D.
Kampilya, Uttar Pradesh
Grey Ware
Gift by Indian Archaeological Society, New Delhi
Acc. No.5.204

305. **Dish**
Kushana-Gupta 200–500 A.D.
Kampilya, Uttar Pradesh
Slipped Red Ware
Gift by Indian Archaeological Society, New Delhi
Acc. No.5.205

6. MEDIEVAL PERIOD

The Zarathusti Lineage: Excavation at Sanjan-2002

306. **Potsherd**
900 A.D.
Glazed Ware
Sanjan, Gujarat
Gift by Indian Archaeological Society, New Delhi
Acc. No.6.01

7. DOCUMENTS

307. **Document of Aurangazeb**
1658–1680 A.D.
Delhi
Persian, Paper
Landgrant
Acc. No.7.01

308. **Document of Asaf Ali Domla**
1797 A.D.
Delhi
Persian, Paper
Landgrant
Acc. No.7.02

309. **Farman of Bahadur Shah I**
1800 A.D.
Delhi
Persian, Paper
Landgrant
Acc. No.7.03

310. **Documents of Jayas**
1800 A.D.
Delhi
Persian, Paper
Land grants
Gift by Dr. S.P. Gupta
Acc. No.7.04

8. ANTIQUITIES AND ART OBJECTS FROM OUTSIDE SOUTH ASIA

311. **Dutch warship on high sea before cloud burst**
1900 A.D.
St.Peterburg, Russia
Oil on Canvas
Gift by Dr. S.P. Gupta
Acc. No.9.01

9. CONTEMPORARY ART

312. **Confronting Dilemmas: Feminine determination**
2000 A.D.
Delhi
Etching on oil canvas
Gift by Dr. S.P. Gupta
Acc. No.10.01

313. **Man and Moon**
2000 A.D.
Delhi
Pastle on canvas
Gift by Dr. S.P. Gupta
Acc. No.10.02

314. **The Process of Creation *Sankhyadarsana***
1959 A.D.
Nagpur, Maharashtra
Pastle colour on Paper
Gift by Dr. S.P. Gupta
Acc. No.10.03

315. **Dancing Peacock**
2000 A.D.
Jaipur, Rajsthan
Pastle on cloth
Gift by Dr. S.P. Gupta
Acc. No.10.04

316. **Reclining Boy-A Fugitive Farewell to Juvenile Quandaries**
2000 A.D.
Delhi
Oil on canvas
Gift by the artist Ms. Poonam Sehgal
Acc. No.10.05

10. TEXTILE ART

317. **Iranian carpet**
Contemporary
Silk
Gift by Dr. S.P. Gupta
Acc. No.11.01

318. **Georgett *Lehnga***
20th Century (Contemporary)
Gift of Mrs. Dayavati Jagdish
Prasad Kesarwani of Kanpur
Acc. No.11.02

Select Bibliography

Agrawala,Vasudeva Saran 1961 *The Heritage of Indian Art.* New Delhi:Publications Divisions.

Agrawala,Vasudeva Saran 1967 Art in the Gupta Period in *The Vakataka-Gupta Age* (R.C. Majumdar and A.S. Altekar, Eds.) pp.423-441 New Delhi: Motilal Banarsidas.

Allchin, F.R. 1963 *Neolithic Cattle-Keepers of South India : A Study of the Deccan Ashmounds.* Cambridge: Cambridge University Press.

Allchin, F.R. 1995 *The Archaeology of Early Historic South Asia.* Cambridge: Cambridge University Press.

Amarendra Nath 1997-98 Rakhigarhi-A Harappan Metropolis in the Sarasvati- Drishadvati Divide, *Puratattva* (28): 39-45.

Amarendra Nath 1998-99 Further Excavations at Rakhigarhi, *Puratattva* (29): 48-49.

Asthana, Shashi 1999 *Mathura Kala.* New Delhi : National Museum.

Badam, G.L. 1984 Pleistocene Faunal Succession in India in the Evolution of East Asian Environment, Vol II. *Palaeobotany, Palaeogeology and Palaeoanthropology* (R.O.Whyte, Ed.) pp.746-775. Hong Kong: University of Hong Kong Press.

Badam, G.L. and Vijay Sathe 1995 Palaeontological Research in India: Retrospect and Prospect, *Quaternary Environments and Geoarchaeology of India* (S. Wadia, R.Korisettar and V.S.Kale, Eds.) pp. 473-495 Banglore : Geological Survey of India.

Bhan, K.K., M. Vidale, and J.M. Kenoyer 1994 Harappan Technology : Theoretical and Methodological Issues, *Man and Environment,* Vol XIX. (1-2): 141-157.

Chakrabarty, D.K. 1997 *The Archaeology of Ancient Indian Cities.* Delhi : Oxford University Press.

Dennell, R.W. H. Rendell and E. Hailwood 1988 Early Tool Making in Asia : Two Million Year Old Artefacts in Pakistan, *Antiquity* 62.

Dhavalikar, M.K.1988 *The First Farmers of the Deccan.* Pune : Ravish Publishers.

Dhavalikar, M.K., H.D.Sankalia and Z.D. Ansari 1988 *Excavations at Inamgaon* (2 vols) Pune : Deccan College.

Dikshit, K.N. 2000 Report of the First Archaeological Campaign at Drupad Kila (Kampilya) in *First International Symposium on Kampilya Project* (B.Marcolongo, Ed.) Padova.

Dikshit, K.N. and Rao Bahadur 1967 Archaeological Remains of the Gupta Period in The Vakataka-Gupta Age (R.C. Majumdar and A.S. Altekar, Eds.) pp.423-441, New Delhi: Motilal Banarsidas.

Filippi, Gian Giuseppe and Bruno Marcolongo 1999 *Kampilya -Quest for a Mahabharata City.* New Delhi : D.K. Printworld.

Gaillard, Claire 1995 An Early Soan Assemblage from Siwaliks: A Comparison of Processing Sequence Between this Assemblage and of an Acheulian Assemblage from Rajasthan. *Quaternary Environments and Geoarchaeology of India* (S. Wadia, R. Korisettar and V.S.Kale, Eds.) pp. 231-245. Banglore : Geological Survey of India.

Gaur, R.C. 1983 *Excavations at Atranjikhera-Early Civilization of the Upper Ganga Basin.* New Delhi : Motilal Banarsidas.

Ghosh, A.1973 *The City in Early Historical India.* Simla : Indian Institute of Advanced Study.

Gupta, P.L. 1969 *Coins.* New Delhi: National Book Trust.

Gupta, S.P. 1972 *Disposal of the Dead and Physical Types in Ancient India.* Delhi: Oriental Publishers.

Gupta, S.P. 1980 *The Roots of Indian Art.* Delhi: B.R.Publishing Corporation.

Gupta, S.P. *The Indus-Saraswati Civilization,* 1996, New Delhi: Pratibha Prakashan.

Gupta S.P. 1999 The Indus -Sarasvati Civilization-Beginnings and Devolopment. *The Dawn of Indian Civilization upto 600 BC* (G. C. Pande, Ed.) pp.269-375 New Delhi: Centre for Studies in Civilization.

Gupta, S.P. and Asthana, S.P. 2002 *Elements of Indian Art,* New Delhi, Indraprastha Museum of Art and Archaeology & D.K. Printworld.

Gupta, S.P., Lal, Krishna & Bhattacharya, Mahua 2002 *Cultural Tourism in India,* New Delhi. Indraprashta Museum of Art and Archaeology & D.K. Printworld.

Indian Archaeology 1975-76 A Review — pp.51-52 Delhi : Archaeological Survey of India.

Indian Archaeology 1994-95 A Review — pp.96-97 Delhi : Archaeological Survey of India.

Janson, H.W. 1985 *A History of Art* London : Thames and Hudson.

Kajale, M D 1991 Current Status of Indian Palaeoethnobotany-Introduced and Indigenous Food Plants with a Discussion of the Historical and Evolutionary Devolopment of Indian Agriculture and Agricultural Systems in General *New light on Early Farming: Recent devolopments in Palaeoethnobotany* (Jane Renfrew Ed.) pp. 155-189 Edinburgh: Edinburgh University Press.

Kajale, M.D. 1996 Palaeobotanical Investigations at Balathal : Preliminary Results. *Man and Environment* Vol XXI (1) : 98-102.

Kennedy, K.A.R. 2000 *God Apes and Fossil Men-Palaeoanthropology in South Asia* pp. 278-323 Michigan: The University of Michigan Press.

Kumar, G.G. Narvare and R.Pancholi 1988 Engraved Ostrich Shell Objects : New Evidence of Upper Palaeolithic Art in India. *Rock Art Research* 5 (1): 43-52.

Lahiri, Nayanjot 1992 *The Archaeology of Indian Trade Routes Upto c. 200 B.C.* Delhi: Oxford University Press.

Lal, B.B. 1997 *The Earliest Civilization of South Asia.* New Delhi : Aryan Books International.

Lal, B.B., Gupta, S.P., Asthana, S.P. (Ed.) *Frontiers of the Indus Civilization.* New Delhi: Indian Archaeological Society & Books and Books.

Majumdar, G.G. and S.N. Rajguru 1966 *Ashmound Excavations at Kupgal.* Pune : Deccan College.

Marcolongo, B. 2001 *First International Symposium on Kampilya Project* : Padova.

Misra,V.D. 1999 A Brief Note on Indian Stone Age Archaeology *The Dawn of Indian Civilization upto 600 B.C.* (G.C.Pande Ed.) pp. 129-138 New Delhi: Centre for Studies in Civilizations.

Misra, V.N. 1987. Middle Pleistocene Adaptations in India *The Pleistocene Old World: Regional Perspectives* (Olga Soffer Ed.) pp. 99-119, New York : Plenum Press.

Misra, V.N. 1989 Stone Age India: an Ecological Perspective. *Man and Environment* Vol XIV (1): 17-64 .

Misra V.N. 1989 Human Adaptations to the Changing Landscape of the Indian Arid Zone During the Quaternary Period *Old Problems and New Perspectives in the Archaeology of South Asia* (J.M.Kenoyer Ed.) pp. 3-20, Winconsin : University of Winconsin.

Misra, V.N.,Vasant Shinde, R.K.Mohanty, Lalit Pandey and Jeewan Kharakwal 1997 Excavations at Balathal, Udaipur District, Rajasthan (1995-1997) With Special Reference to Chalcolithic Architecture. *Man and Environment,* Vol XXII (2): 35-60.

Murty, M.L.K. 1989 Pre-Iron Age Agricultural Settlements in South India : An Ecological Perspective. *Man and Environment,* Vol XIV(1): 65-81.

Paddayya, K. 1989 The Acheulian Culture Localities along the Fatehpur Nullah, Baichbal Valley,Karnataka. in *Old Problems and New Perspectives in the Archaeology of South Asia* (J.M.Kenoyer, Ed.) pp. 21-28 Winconsin : University of Winconsin.

Paddayya, K. 1973 *Investigations into the Neolithic Culture of the Shorapur Doab, South India,* Leiden.

Paddayya, K. 1993 Ashmound Investigations at Budhihal, Gulbarga District, Karnataka *Man and Environment,* Vol XVIII, (1): 57-87.

Paddayya, K., Richa Jhaldiyal and Michael D. Petraglia 1999-2000 The Significance of the Achulian site of Isampur, Karnataka in the Lower Palaeolithic of India, *Puratattva* (30) 1-24.

Pal, J.N. 2000 Mesolithic and Neolithic Societies of the Vindhyas and the Middle Gangetic Plain, *Social History and Social Theory* (V.D.Misra and J.N.Pal, Eds.) pp.7-13, Allahabad : University of Allahabad.

Pappu, R.S. 2001 *Acheulian Culture in Peninsular India.* New Delhi: D. K. Printworld.

Prasad, Kameswar 1984 *Cities, Crafts and Commerce under the Kusanas.* Delhi: Agam Kala Prakashan.

Ray, Niharranjan 1975 *Maurya and Post-Maurya Art.* New Delhi : Indian Council of Historical Research.

Rendell, H.M.,E.A.Hailwood and R.W. Dennel 1987 Magnetic Polarity Stratigraphy of Upper Siwalik Sub-Group, Soan Valley, Pakistan: Implications for Early Human Occupance of Asia *Earth and Planetary Science Letters* 85: 488-496.

Sankalia, H.D., B.Subbarao and S.B.Deo 1958 *The Excavations at Maheshwar and Navdatoli* 1952-53. Pune and Baroda : Deccan College and M.S. University.

Sankalia, H.D., S.B. Deo, Z.D. Ansari 1969 *Excavations at Ahar.* Poona : Deccan College.

Sankalia, H.D., S.B.Deo, Z.D. Ansari 1971 *Chalcolithic Navdatoli.* Poona : Deccan College.

Sankalia, H.D.1974 *Prehistory and Protohistory of India and Pakistan.* Poona : Deccan College.

Sharma,A.K.1982 Gufkral 1981: An Aceramic Neolithic Site in the Kashmir Valley, *Asian Perspectives* 25 (2): 24-41.

Sharma, T.C. 1981 The Neolithic Pattern of North-Eastern India, *Madhu: Recent Researches in Indian Archaeology and Art*

History (M.S. Nagaraja Rao, Ed.) pp. 41-52, Delhi: Agam Kala Prakashan.

Sivaramamurti, C. 1970 *Indian Paintings*. New Delhi: National Book Trust.

Srivastava, A.L 1994 The Sources in *The Mughal Empire* (R.C. Majumdar, J.N. Chaudhari and S. Chaudhari eds.) p. 13 Bombay : Bharatiya Vidya Bhavan.

Sonakia, A.1984 The Skull Cap of Early Man and Associated Mammalian Fauna from the Narmada Valley Alluvium, Hoshangabad Area, Madhya Pradesh, India *Geological Survey of India Records* 133 (6).

Sonawane, V.H. and P. Ajithprasad 1994 Harappan Culture and Gujarat, *Man and Environment*, Vol XIX (1-2): 129-139.

Thomas, P.K. 1975 Role of Animals in the Food Economy of the Mesolithic Culture of Western and Central India in *Archaeozoological Studies* (A.T. Clason, Ed.) pp. 322-328 Amsterdam.

Thomas, P.K. 1989. Utilization of Domestic Animals in Pre- and Protohistoric India, *The Walking Larder: Patterns of Domestication, Pastoralism and Predation* (J.Clutton-Brock, Ed.) pp.108-112, London : Unwin Hyman.

Thomas, P.K. and P.P. Joglekar 1994 Holocene Faunal Studies in India, *Man and Environment*, Vol XIX (1-2): 179-203.

Thomas, P.K., P.P Joglekar, V.D. Misra, J.N. Pandey and J.N. Pal 1996 Faunal Evidence for the Mesolithic Food Economy of the Gangetic Plain with Special Reference to Damdama, *The Prehistory of Asia and Oceania, Colloquium XXIII, Bioarchaeology of Mesolithic India : an Integral Approach* (Gennadii E. Afanasev, Serge Cleuziou, John R. Lukacs and Maurizio Tosi, Eds.) pp.255-266, Forli Italia : A. B.A.C.O. Edizioni.

Thomas, P.K. and P.P. Joglekar 1996 Faunal Remains From Balathal, Rajasthan : A Preliminary Report, *Man and Environment*, Vol XXI (1) pp.91-97.

Tripathi, Vibha 1999 Early Iron Technology and its Socio-Economic Impact in *The Dawn of Indian Civilization upto 600 B.C.* (G.C.Pande, Ed.) pp.493-508. New Delhi: Munshiram Manoharlal.

Vallianatose, Helen 1999 *Prlude to Palaeodiet : A Histological and Elementary Study of Diagenesis Among Early Holocene Skeletons from North India*, pp.32-52 Allahabad : University of Allahabad.

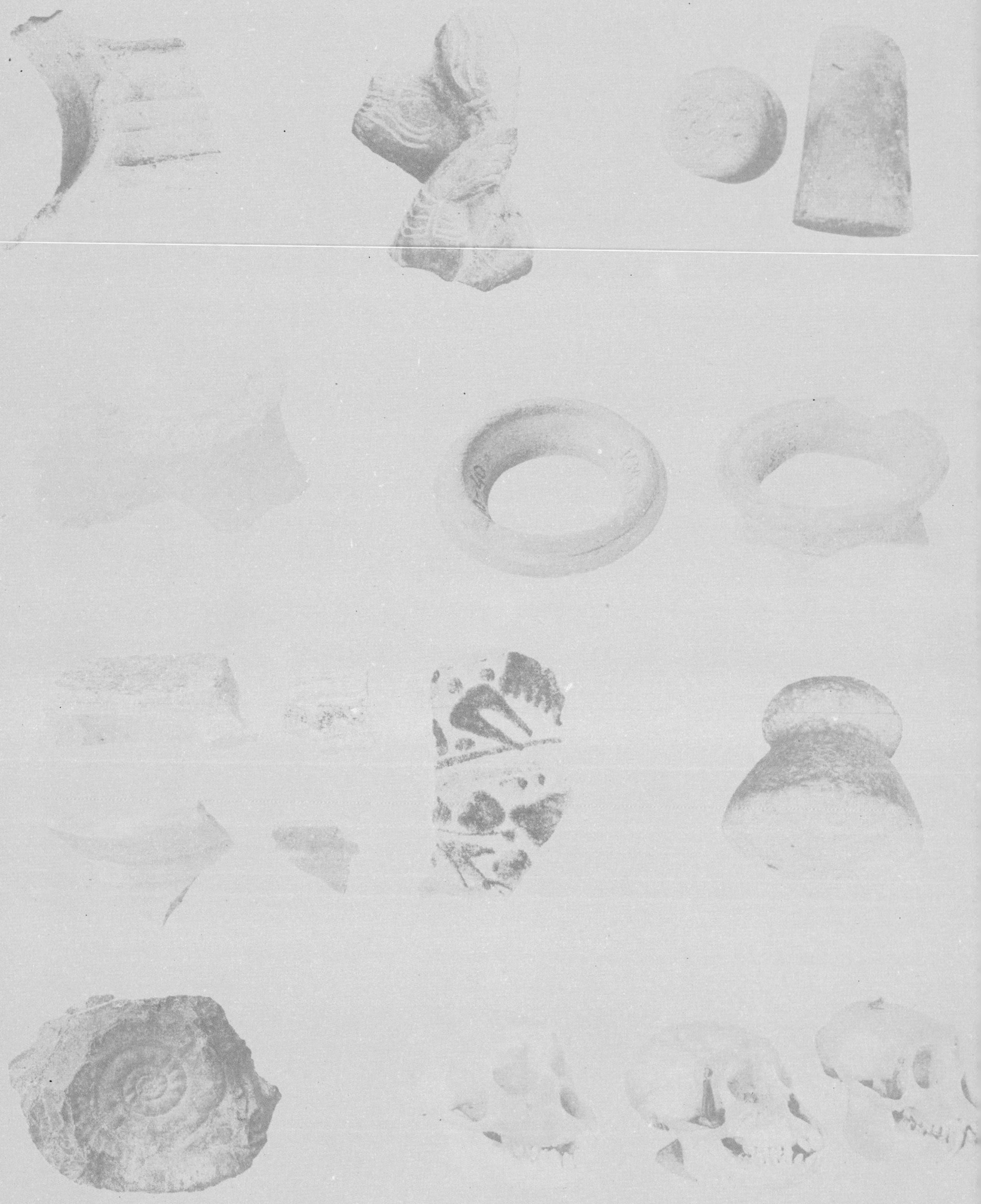